Technology and Teaching English Language Learners

Mary Ellen Butler-Pascoe
Alliant International University

Karin M. Wiburg
New Mexico State University

08174

Boston • New York • San Francisco
Mexico City • Montreal • Toronto • London • Madrid • Munich • Paris
Hong Kong • Singapore • Tokyo • Cape Town • Sydney

Series Editor: *Aurora Ramos Martínez*
Editorial Assistant: *Beth Slater*
Marketing Manager: *Amy Cronin*
Production Editor: *Christine Tridente*
Composition Buyer: *Linda Cox*
Editorial Production Service: *TKM Productions*
Electronic Composition: *TKM Productions*
Manufacturing Buyer: *JoAnne Sweeney*
Cover Administrator: *Kristina Mose-Libon*

Between the time Website information is gathered and published, some sites may have closed. Also, the transcription of URLs can result in unintended typographical errors. The publisher would appreciate notification where these errors occur so that they may be corrected in subsequent editions.

Library of Congress Cataloging-in-Publication Data

Butler-Pascoe, Mary Ellen.
   Technology and teaching English language learners / Mary Ellen Butler-Pascoe, Karin M. Wiburg.
      p. cm.
   Includes bibliographical references and index.
   ISBN 0-205-32677-3
      1. English language--Study and teaching--Foreign speakers. 2. English language--Study and teaching--Technological innovations. 3. Information technology. I. Wiburg, Karin M. II. Title.

PE1128.A2 B89 2002
428'.0071--dc21   2002024881

Printed in the United States of America

10 9 8 7 6 5 4 3 2 1   RRD-IN   08 07 06 05 04 03 02

Hyper Studio® and all of its screen images is a registered trademark of Knowledge Adventure, Inc. and is used under license.

Netscape Communicator browser window © 1999 Netscape Communications Corporation. Used with permission. Netscape Communications has not authorized, sponsored, endorsed, or approved this publication and is not responsible for its content.

Dedicated to the memory
of

My brother, Emmett William Butler III—Billy,
who though he could not speak with words,
taught me early in life how to use sounds, signs, and visuals
to communicate with others.

Mary Ellen Butler-Pascoe

and

My father, Dr. Park Hays Miller, Jr.,
who while a busy scientist still found time
to read me bedtime stories and act out fairy tales
around our living room table.

Karin M. Wiburg

Contents

Preface

Over the years we have taught many teachers numerous methods for teaching English language learners; we have also taught them how to use computers in education. Seldom, however, have we had the opportunity to connect in substantive ways technology use to methods for teaching English, as well as methods for helping language learners master content. There are many reasons for this frustrating division between our work as language teachers and technology instructors. Both in the foreign language field and in TESOL (Teaching English to Speakers of Other Languages), there are a lack of rich instructional models and resources for integrating technology with language learning. This may reflect a deeply ingrained bias in traditional educational systems toward dividing everything into specific fields and isolated topics. Although there are exceptions, in most colleges and K–12 schools, faculty teaching English language learners and those teaching computer and media classes are not likely to be working together.

In the humanities fields there may also be a limited perception related to the word *technology*. We define *technology* as tools and processes associated with using those tools that shape human activity. Among those who embrace a holistic and humanistic approach to education, and we would place most TESOL educators in this camp, there is an understandable backlash against the notion of a technocratic curriculum—one in which technology is used as an end rather than a means for teaching and learning. Their skepticism is especially understandable when one considers the failures of earlier technologies that promised to be the panacea for foreign language teaching. Both the language labs and the automatic machine translation of the 1950s and 1960s failed to live up to the expectations of linguists, language teachers, and school administrators (Moses, 1991). The earliest drill-oriented computer programs designed for language learning reflect a narrow, technocratic approach and influenced educators to discount the power of technology without considering its communicative power.

We find a separation between technology and language learning especially ironic, because both fields share a number of common beliefs about learning and teaching. Theories addressing the cognitive and developmental processes involved in second language acquisition have received wide attention and have had a significant impact on methodology of Teaching English to Speakers of Other Languages. Pedagogy has moved from the behavioristic audio-lingual method of the 1960s to current approaches focusing on the learning process, the student's role in that process, and the sociocultural context of the learning. In a similar fashion, educational technology has moved from a traditional emphasis on behaviorally based instructional delivery systems to the design of student-centered, problem-based learning environments based on sociocultural constructivist theory.

With such overlapping theoretical frameworks, the technology and TESOL disciplines are ideal partners for providing effective second language teaching. Educators from both fields are now called on to collaborate in broader pedagogical discussions that recognize the impact of technology on second language learning and to assist teachers to discover ways in which they can utlilize technology to meet the needs of English learners.

Our experience confirms what recent research says about the lack of access to technology for bilingual and TESOL teachers (Wetzel and Chisholm, 1998), both pre-service and in-service. Wiburg, in her work with teachers in bilingual Latino majority schools in southern New Mexico, has found that bilingual and ESL (English as a Second Language) teachers are often the last to be given computer access or training related to technology use. Butler-Pascoe (1995), in her work with TESOL graduate students, has found that it is common for these teachers to have inadequate training or access to the resources needed to infuse technology into their teaching. This book is our attempt to change this situation. It specifically addresses the use of technology within well-developed second language acquisition theories and practice. It offers concrete examples and models for enhancing language learning environments through technology.

Special features of each chapter include the use of guiding questions, real-world examples from classroom situations with which the authors are familiar, and a discussion of the attributes of these learning environments that account for their success with English language learners. Each chapter concludes with a summary of key points, additional teaching activities, a list of technology resources used in the chapter, and, when appropriate, additional resources for teachers. Although there are many similarities in the educational philosophy of the TESOL and educational computing fields, practice and research remain divided. This book shows how technology can be used to effectively support second language learning.

Acknowledgments

We thank our graduate students at New Mexico State University and at Alliant International University in San Diego, California, for their help in reading and critiquing these chapters and helping us modify many of the chapter activities. We give a special thanks to AIU doctoral students Andre Boyer, Tien-Tsai Chiang, Faou Dabaji-Shanteau, Margaret Don, Mio Hasagawa, Bailong Jiao, Joann Jurchan-Rizzo, Kenneth Kelch, Todd Morano, Eliana Santana, and Antoinette Schooler, who also assisted us in identifying exemplary software and websites. Thank you to Dr. Ana Huerta-Macias and Manuel Bustamante at New Mexico State for reading and critiquing the initial drafts of the book. We also acknowledge the numerous teachers and administrators who welcomed us into their classes and schools to share their exciting explorations into using technology with their English language learners.

We are grateful to Ann Kinsey for her invaluable expertise and technical assistance in preparing the numerous software and website screen shots included in the book. Thank you, too, to our editors at Allyn and Bacon, Aurora Martínez, Beth Slater, and Christine Tridente, for their guidance and assistance in the completion of this book. We also thank Lynda Griffiths of TKM Productions for her patience and care in steering the book through all the production stages. We are grateful to the following reviewers for their comments and suggestions: Sue Atkinson, Rice University/University of Houston; Sharla Jones, Northwest Vista College; and Buenaventura Torres-Ayala, University of Texas at San Antonio.

Finally, we express our appreciation to our friends and families for their support throughout the writing of this book. We give a special thanks to our husbands, Marv Wiburg, who not only provided moral support but technical assistance as a librarian at NMSU, and Larry Pascoe, who provided both endless support and a haven for peace and reflection on his sailboat, aptly named *Sabbatical.* Also, Mary Ellen Butler-Pascoe expresses her gratitude to her parents, Margaret Lucille Butler and Emmett William Butler, Jr., for their lifelong support, encouragement, and belief in her.

References

Butler-Pascoe, M. E. (1995). A national survey of the integration of technology into TESOL master's programs. In Del Anna Willis, Bernard Robin, and Jerry Willis (Eds.), *Technology and Teacher Education Annual, 1995.* San Antonio, TX: Association for the Advancement of Computing in Education (AACE).

Moses, Y. M. (1991). Listening interactively. *Computer Education* 17, 293–300.

Wetzel, K., and Chisholm, I. (1998). An evaluation of technology integration in teacher education for bilingual and English as a second language education majors. *Journal of Research on Computing in Education* 30(4): 379–396.

1

Introduction

As a teacher educator, I first began to see the promise of technology not just as an interesting add-on to education, but as a fundamental tool for restructuring classroom learning, when I went to visit a middle school in California near the Mexican border. The school had about 90 percent underrepresented students, with the largest population being African American, followed by Hispanic and Asian American students. Teachers, with the help of parents and the community, ran this public school, and had special permission to reorganize the roles of teachers and administrators. All administrators did some teaching, and teachers had a couple of half days per week to counsel with parents and students and plan curriculum together. Four educators worked collaboratively to lead families of 60 students. Technology was an essential part of this restructuring—the tool that made the thematic units and continuous communication work. Each family of 60 students had 15 computers that were used for learning activities throughout the school day.

When I entered the classroom during my first visit, students, working in pairs or small groups, were using a multimedia program to explore and develop questions about whales. I sat down next to a boy and began to ask him about his work. The boy's partner told me matter-of-factly that the student I was talking to didn't speak English, but he would soon. With the support of peer learning and the multimedia program, the two students were operating at a high conceptual level, even though one of the students was just learning English.

—Karin Wiburg

As the director and instructor of a large university English as a Second Language (ESL) program in California in the 1980s, I remember well the early successes and frustrations of integrating computers into our writing program. We held our writing classes in the computer labs where students brainstormed ideas and composed, revised, peer edited, and published their compositions on the computers. Despite the all-too-frequent technical difficulties, the advantages of using computers with our recently adopted writing-as-a-process approach were obvious from the beginning. Word processors made it possible for students to easily correct errors and revise their compositions, avoiding tedious rewrites. The instructors were able to read the students' writing on their computer monitors and make suggestions or ask for clarifications while the students were in the process of writing. Even students in the lower-level classes marveled at the writing they were capable of producing with the assistance of computer-generated prompts. With the hit of one key, all the prompts disappeared, transforming the students' responses to the electronic prompts into well-formulated paragraphs.

As optimistic as I was about the potential of technology in assisting second language learners in developing their English skills, I was most struck by the role it could play in meeting the affective needs of these students. I will never forget the look of pride on the face of one of our graduate ESL students as he pointed out his essay displayed on the classroom's Writers' Bulletin Board and quietly said, "That one is mine." I had observed him earlier that week in the computer lab revising his essay and was somewhat amazed to note how many hours he had spent there after a long day of classes. In later conversations with this student, I began to understand more clearly why he was so attracted to the computer lab. First, he explained that he felt more a part of the broader university community in the computer labs than in the more isolated ESL classrooms. In the labs he could interact with American students and other friends from his country who were already studying in degree courses. He described the pride he felt when he produced a professional-looking paper in contrast to his often illegible handwritten assignments. This seemed to be a special benefit to ESL students like himself, who were struggling to use an alphabet different from that of their native language. He also reported that with the computer-based grammar programs, he could make mistakes, get feedback, and figure out the correct answer without the embarrassment that he sometimes experienced in class. Additionally, learning to word process and use other computer applications while improving his language skills gave him a strong sense of accomplishment.

In subsequent years, research would confirm that the experiences of this student were some of the frequently cited positive effects of computer-assisted ESL writing environments, but my conversations with this one student over a decade ago were compelling enough for me to be convinced that technology would play a substantive role in the future of second language teaching.

—Mary Ellen Butler-Pascoe

Chapter Overview

We began this chapter by reflecting on the first time we each experienced the tremendous potential of technology for learning and especially second language learning. We felt it was appropriate to begin by sharing these early 1980s experiences with you. This chapter continues with an historical overview of the uses of technology in second language teaching. It then describes the current status of technology use in programs serving English language learners (ELLs) from elementary school through college, considers the problem of misuses of technology with this population, and looks at the promise of technology for supporting the multiple dimensions of rich language learning environments. Both in this chapter and in the book, technology is considered in its dual role of assisting language learning directly as well as providing support for mastering academic content. This chapter calls for increased professional development to assist teachers in utilizing technology in their teaching. The chapter includes an overview of the organization of the rest of the book and concludes with a summary of the key ideas of the chapter.

A Historical Overview

> *How have the uses of technology evolved over the last several decades in terms of serving English Language Learners (ELLs)?*

The use of technology in the language learning classroom is not new. Pablo Friere, as part of his development of adult literacy learning circles in Brazil, used audiovisual materials. Sayers and Brown (1998) write about the early integration of technology and literacy:

> Literacy instruction in Freire's campaigns was divided into two parts: pre-literacy and a literacy-building phase. In the pre-literacy phase, slides were created that relied entirely on graphic, non-written representations, depicting culture as a vital social process in which the community plays an active, determining role. During the literacy-building phase, the slides used both graphic and written representations of key community concerns called "generative themes" that literacy workers had identified after weeks of research with local residents. (p. 24)

Unfortunately, such culturally sensitive uses of technology hadn't gained a foothold in schools in the United States before they were besieged by behaviorally oriented computer-assisted learning programs. For more than a decade beginning in the mid-1960s, computer assisted instruction (CAI) designed for use in language teaching structured learning according to the behaviorist model (Stevens, 1989). This stimulus-response model provided sequential instruction with feedback, frequent reinforcement, branching, and self-pacing. Such drill and practice mode of delivery was perfectly matched to the teaching of linguistic patterns espoused by the structural linguists and proponents of the audio-lingual method of second language teaching of that era. Computers were introduced in schools at a time when behavioral objectives dominated the curriculum (Norton and Wiburg, 1998). Students were taught in isolated skill sequences and seldom assisted in synthesizing these pieces of learning. Early uses of technology in schools mirrored what often happens when new technologies are invented. The potential of these technologies to do things differently was rarely explored. Instead, the technologies were used to make existing practices more efficient. Coughlin (1989) reports Underwood's description of early computer-assisted language learning (CALL) in this regard: "The tendency was rather to try to push and squeeze current language learning materials to fit the computer, to 'computerize' our lab exercises, or imitate unabashedly the teaching machines or programmed instruction of the recent past" (p. 71).

Thus, if computers were used at all for language learning, they were primarily used as drill and practice teaching machines. The results of this type of intervention were mixed. A classic six-year, in-depth study by Hativa (1988) involving the effect of computer-assisted instruction in arithmetic on elementary students' learning sheds light on the impact of CAI on learning for different populations. She reported a differential impact of CAI programs on lower-achieving as compared to higher-achieving students, with higher-achieving students receiving more benefit from the use of CAI. Students who were not doing well in mathematics tended to get caught in repetitive loops as a result of making the same mistake over and over and became increasingly discouraged.

Roblyer (1989) did a meta-analysis of 38 published and unpublished studies and 44 dissertations on the impact of computer-based instruction on student learning. Generally, positive effects were found at all grade levels; however, for ESL students, the effectiveness was low overall and even negative in studies involving Hispanic students.

A more recent study, which examined the relationships between technology, academic achievement, and pedagogy, confirms that isolated drill and practice might not be the most effective way to improve student achievement. Wenglinsky (1998) used test scores from the 1996 National Assessment of Educational Practices to investigate these relationships:

> Eighth graders whose teachers used computers mostly for "simulations and applications"—generally associated with higher-order thinking—performed better on the NAEP than did students whose teachers did not. [And] eighth graders whose teachers used computers mostly for drill and practice—generally associated with lower-order thinking—performed worse.

This should not be taken to mean that drill and practice programs are never useful in the second language classroom. In fact, as a result of the increasing multimedia capability of computers, some of the most exciting new work in the use of technology involves the development and implementation of new multimedia tutorial systems (Cummins, 1998). These systems provide user-controlled and -supported practice in using multiple sources of text in the target language and are showing positive results for language learning. In addition, even traditional programs that reinforce grammar, spelling, and vocabulary learning can provide useful assistance for language learning if used as part of a communicative approach. Though many of these types of programs have the disadvantage of focusing on form over function, such software can be valuable in reinforcing class instruction and providing focused practice of specific skills. Pronunciation programs allow second language learners to visually compare the voice patterns of their speech with that of a native speaker. Drill and practice software can be programmed to adapt to the language proficiency level of each student, supplying corrective advice and self-paced practice in grammar and vocabulary development. With individualized reading programs, students can select the difficulty level of the text as well as the speed of timed readings. Games provide additional motivation to individualized instruction by challenging students to move to the next level of mastery. Record-keeping features assist the teacher and students in assessing the students' progress and designing future plans of study.

By the 1970s, psychologists and educators began to recognize the importance of the individual in the learning process. As the premises of the humanistic movement filtered into education and second language methodologies such as Curran's Community Language Learning (Curran, 1972, 1982), CALL courseware was adapted to a more humanistic design based on intrinsic motivation, and interactivity.

Linguists and language teachers of the 1970s and 1980s began to turn their attention to the function of language and to its communicative nature. With the emergence of the Communicative Language Teaching (CLT) and the writing process approaches, communicative uses of technology were developed. Word processors, on-line databases, and telecommunications offered unique opportunities to engage English language learners in functional uses of language by providing them a collaborative learning environment, authentic audiences, and real-world tasks (Phinney, 1989; Cohen and Riel, 1986).

In the 1980s and 1990s, with a focus on meeting the cognitive and academic language proficiency needs of second language learners, task-based and content-based teaching became widely accepted pedagogical practices in second language teaching (Nunan, 1999; Snow and Brinton, 1988). Just as the word processor had so perfectly meshed with the changing paradigm in writing from an emphasis on product to process, Internet resources and CD-ROM databases as well as simulation and authoring software ideally supported content- and task-based instruction. Once again, technology and second language acquisition theory and pedagogy evolved in parallel directions. The microcomputers of the 1980s had placed significant computing power into the hands of the individual. As networks and the capacity of computers grew in the 1990s, the computer became a powerful communication tool to support communication of not only text but also graphics, video, and sound, and to connect learners to increasingly rich learning resources available via the World Wide Web. As Dede (1996) observed, the developed word had moved from the age of information to the age of communication with learning environments in which students were not just receivers of information, but had the capability to create new information using networked computer systems.

Technology Access of English Language Learners

Are the estimated 2 million non-English speakers currently in U.S. classrooms receiving equitable access to computers?

In her introduction to the section on diversity in *Technology and Teacher Education Annual* (Carey, Carey, Willis, and Willis, 1993), Harrington suggests that educators' assumptions about the use of technology with certain groups served to place some students at a disadvantage. Skeele (1993) notes that less frequent educational computer use by groups other than white males or high-ability students had been noted in the research for some time. She suggested that it is "indisputable that the classroom computer is not shared equally" (p. 15). Further, it is not just access to computers that is important, but the kinds of uses to which students are introduced. For example, students from higher economic backgrounds tend to *direct the computer*, whereas students from lower socioeconomic backgrounds are often *directed by it* (Dutton, Peltu, and Bruce, 1999).

The situation has not improved in recent years. Chisholm (1998) reported on a study (Trotter, 1997) that shows that schools with high populations of poor and minority students continue to have more students per computers than richer, mainstream schools. Children in the schools of lower socioeconomic districts also have less access to the Internet, to multimedia, to CD-ROMs, and to cable TV than children at more affluent schools (Coley et al., 1997). Chisholm (1998) also reported that teachers of language minority students continue to use technology for primarily electronic drill and practice activities rather than for higher-end uses such as productivity and research.

Hunt and Pritchard (1993) sought to determine whether the limited use of computers by language minority students was due to a lack of availability of computers or a problem with teachers not knowing how to use the technology with second language learners. To answer this question, they conducted a 1992 study in which they deliberately studied computer-rich schools with large populations of language minority students. A survey was given to 12 school districts in Fresno, California, asking teachers about their access to technology; how they modified instruction for language minority students; under what conditions their students used computers; and what support they received to assist them to use technology with language minority students. Approximately 20 percent of the teachers who returned the surveys were chosen for follow-up observations based on the high percentage of language minority students in their classrooms and their reported access to technology.

The teachers in this study all reported modifying instruction for limited English speakers but *none* of the modifications involved using technology. Although half the teachers participating in the study (*N* = 177) had regular classroom access to computers, 60 percent of these teachers who used technology regularly with their students reported *never using computers with language minority students*. The other 40 percent who did use computers with language minority students had these students doing drill and practice programs in language arts and mathematics. This study emphasizes the need to integrate technology into teaching in such a manner as to strengthen the instructional strategies that are being utilized by TESOL teachers. The purpose of this book is to accomplish just that.

The Power of Multimedia and the Internet

How have the Internet and the increasing multimedia capability of computers improved language learning opportunities?

Research in second language acquisition (Krashen, 1989) has clearly suggested the need of comprehensible input in order for second language learning to take place. Perhaps the single most important role of the second language teacher is to act as a facilitator in providing this intensive input. Traditionally, teachers have relied heavily on the use of pictures, realia, and gestures to convey meaning to beginning language learners. The computer, with its Internet and hypermedia capabilities, is a powerful addition to second language teachers' resources. Computers utilize a multisensory collection of text, sound, pictures, video, animation, and hypermedia to provide meaningful contexts to facilitate comprehension. Technology is equally important in the sheltered, academic-area classrooms where its ability to provide comprehensible input serves as a scaffold to support students as they study academically challenging subject matter (Bruner, 1986).

Using multimedia, students can, for instance, read and listen to a story before writing and recording their own versions of a similar story. Programs with theme-based vocabulary embedded in context assist the learner in focusing on meaning before practicing form. Multimedia provides the multiple modalities needed to meet the needs of students with different learning styles and strategies. The aural, visual, tactile, and kinesthetic learners have access to a variety of computer-based activities that are well suited to their preferred learning styles. As students perform diverse tasks with the computer, they broaden their repertoire of metacognitive, cognitive, and affective learning strategies (Bickel and Truscello, 1996). Research by Falk and Carlson (1991) indicates that use of computer-based multimedia leads to enhanced learning on criteria such as acquisition of content, development of skills, efficiency of learning, and satisfaction with instruction.

Bruder, Buchsbaum, Hill, and Orlando (1992) report on the work of Rich Miyagawa, a high school teacher at Blair High School in Pasadena, California, who has 312 Hispanic, Vietnamese, Chinese, Japanese, Filipino, Indonesian, and Polish students in his program using a common language—multimedia—to interact with concepts from the core curriculum while learning English. Miyagawa pairs incoming students with little knowledge of English with a second student who speaks their native language. Within a few days these newcomers are participating in the development of multimedia projects in high school content areas and beginning to try out their English. He reports rapid growth in English writing and reading skills to the extent that his students are now responsible for electronically publishing the school newspaper.

Research by Mergendoller and Pardo (1991) at the Davidson Middle School in San Rafael, California, exemplifies the sort of interactive, multicultural, multimedia technology environments possible. This report describes the second year of a program in which children from different cultural backgrounds and with differing abilities and perspectives work together using technology to enhance their thinking and learning. Children work in heterogeneous groups using a variety of technologies, including videodisc, camcorders, and computers, within an integrated English, history, and multimedia course. Observations of this eighth-grade class suggest some of the reasons the program has been successful in supporting students whose first language is not English. Factors include (1) a well-defined student-centered approach to teaching; (2) the use of complementary staff expertise through team teaching; (3) a schedule that provides longer class periods for student work and instruction; (4) a constant attempt to tailor class assignments and instructional interactions to encourage student interest and motivation; and (5) a wide range of tasks that vary in their cognitive, social, and procedural complexity. In addition, time and support were provided for teachers to become their own multimedia curriculum developers (Connelly and Clanandin, 1988).

In more recent times, multimedia learning environments have moved to the World Wide Web, where it is becoming easier for students to participate in multimedia and hypermedia learning environments. Li and Hart (1996) found that multimedia qualities of the World Wide Web could be utilized to create an electronic ESL magazine for intermediate English language learners that has substantial advantages over its paper counterpart. The communications between editors and writers and the posting of new material can be done more quickly and with less effort. Color pictures, audio, and even video can be just as readily and economically presented as text, and, most important, the electronic version can build a wide audience without large promotional expenses.

Willetts (1992), in a review of technology and second language learning, noted that although the computer has many advantages for enhancing language learning, connecting it to other technologies multiplies its benefits. Different types of technologies support different aspects of language learning—for example, audiocassettes for listening skills. Interactive videodisc systems provide an ideal environment for practicing all language skills, including speaking, listening, writing, and reading.

In their visionary book, *Brave New Schools,* Cummins and Sayers (1997) demonstrate the power of the Internet to build not only technological literacy but also cultural and critical literacy. Cultural literacy, according to the authors, "focuses on the particular content or knowledge that is required to understand texts or social situations" (p. 88), whereas critical literacy focuses literacy learning around issues related to power. Work in critical literacy was the focus of Friere's cultural circles, mentioned earlier in the chapter. The authors go on to describe eight global learning projects in which multilingual and multinational teachers and students develop cultural and critical literacy as they collaboratively address pressing world problems, such as the need to deal with racial and religious prejudice. One example involving how the words of a teenager living in a Croatian refugee camp are received and reacted to by many different young people around the world demonstrates the power of authentic audiences and real problems for building literacy.

Although many teachers of second language learners may not want to begin by using the Internet to participate in large, global projects, there are many opportunities to participate in smaller projects and even to simply share collaborative work with one other teacher. English learners from two different communities can, for example, use computer applications such as spreadsheets to gather and analyze pollution conditions in their communities. They can then employ the Internet to discuss their findings and publish a collaborative report with students from different parts of the world, or sister schools across continents can communicate electronically simply to discuss daily happenings in their schools and communities.

In summary, technology can provide students with language experiences as they move through the various stages of language acquisition. Beginning with the use of multimedia to provide comprehensible input in the preproduction stage, students progress to programs that require limited responses, and in the more advanced stages, use their second language as they manipulate technology to solve a problem, complete a task, or communicate with real audiences around the world. Not only telecommunications activities but also interactive video and simulation programs of real-life experiences foster critical thinking and problem solving. It is through such technology-based experiences that students develop communicative competence by using English both productively and receptively in unrehearsed contexts.

Progress has been made recently in the area of integrating technology to better serve diverse students, including the second language learner. Chisolm (1996), for example, has developed a set of principles for integrating technology in the multicultural classroom. As the demographics of classrooms change and include growing numbers of students for whom English is not their first language, teachers face the increasingly complex task of integrating technology with principles of second language learning and multicultural education. This book is an attempt to make the complexity of this task easier for practicing teachers, pre-service students, and the university educators who teach them. In conclusion, the use of technology to support research, communication, and productivity has great potential for assisting language learning. The benefits of computer-based technology for second language instruction constitute a compelling argument for comprehensive teacher education in the classroom use of technology.

Classroom Scenarios

What do exemplary classrooms utilizing technology for language learning look like?

In the following section, we share our experiences in working with evolving learning environments at different educational levels: an elementary bilingual multiage classroom; a middle school social studies classroom in a low-income border school, and two academic writing classes for English language learners at a small private university. Following these scenarios we will examine what attributes all of these classrooms have in common as they relate to effective second language teaching strategies supported by technology. Throughout the book we will use scenarios to help the reader visualize the effective use of technology for learning.

Computers Are Elementary

In Cissy Lujan-Pincomb's bilingual class, all of her third-, fourth-, or fifth-grade students are either *techno-pals* or *techno-pros*. Techno-pros are students who have mastered the use of technology to complete challenging assignments involving the use of spreadsheets, Internet searches, desktop publishing, and multimedia tools to demonstrate their knowledge of the elementary curriculum. They will partner with students new to technology—the techno-pals. Of course, as these experienced student technology teachers move on to middle school, their students will complete the performance tasks assessments that will allow them to become the official techno-pros ready to mentor new students. Every student has a computer partner and the teacher has enough skilled students that using the computer becomes a class responsibility, not something she has to do while facilitating learning for both her English- and Spanish-speaking students.

Ms. Lujan-Pincomb has mastered the complex task of providing a rich and challenging learning environment to her multiage bilingual students through the use of technology and a project-center approach to learning. At the root of her success is the educational philosophy and practice she developed long before she discovered computers. She believes that learning occurs in a social context and that children learn best when they are allowed to construct meaning through challenging individual and group work. She uses a student-centered, task-based approach, where the emphasis is on completing work to solve problems. The classroom activities require cooperation and avoid the competitive, individualistic focus of traditional test-based classrooms.

The students were studying insects. They all had to pretend they were out of the classroom and had discovered a new insect. The task of the techno-pros was to help their pals use KidPix software to draw their insects with all the appropriate parts, label the parts, and name their insect. As part of an action research project, Lujan-Pincomb (1998) recorded the comments of the techno-pals: "Wow!" "I really like my rainbow bug"; "My bug has compound eyes and the proboscis is so cool." Later in the week the techno-pros helped their partners explore the Iowa State University Entomology website and find three answers to questions they had about a real insect. They were also supposed to print a picture of their insect if they could find one.

Ms. Lujan-Pincomb asked the techno-pals how their lesson on the computer was. One pal replied, "It was cool. I found a neat picture of my mosquito. I did not know they saw your skin and put their spit in you so it won't clog the blood." Her techno-pro commented, "It's not clog, it's clot. It is saliva, not spit, that keeps your blood from clotting."

Ms. Lujan-Pincomb debriefed her techno-pros after a teaching session asking how it went that day working with the Internet:

"I thought it was perfect until my pal thought we were on Grolier's or something."

"Yeah, how do you explain that it's not like a CD or something?"

"I told my pal it was like a phone call to someone real far, but better, because you always get a picture with the words, and they are always at home."

"They didn't get to talk to the astronauts like we did, or R. L. Stien, so they don't know how it works. Hey, Ms. Pincomb, that's it. Can we do like a chat with an expert or email or something so they get it?"

What rich language and learning for an elementary bilingual classroom!

Multimedia at the Middle School

In Sheila Hills's seventh-grade class at Sierra Middle School in Las Cruces, New Mexico, a fourth of her students speak only Spanish, a fourth speak only English, and the other half, as is typical in this border community, speak both English and Spanish at varying developmental levels. Yet all of her students speak a common language—multimedia. Juan, who arrived in the middle school yesterday, sits with his new friend, Sam, and two other students from Mexico, who had been in the school's technology-enhanced sheltered English program for several months and now have a good grasp of beginning English.

This group of four, like the other groups of children, is gathered around one of the five computers in the classroom. Their task is to use a computer-based multimedia authoring program called *Point of View* to create an original presentation on the first president of the United States. The program contains images of Washington's childhood, his years of schooling and adolescence, as well as the years spent fighting in the revolution and establishing the first presidency.

Juan and the three others in his group browsed through many different images related to Washington's life and work. They had to decide what images to use and in what order. Thinking and practice in English occurred continuously. As the students worked together, they began to value each other's strengths, seeing that they could be used to complete the assigned project—a slide show on Washington using a multimedia tool. It was soon apparent that some students were especially good at the technology, able to use the program efficiently, while others could draw, write, or organize the group activity to meet their goal. Unlike traditional classrooms in which teachers hope for similar levels of abilities in their students, the instructional model that emerged around multimedia valued diversity and required cooperation, not competition.

Because the school supported bilingual approaches, students in the group who are more comfortable in Spanish can create text boxes and type in Spanish, while a second text box presents the same information in English, supporting literacy in both languages. Students used a microphone to add sound and voice narrative, and adding their own drawings as well as graphics from other programs. They have an evaluation rubric that they used during the process to make sure they met all the goals: Were there interactive buttons that worked? Was the information accurate, spelled correctly and grammatically correct? When possible, was more than one point of view represented? The teacher had developed the first rubrics for the students, and as they gained experience in assessing their work, she asked them to help develop assessment rubrics for new projects. The students were all actively involved in the learning task, which required thinking and communication without demanding high initial levels of English.

A few weeks earlier, one of us had been in this same classroom as students were finishing up a paired task involving creating a multimedia map presentation related to their chosen inventors that they had researched. The task involved researching an inventor using both print and previously chosen Internet sites. Students then used a multimedia program that contained maps to create a presentation that showed where their inventor was born and had lived and worked and included links to different pages that showed off her or his inventions and their importance in the world. The same intense concentration was present, as well as a willingness to stay in during lunch and work through recess. What was most amazing to the teacher was the number of students who asked to go to the library and to get additional print information about their inventor. Many of these were students who did not usually want to spend time in reference books.

Like the teacher in the first scenario, both of these teachers were also participating in a university/public school professional development project in which teams of teachers with the help of university professors and graduate students assisted themselves in designing rich learning environments for their students using technology. We had also observed this classroom prior to the professional development intervention about a year before. At that time this same teacher was still using a lecture approach, although attempting to shelter instruction as much as possible for her English language learners. Many of the students, especially the ones who didn't understand English, were restless and doing other things like drawing in their notebooks or looking out the window. What a difference expanded instructional strategies and a project-based approach to learning and technology were making.

About These K–12 Teachers

The teachers mentioned in these first two scenarios, Cissy Lujan-Pincomb and Sheila Hills, were both part of the Nuestra Tierra Project, a two-year effort supported by former phone company USWEST in which teachers and university researchers worked together to see what would happen if teachers were fully supported in integrating technology in their classrooms in constructivist and culturally relevant ways. Teachers reported increased use of expanded instructional strategies, confidence in using the technology, and increased use of student and community resources in the curriculum. In-depth interviews over the project detailed the teachers' growth from anxious computer users to confident technology integrators. Detailed findings from that project can be found in Wiburg, Montoya, and Sandin (1999).

Combining Collaborative Projects and Individualized Practice

The next two scenarios take place in computer-assisted ESL writing classes at a small private university. The international students in Maru Mercado's intermediate-level ESL writing class are there to improve their English skills in order to begin undergraduate or graduate degree programs at the university. Some students are composing or revising their compositions on the computers located on each desk, while others are writing letters that they will send electronically to university ESL students in Mexico. Through this exchange they hope to learn more about Mexican culture while increasing their grammar and writing skills. Today they are asking their Mexican email pals for more specific details about the Mayan culture that they had described in their last message.

Another small group of students gather around one computer as they explore an on-line database on the Mayan Empire. Working with this interactive program, each student has adopted the character of either a member of an archeological expedition in the Mayan region or a native of that area. The students can be heard debating issues about preserving Mayan artifacts from the perspectives of the characters they are playing. Their research will be material for a class play and for a pamphlet on the Mayan people that their class is designing, writing, and publishing as part of the writing process they engage in each week. Outside of class, students work at their own speed and competency level with grammar software that focuses on the specific grammar errors they made in their writing.

This computer-supported writing and grammar class provides students both a functional environment where they work collaboratively on tasks using telecommunications, on-line databases, and word processing, and that provides opportunities for individualized computer-based skill development. Ms. Mercado realizes that her students write more clearly and in more detail when communicating with a real audience of their Mexican peers than when they are just doing a writing assignment to turn in to her. Her students have discovered that they will have to give additional explanations to their electronic pen pals if the meaning of their writing is not clear to them the first time. Ms. Mercado also recognizes that when her students are engaged in a task-based research project, they not only use English in their final report but they must also constantly communicate and negotiate with each other in order to complete the project.

The interesting thing about the use of grammar software in this class is that the specific software selections grew out of the teacher's individual diagnosis of each student's writing during the revision and editing stages of the writing process. Students are therefore able to practice problematic structures that appear within the context of their own writing and avoid the tedium or stress of learning the "grammar rule of the day," which they may already know or may not yet be ready to tackle.

Word Processing and Language Negotiation

In another intermediate writing class next door, Geoffrey Walker is showing his students a brochure on cultural and entertainment attractions in San Diego that his writing class from the previous quarter had published. He is explaining to his students that their class will be producing the same kind of publication to send back to relatives in their home countries. He shares with them a wide assortment of pamphlets he has brought to class on each of the various attractions in the city. As the students discuss the sights of San Diego, they share information about the main points of interest and cultural and entertainment events in their native hometowns. The students are quite engaged in these materials as they divide into groups of four, with each group being assigned one particular attraction to report on. Each group will have to read its pamphlet and decide which key features to present. With limited space allotted for each attraction in the class brochure, the groups must read for main ideas and summarize the material from their pamphlet that they want featured in the brochure. Each group will also select or draw a picture that best depicts their attraction to scan into the final brochure on San Diego. Over the next week, the students will compose on the word processor, do peer reviews of each other's writing on the computer, and desktop publish their final products.

Mr. Walker understands the importance of students having to use the language in order to accomplish a task. In the process of working collaboratively and negotiating with each other about the form and content of their writing, they are using and improving all of their language skills.

In both of these college writing classes, the students are evaluated on work they accomplish at each stage of their writing, from the initial brainstorming with computer-generated prompts to the desktop publishing of their compositions.

All four of these scenarios demonstrate insights into successful teaching practices utilizing technology for English language learners. While these examples range from K–12 through college level, they contain common attributes of successful technology-enhanced language learning environments.

Designing Learning Opportunities for Second Language Learners

What do the environments described in these scenarios have in common? What attributes seem to exist across these different settings that relate to learning language and content with the support of technology?

Having read the scenarios and knowing that research findings supported their effectiveness, what do you think were the important factors in the successful use of technology in these classrooms? You, as a reader, might want to take a few minutes to write down on a piece of paper your perceptions of what seemed important for learning and language development. In the following section we will reflect on the classroom scenarios and describe what we consider to be essential attributes in the design of language learning environments.

Attributes of a Successful Technology-Enhanced Language Learning Environment (TELLE)

We recognize that these attributes are overlapping, but we focus on them individually in order to provide a framework for the development of teaching strategies.

1. Provides interaction, communicative activities, and real audiences. Students working on group projects in Mr. Walker's and Ms. Mercado's college ESL classes were engaged in tasks that required that they interact with materials, the computer, and each other. When students in Ms. Mercado's class communicated electronically with students in Mexico, they discovered how precisely one needs to communicate one's ideas, especially when describing places and events that are unfamiliar to the reader. In the process of writing to a real audience from a different culture, they had to provide details in order to accurately communicate their messages. When students in this same class used an on-line database for background information on the Mayan culture, interactive features of that program allowed them to select questions that they wanted answered on that topic.

Mr. Walker's students had to negotiate with each other about which features of their cultural or entertainment attractions they wanted to present in the class brochure. In making these choices, they were forced to express their opinions and give feedback to others in the group—two important ingredients of interaction and communication. Chapter 2 explores the role of interaction and authentic audiences in communicative language teaching.

2. Supplies comprehensible input. English language learners need to be exposed to a sufficient amount of language that is understandable to them. While the four walls of a traditional classroom can limit the exposure students receive, technology capabilities can play a major role in expanding their language experiences. In some cases, like with the middle school students, the input was made more comprehensible through the use of a well-designed multimedia authoring program such as the point-of-view presentation on President Washington. The on-line database on the Mayan Empire brought information into the classroom that students would not otherwise be exposed to, and through the use of maps, pictures, and other graphics, did it in a manner that made the material comprehensible to the students. Students at the elementary school had the opportunity to explore pictorial websites that helped them learn about insects. The key role comprehensible input plays in language acquisition is more fully discussed in Chapters 2 and 4.

3. Supports development of cognitive abilities. Technology offers students new tools that encourage cognitive development. In the university ESL classes, students used cognitive skills to research their topic, rewrite their information from essay to a play format, design layouts for their brochures, and write, peer edit, and publish their final products. Students in Ms. Lujan-Pincomb's class developed research skills as they electronically explored Iowa State's Entomology website to find answers to their questions on insects. In a debriefing session with her students about their learning, the techno-pros reflected on how they explained to their peers exactly what the Internet was and how it operated. These students were using their metacognitive skills to analyze how their friends learned this concept. Using technology to support development of cognitive skills and promote critical thinking and inquiry-based learning is fully explored in Chapters 3, 5, and 6.

4. Utilizes task-based and problem-solving activities. Task-based learning requires students to share information and work collaboratively to complete a project or solve a problem. In each of the classroom scenarios, the students were engaged in task-based learning that encouraged language use. The elementary students worked in pairs on the task of drawing insects and labeling their parts. The middle school students used an authoring program to design a multimedia map presentation showing the homelands of selected inventors. One class of college students conducted research, produced a pamphlet, and wrote a play on the Mayan people, while their peers in another class collaborated on a brochure describing the various tourist sights in San Diego. Chapters 2 and 6 discuss task-based, problem-solving, and inquiry-based language learning in detail.

5. Provides sheltering techniques to support language and academic development. In all of these examples the teachers used a variety of different sheltering strategies. Ms. Lujan-Pincomb used drawing software to help her students *re-present* their bugs in an alternative form. She used an organized website about insects to provide contextualization for their searches for insect information. Students in Sheila Hills's classroom used multimedia as a form of text *re-presentation*, improved their metacognitive abilities as they made decisions about which images and text to use and in which order, and used a commercial program to provide a multimedia context for the life of the first president.

Mr. Walker modeled for his ESL students exactly what their final brochure on attractions in San Diego would look like. Although this class would be describing different sights than the last class, by showing the students the brochure created by a previous class, he helped them develop a mental picture of the final product they would be creating. Thus, his students were better able to clearly understand the task and the role each group would play in the class project. This teacher also bridged to the prior knowledge of the students by asking them to describe cultural sites and entertainment events in their own countries. Notice that all of this support was given to students before they even began reading or writing. Ms. Mercado encouraged her students to use and present the same language in more than one form. For example, students transformed the on-line text that they were reading about the Mayans into a play in which each student took on the role of a character at a Mayan archeological site. These and other sheltering strategies are explored in Chapter 3.

6. Is student-centered and promotes student autonomy. The technology-enhanced environment and the curriculum support student autonomy and developmental growth through each stage of language development. Vygotsky's zone of proximal development is well supported in the case of Ms. Lujan-Pincomb's classrooms where slightly more capable students help younger students modify their language.

The computer offers teachers the ability to individualize grammar assignments based on errors made in each student's writing. Ms. Mercado used a wide assortment of grammar software to personalize assignments in order to address the particular needs of each student in her university-level writing class. Students had the autonomy to work with these programs at their own speed and level outside of class time. The Spanish-speaking students in Ms. Lujan-Pincomb's class were able to use multimedia to create text boxes in Spanish and a narrative in their native language as well as English. Aspects of student-centered learning are fully explored in Chapters 2 and 7.

7. Facilitates focused development of English language skills. Successful language learning classes promote the development of all English language skills— listening, speaking, reading, and writing—and provide opportunities for focused practice of these skills. This is especially true for higher-level and college ESL students who frequently have to be concerned with the rate of language skill acquisition as well as proficiency level. The university ESL classes mentioned in the scenarios used the writing-process approach to developing all language skills with emphasis on writing. This process is greatly facilitated by computer functions that allow students to compose, peer edit, and easily revise and edit their writing. Students can use selected software to improve troublesome grammar structures and practice paragraph and essay construction.

In Mr. Walker's class, students practiced the academic tasks of determining main ideas, paraphrasing, and summarizing. These are typically difficult skills for intermediate and advanced ESL students to develop. By limiting the space available for each group's writing submission to the class brochure, the teacher clearly demonstrated the function of these skills in a real-life situation. The tasks that these students were working on required intense listening and speaking practice focused around the computer as students questioned, clarified, and negotiated, in order to complete the class projects. Chapters 4 and 5 examine how technology facilitates focused development of English language skills.

8. Uses multiple modalities to support various learning styles and strategies. Because of the variety of ways in which learning can occur, students with different learning styles employ a wide array of strategies as they approach the complex task of learning a second language. Teachers need to design learning environments that utilize technology to support multiple ways of learning and demonstrating knowledge, much in the same way as the teachers featured in the scenarios. With its multimedia capabilities, technology offers aural, visual, tactile, and kinesthetic learners a variety of computer-based activities that are well suited to their preferred learning styles. For instance, Ms. Lujan-Pincomb's elementary

ments characterized by the attributes presented in this chapter and described more fully in later chapters.

Overview of the Rest of the Book

The rest of the book is organized around the various approaches and strategies used in the second language learning classroom. Each chapter begins with a chapter overview followed by a theoretical framework that integrates language acquisition and learning technology theories relevant to the chapter topic. Guiding questions and sample activities utilizing technology and demonstrating applications of theory are used throughout the chapters. Key ideas in each chapter are summarized, followed by suggested additional teaching activities and a list of resources that support the instructional approaches in the chapter.

The remainder of the chapters (2 through 8) discuss a variety of theories, approaches, and instructional practices of second language teaching that are supported through integration with technology.

Chapter 2 describes the communicative approach to language instruction and explores ways in which technology supports task-based learning.

Chapter 3 examines the integration of technology in content-based teaching to support the academic development of English language learners.

Chapter 4 demonstrates the use of technology to provide focused practice for the development of oral communication skills in English.

Chapter 5 explores the use of technology to teach reading and writing skills and examines a variety of software and websites available for this purpose

Chapter 6 discusses utilizing technology to promote critical thinking and inquiry-based learning.

Chapter 7 addresses the role of culture in language learning and the use of technology to develop communities of learners and facilitate learning in multicultural and multilingual settings.

Chapter 8 studies computer-supported assessment methods for second language teaching.

Conclusion

We began the chapter with two experiential life stories that were turning points in terms of realizing in a deep way the potential of technology for language learning. A historical overview of technology and its use and misuse in language learning classrooms was provided followed by a discussion of current uses of technology for second language teaching. Four classroom scenarios at various levels provided a rich context for discussing the desired attributes of technology-enhanced language learning environments. Twelve attributes considered essential to the success of technology-enhanced learning environments were discussed, citing examples from classroom scenarios in Chapter 1.

Summary of Key Ideas

1. Historically, theories and practices of second language teaching and developments in technology and educational computing have paralleled and complimented each other.

2. There have been many changes in the use of technology in language learning classrooms. The general direction of the change was from a behaviorally based computer as a teaching machine to the use of computers as communication devices.

3. Information-management tools (word processing, telecommunications and databases, on-line and off-line) and computer-based multimedia and Web environments show promise as successful learning environments for second language learners.

4. Research suggests that drill and practice software is not always effective with second language learning students. However, programs that provide focused practice based on the individual learner's particular needs can facilitate language development.

5. With the growth of multimedia capability, learner-controlled hypermedia environments have much to offer the language learner.

6. Scenarios are provided as a way of showing rich language learning environments in which students range from young children to college level.

7. Twelve attributes considered essential to the success of technology-enhanced language learning environments are discussed, citing examples from classroom scenarios in Chapter 1. Such environments
   a. Provide interaction, communicative activities, and real audience
   b. Supply comprehensible input
   c. Support development of cognitive abilities
   d. Utilize task-based and problem-solving activities
   e. Provide sheltering techniques to support language and academic development
   f. Are student-centered and promote student autonomy
   g. Facilitate focused development of English language skills
   h. Use multiple modalities to support various learning styles and strategies
   i. Support collaborative learning
   j. Meet affective needs of students
   k. Foster understanding and appreciation of the target and native cultures
   l. Provide appropriate feedback and assessment

8. Research indicates that teachers do not have the training needed to integrate technology into their teaching. A strong professional development program is needed to prepare teachers to design effective experiences for second language learners using technology.

References

Bickel, B., and Truscello, D. (1996, Autumn). TESOL technology: New opportunities for learning: Styles and strategies with computers. *TESOL Journal 6*, (1): 15–19.

Bruder, I., Buchsbaum, H., Hill, M., and Orlando, L. (1992). School reform: Why you need technology to get there. *Electronic Learning* 11(8): 22–28.

Bruner, J. (1986). *Actual Minds, Possible Worlds.* Cambridge, MA: Harvard University Press.

Bull, G., and Cochran, P. (1991, April). Learner-based tools. *The Computing Teacher.* International Society for Technology in Education, Oregon.

Butler-Pascoe, M. E. (1995). A national survey of the integration of technology into TESOL master's programs. *Technology and Teacher Education Annual* (pp. 98–101). Charlottesville, VA: Association for the Advancement of Computers in Education.

Carey, D., Carey, R., Willis, D., and Willis, J. (Eds.). (1993). *Technology and Teacher Education Annual.* Charlottesville, VA: Technology and Teacher Education Annual.

Chisolm, I. M. (1998). Six elements for technology integration in multicultural classrooms. *Journal of Information Technology Education* 7, 247–268.

Cohen, M., and Reil, M. (1986, August). Computer networks: Creating real audiences for students' writing. La Jolla, CA: UCSD, *Interactive Technology Laboratory Report no. 15.*

Coley, R. J., Cradler J., and Engel, P. K. (1997). Computers and classroom: The status of technology in U.S. schools. ETS Policy Information Report. [On-line]. Available: http://www.ets.org/research/pic/compclass.html.

Collis, B. (1990). *The Best of Research Windows: Trends and Issues in Educational Computing.* Eugene, OR: International Society for Technology in Education.

Connelly, M., and Clanindin, J. (1988). *Teachers as Curriculum Planners: Narratives of Experience.* New York: Teachers College Press.

Coughlin, J. M. (1989). *Recent Developments in Interactive and Communicative CAL: Hypermedia and "Intelligent" Systems.* Washington, DC: Center for Applied Linguistics. (ERIC Document Reproduction Service No. ED 313909).

Cuban, L. (1986). *Teachers and Machines: The Classroom Use of Technology since 1920.* New York: Teachers College.

Cummins, J. (1998). Using text as input for computer-supported language learning. *CAELL Journal, 9* (1): 3–10.

Cummins, J., and Sayers, D. (1997). *Brave New Schools.* New York: St. Martin's Press.

Curran, C. (1972). *Counseling-learning: A Whole Person Model for Education.* New York: Grune and Stratton.

Curran, C. (1982). Community language learning. In Robert W. Blair (Ed.), *Innovative Approaches to Language Teaching.* Rowley, MA: Newbery House Publishers.

Dede, C. (1996). Emerging technologies and distributed learning. *American Journal of Distance Education* 10 (2): 4–36.

Dell, A., and Disdier, A. (1994). Teaching future teachers to enhance teaching and learning with technology. In J. Willis, Bernard Robin, and D. Willis (Eds.*), Technology and Teacher Education Annual, 1994* (pp. 178–182). Charlottesville, VA: Association for the Advancement of Computing in Education.

Dutton, W. H., Peltu, M., and Bruce, M. (1999). *Society on the Line: Information Politics in the Digital Age.* New York: Oxford University Press.

Dutton, W. H., Rogers, M. E., and Jun, S. (1987). Diffusion and social impacts of personal computers. *Communication Research* 14 (2): 219–250.

Educational Testing Services (ETS). (1989). *TOEFL Test of Written English.* Princeton, NJ.

Falk, D., and Carlson, H. (1992, September). Learning to teach with multimedia. *T.H.E. Journal,* 96–101.

Fazzinni, (1990). Using the computer to increase academic, vocational, and skills of jr. high occupational students. In A. Freedman (Ed.), *Yes, I Can Action Projects to Resolve Equity Issues in Education.* Eugene, OR: International Society for Technology in Education (ISTE).

Fosnot, C. (1989). *Enquiring Teachers Enquiring Learners: A Constructivist Approach to Teaching.* New York: Teachers College Press.

Fulton, K. (1993). Teaching matters: The role of technology in education. *Technology and Teacher Education Annual 1993.* Charlottesville, VA: Association for the Advancement of Computers in Education.

Hativa, N. (1988). Computer-based drill and practice in arithmetic: Widening the gap between high-achieving and low-achieving students. *American Educational Research Journal* 25 (3): 366–397.

Hunt, N., and Pritchard, R. (1993). Technology and language minority students: Implications for teacher education. In D. Carey, R. Carey, D. Willis, and J. Willis (Eds.), *Technology and Teacher Education Annual, 1993* (pp. 25–27). Charlottesville, VA: Association for the Advancement of Computing in Education.

International Society for Technology in Education (ISTE). (1999). *Will New Teachers Be Prepared to Teach in a Digital Age? A Publication of the Milken Exchange on Education Technology.* Eugene, OR: Author.

Johnson, D. (1985). *Using Computers to Promote Development of English as a Second Language.* Unpublished report. New York: Carnegie Corporation.

Krashen, S. (1989). *Language Acquisition and Language Education.* New York: Prentice-Hall International.

Levy, D., Navon, D., and Shapira, R. (1991). Computers and class: Computers and inequity in Israeli schools. *Urban Education* 25 (4): 483–499.

Li, R. C. (1997). Getting started in distributing multimedia ESL materials on the Web. In T. Boswood (Ed.), *New Ways of Using Computers in Language Teaching* (pp. 196–198) Alexandria, VA: TESOL.

Li, R., & Hart, R. S. (1996, Winter). What can the world wide web offer ESL teachers? *TESOL Journal:* 5–10.

Lujan-Pincomb, C. (1998). Unpublished action research report. New Mexico State University.

McCloskey, M. (1992). Turn on units: English as a second language content area curriculum in math, science, and computer science for grades K–6. (ERIC Document Reproduction Service No. ED 347090).

Mehan, H., Miller-Souviney, B. and Riel, M. (1986). Knowledge of text editing and the development of literacy skills. In T. Cannings and S. Brown (Eds), *The Information Age Classroom: Using the Computer as a Tool.* Irvine, CA: Franklin, Beedle, and Associates.

Mergendoller, J., and Pardo, Elly. (1991). An evaluation of the MacMagic program at Davidson Middle School. (ERIC Document Reproduction Service No. ED 351143).

Meskill, C. (1991). Language learning strategies advice: A study of the effects of on-line messaging. *System* 19 (3): 277–287.

Moses, Y. M. (1991). Listening interactively. *Computer Education* 17: 293–300.

Nord, J. (1986). Language as an interactive process. *Nagoya University of Commerce Bulletin* 31: 275–316. (ERIC Document Reproduction Service No. ED 284419).

Norton, P., and Wiburg, K. (1998). *Teaching with Technology.* Ft. Worth, TX: Harcourt-Brace.

Nunan, D. (1999). *Second Language Teaching and Learning.* Boston: Heinle and Heinle Publishers.

Office of Technology Assessment (OTA). (1995). *Teachers and Technology: Making the Connection.* (Publication No. OTA-HER-616). Washington DC: U.S. Government Printing Office.

Phinney, M. (1989). Computers, composition, and second language teaching. In M. Pennington (Ed.), *Teaching Languages with Computers: The State of the Art.* La Jolla, CA: Athelstan Publishers.

Riel, M. (1985). Quoted in H. Mehan, Computers in classrooms: A quasi-experiment in guided change. Final Report. (ERIC Document Reproduction Service No. ED 292460).

Roblyer, M. D. (1989). The impact of microcomputer-based instruction on teaching and learning: A review of recent research. (ERIC Clearinghouse on Information Resources EDO-!R-89-10).

Sampson, D., and Gregory, J. (1991). A technological primrose path? ESL students and computer-assisted writing programs. *College ESL* 1 (2): 29–36.

Sayers, D. (1991). Cross-cultural exchanges between students from the same culture: A portrait of an emerging relationship mediated by technology. *Canadian Modern Language Review* 47 (4): 23–24.

Sayers, D., and Brown, K. (1998). Freire, Freinet and engaged distancing. *CAELL Journal* 9 (1): 23–24.

Skeele, M. (1993). Technology and diversity: Resolving computer equity issues through multicultural education. In D. Carey, R. Carey, D. Willis, and J. Willis (Eds.), *Technology and Teacher Education Annual, 1993* (pp. 14–18). Charlottesville, VA: Association for the Advancement of Computing in Education.

Snow, M., and Brinton, D. (1988). Content-based language instruction: Investigating the effectiveness of the adjunct model. *TESOL Quarterly* 22: 4.

Staples, K., and Lathrop, A. (1993) Subject-matter technology resources for limited English-proficient students. Available from the California Computer Software Clearinghouse, California State University, Long Beach, 1250 Bellflower Boulevard, Long Beach, CA 90840 or on-line from CORE (California On-line Resources in Education).

Stevens, V. (1989). A direction for CALL: From behavioristic to humanistic courseware. In M. Pennington (Ed.), *Teaching Languages with Computers: The State of the Art*. La Jolla, CA: Athelstan Publishers.

Tella, S. (1992). Talking Shop via e-mail: A thematic and linguistic analysis of electronic mail communication. Research Report 99. Available from University of Helsinki, Department of Teacher Education, Ratakatu A,00120 Helsinki, Finland and ERIC Document Reproduction Service No. ED 352015.

Trotter, A. (1996, June). The great divide. Closing the gap between technology haves and have nots. Electronic School. [On-line]. Available: http://www.electronicschool.com/o696fl.html.

Underwood, J. (1989). On the edge: Intelligent CALL in the 1990s. *Computers and the Humanities* 23: 71–84.

Wetzel, K., and Chisholm, I. (1998). An evaluation of technology integration in teacher education for bilingual and English as a second language education majors. *Journal of Research on Computing in Education* 30 (4): 379–397.

Wetzel, K., and Chisholm, I. (1998). An evaluation of technology integration in teacher education for bilingual and English as a second language education majors. *Journal of Research on Computing in Education,* 30: 379–397.

Wenglinsky, H. (1998). *Does It Compute? The Relationship between Educational Technology And Student Achievement in Mathematics*. Princeton, NJ: Educational Testing Service. Accessed March 6, 2002 from ftp://ftp.ets.org/pub/res/technolog.pdf.

Wiburg, K., Montoya, N., and Sandin, J. (1999) Nuestra Tierra: A university/public school technology integration project. *Journal of Educational Computing Research 21* (2): 183–219.

Wiggens, G., and McTighe, J. (1998). *Understanding by Design*. Alexandria, VA: Association for Supervision and Curriculum Development.

Willetts, K. (1992). Technology and second language learning. *ERIC Digest*. (ERIC Document Reproduction Service No. ED 350883).

Woodrow, J. (1993). The implementation of computer technology in pre-service teaching. In D. Carey, R. Carey, D. Willis, and J. Willis (Eds.), *Technology and Teacher Education Annual 1993* (pp. 368–373). Charlottesville, VA: Association for the Advancement of Computing in Education.

2

Communicative Language Teaching

Chapter Overview

Communicative language teaching (CLT) has a plethora of definitions according to the particular researchers and practitioners you consult, but there are some widely accepted principles and characteristics on which most proponents of this approach agree. The primary goal of CLT is to help students develop communicative competence in the target language. It focuses on the structural and communicative aspects of language and values the use of language for purposeful communication.

The following chapter discusses the theoretical construct of communicative competence, investigates various interpretations and principles of communicative language teaching as contrasted with the structural methods that preceded it, and considers ways in which technology, ranging from tape-recorders to websites, can be used to support this highly interactive approach to language teaching. Numerous classroom applications are provided along with an in-depth description of the use of technology to support the communicative elementary schools in the United States and the Netherlands.

Communicative Competence

Communicative competence has been a widely discussed construct in the second language acquisition literature since the early 1970s and provides the theoretical framework for communicative language teaching (CLT). Hymes (1971, 1972) first proposed the term *communicative competence* to characterize appropriate use of language in social contexts, while Savignon (1972, 1983) used the term to distinguish between a language learner's mastery of isolated grammar rules and the more complex ability to negotiate meaning and interact with other students (Savignon, 1991).

In their seminal work on this topic, Canale and Swain (1980) defined four components of communicative competence that are required to allow the second language learner to communicate effectively with other speakers of the target (L2) language. The first, *grammatical competence*, refers to the learner's knowledge of the structure of the language, and the second, *discourse competence*, allows the language learner to use knowledge of that grammar system to connect sentences in a meaningful manner. The last two components of communicative competence give insight into the more functional aspects of the language. *Sociolinguistic competence* is based on the knowledge of the social and cultural rules of the L2 environment, whereas *strategic competence* provides strategies such as repetition, hesitation, fillers, guessing, and body language, which serve to compensate for any breakdown in communication.

What are some other views of communicative competence?

Littlewood (1981) further identified four related domains of skill that he claimed constituted a learner's communicative competence. According to Littlewood, the learner must (1) develop a high-skill level in manipulating the linguistic system; (2) be able to recognize the communicative functions of the linguistic forms she or he uses; (3) be capable of communicating meaning in concrete situations and using feedback to evaluate his or her success in conveying his message; and (4) be able to distinguish and use socially acceptable forms of the language.

Over a decade later, Brown (1994) offered a similar definition. He suggested that in its primary form, communicative competence consists of (1) organizational competence (grammatical and discourse); (2) pragmatic competence (functional and sociolinguistic); (3) strategic competence; and (4) psychomotor skills (for example, pronunciation). Brown's (1994) definition of communicative competence is best explained by his observations about its application to classroom practice:

> Given that communicative competence is the goal of a language classroom, then instruction needs to point toward all of its components: organizational, pragmatic, strategic, and psychomotor. Communicative goals are best achieved by giving due attention to language use and not just usage, to fluency and not just accuracy, to authentic language and contexts, and to students' eventual need to apply classroom learning to heretofore unrehearsed contexts in the real world. (p. 29)

What is the potential of technology to support communicative competence?

Technology applications are uniquely suited to support communicative competence (Brown, 1994; Canale and Swain, 1980; Littlewood, 1981; Savignon, 1991). While specific applications provide support for all aspects of communicative competence, including grammatical and discourse competence, new electronic learning environments seem especially appropriate in the areas of pragmatic and strategic competence (Brown, 1994). Furthermore, they fit perfectly with Littlewood's requirements for strategies that help students to recognize the communicative functions of the linguistic forms they use, communicate meaning in concrete situations, and use feedback to evaluate their success in conveying messages.

In short, technology provides powerful contexts for communicative language, whether it involves students gaining cultural literacy (Cummins and Sayers, 1995) through participation in electronic global communities, or the use of rich multimedia environments in which language learners can interpret and create functional conversations and presentations using a variety of media (Buell, 1999) and then evaluate their communication in terms of social appropriateness. Computer-enhanced language learning environments provide multiple opportunities for completing authentic tasks and interacting with authentic audiences. In Egbert and Hanson-Smith's (1999) recent edited book on computer assisted language learning (CALL) environments, about half of the chapters are organized around the use of technology to support interaction, authentic audiences, and authentic tasks—important attributes of communicative language learning environments.

As computers have moved from data processing devices to communicative tools and knowledge environments, growth has occurred in the use of computers for electronic collaborations. Bonk and King (1998) provide an entire taxonomy for computer-based collaborative tools ranging from electronic mail to asynchronous bulletin board systems to synchronous chat rooms. The potential of the computer for language learning is growing as more and more sophisticated tools are being developed to support electronic discourse. Growth is perhaps strongest in the area of communicative language teaching.

Communicative Language Teaching

What changes in theory and methodology of second language teaching led to communicative language teaching?

Regardless of the exact definition of communicative competence, it has become the theoretical foundation for a family of second language teaching approaches that came to be known as communicative language teaching (CLT). As we explore the evolution of communicative language teaching to its present interpretations, we must first examine what is variously termed the notional approach, functional approach, or notional-functional approach that served as a precursor to CLT.

In the 1970s, educators began noticing that many students could produce accurate sentences in the classroom, but could not use them to communicate their ideas in authentic settings. Applied linguists such as Candlin (1976) and Halliday (1973) began to challenge the structural view of language that had so dominated language teaching in the1960s in the form of the audio-lingual method (ALM) and structural curricula. They instead advocated for language teaching to focus on the functional and communicative aspects of language. British linguist D. A. Wilkins (1976) suggested two types of meanings that could serve as the basis for a communicative approach and syllabus: notional meanings that included categories such as duration, location, quantity and frequency, and functional meanings that encompassed categories such as requests, introductions, greetings, and apologies (Johnson and Morrow, 1981). While the notional syllabus overcame many of the problems of the structural syllabus, its application had limitations in developing communicative competence. Widdowson (1979) warned that communication does not occur through notions and functions that are presented as self-contained units of meaning, but rather in situations in which meanings are negotiated through interaction. He saw communicative competence as a "set of strategies or creative procedures" (p. 248) that the learner uses to apply his or her linguistic knowledge in various contexts. He found the notional syllabus lacking in that it left it up to the learner to develop these creative strategies on his or her own. The notional syllabus, according to Widdowson, addressed the components of discourse rather than dealing with the actual discourse itself. He advocated for a more participant view of language that would be centered on the learner and the language he or she used. Since the mid-1970s the notional-functional approach has evolved into the more comprehensive communicative language teaching approach that has as its primary goal the development by the learner of communicative competence in the target language.

What is the communicative language teaching (CLT) approach?

The communicative language teaching approach has been interpreted in various forms over the last three decades depending on the instructional setting and student population. Unlike other methods and approaches in second language teaching, there is no single authority, definitive text, or universally accepted model of CLT. Nonetheless, there are now some widely accepted principles and practices that characterize communicative language teaching. Brown (2000) outlined four fundamental features of CLT:

1. Classroom goals are focused on *all* the components of communicative competence and not restricted to grammatical or linguistic competence.
2. Language techniques are designed to engage learners in the pragmatic, authentic, functional use of language for meaningful purposes. Organizational language forms are not the central focus but rather aspects of language that *enable* the learner to accomplish those purposes.
3. Fluency and accuracy are seen as complementary principles underlying communicative techniques. At times, fluency may have to take on more importance than accuracy in order to keep learners meaningfully engaged in language use.
4. In the communicative classroom, students ultimately have to use the language, productively and receptively, in *unrehearsed* contexts. (p. 266)

To support these principles, CLT utilizes techniques that engage students in authentic, functional uses of language to accomplish real-world tasks. Students are required to negotiate meaning and use language creatively in spontaneous contexts. According to applied linguists Johnson and Marrow (1981), emphasis is placed on purposeful use of language through communicative activities that (1) utilize information gaps in which information that is known to one person is unknown to another; (2) allow speaker autonomy to make choices about what he wishes to say and how; and (3) provide feedback from the interlocutor that allows the speaker to assess whether her or his message was understood.

The CLT approach to language pedagogy represented a clear break in many regards from the more structural approaches to second language pedagogy that had preceded it. During this same time span, the use of the computer as a teaching machine and drill and practice provider has changed to the use of the computer as an interactive communication tool and stimulus for interaction. As Seedman (1995) advocated, the focus in computer-assisted language learning materials is shifting from the software itself to the interaction the software promotes. Thus, computers have become increasingly powerful allies in communicative language teaching. Similarly, the Internet is viewed not only as a provider of skill development websites but as a resource for Web-based, communicative projects. The remainder of this chapter looks at the role technology can play in enhancing communicative language teaching.

How can technology support communicative language teaching?

Different technologies have always played an important role in supporting language teaching beginning in the early days of language labs and instructional television. Graphical images and film clips have long been used extensively for providing stimuli and context for language teaching. Computers are now greatly expanded communication tools, both in terms of their use as part of networked resources and communities, and in terms of an expansion of the types of communicative media available. There is a merging of traditional media technologies (film, video, radio, television), many of which have always been powerful partners for language teaching, with increasingly powerful computers and networks. Expanded and accessible multimedia networked environments provide images, video, sound, and graphics, as well as print, and are becoming more easily available and controllable by teachers and learners. Massive amounts of information are available on virtually any topic, and students can interact with each other around the globe via the World Wide Web. Today's computer-based technologies—including multimedia, email, discussion boards, electronic databases, chat rooms, and teleconferencing capabilities—are ideally suited to support a communicative language teaching approach.

A variety of simple exercises using videos and a VCR exemplify the excellent fit between technology use and strategies for communicative language teaching. Students learning English can be shown an opening scene in an adventure movie, such as *The River Runs Through It*. Then the teacher asks the students to predict what might happen after a certain scene—for example, when the boys launch a boat from the top of a waterfall. She or he can then show the next scene with or without sound and ask for further predictions. One group can be shown the video without sound and asked to make predications about what might be said, while a second group listens only to the sound and tries to figure out what images might be happening in the movie. Other movies show common social interactions, scenes with parents and children interacting, arguments, scenes in school, confirming that all sorts of possibilities exist for observing and analyzing social language via video. Eventually students can make their own videos involving language interactions in social settings and then watch them again and again and even reshoot the scenes in order to analyze the appropriateness of their messages.

Linguists, including Nunan (1988) and Quinn (1984), have provided comparisons of the characteristics of traditional, structural methodologies and communicative approaches. Table 2.1 expands such comparisons to include the many ways in which technology supports the transition to communicative language

TABLE 2.1 *Comparison of Structural Methods and Communicative Language Teaching with Technology Support*

	Structural Methods	Communicative Language Teaching (CLT)	Technology Support of CLT
View of Language			
View of Language	• Structural view of language • Focus on linguistic competence	• Views language as communication • Focus on all aspects of communicative competence: grammatical, discourse, sociolinguistic, and strategic	• Real-life communication with authentic audiences • Email and keypals • Interactive videos • Electronic mail lists • Web discussion boards • Chat rooms • Desktop publishing • Teleconferencing
Language Emphasis	• Linguistic structures and form	• Meaning and form of language	• Combination of collaborative Web-based projects and skill-based software • Form-focused practice within the context of meaningful experiences
Language Skills Emphasized	• Reading and writing	• All skills: listening and speaking, reading and writing	• Interactive videos • Pronunciation software • Teleconferencing • Word processing and desktop publishing of writing • Grammar software and websites • Electronic databases as reading and research resources

TABLE 2.1   *Continued*

	Structural Methods	Communicative Language Teaching (CLT)	Technology Support of CLT
Nature of Discourse	• Drills, exercises, memorized dialogs	• Authentic oral and written language	• Keypals, email, and Web-based local and global projects • Bulletin board discussions • Multimedia presentations • Presentation programs, e.g., *PowerPoint* • Authoring programs, e.g., *Hyper Studio*

Learning Environment and Interactions

	Structural Methods	Communicative Language Teaching (CLT)	Technology Support of CLT
Roles of Teacher/ Student	• T—Presenter of lessons • S—Recipient of information and structured practice	• T—Facilitator of learning • S—Active participant in in one's own learning	• T—Classroom manager and facilitator of technology-enhanced learning • S—User of technology
Classroom Format	• Teacher-fronted	• Pairs, small groups, learning stations	• Task-based/computer-based learning centers • Collaborative pair and small group computer-based projects • Peer and cross-age tutoring with student techno-experts
Learning Environment	• Classroom	• Classroom linked to outside community and world	• Technologically linked to the world through the Web • Technology as source of authentic materials beyond classroom
Nature of Student Interaction	• Primarily student to teacher; also teacher-directed student/ student interactions	• Collaborative with all students and teacher	• Collaborative with students and teachers in classrooms around the world • Increased student autonomy through electronic resources • Student-centered environment

Curriculum, Materials, and Activities

	Structural Methods	Communicative Language Teaching (CLT)	Technology Support of CLT
Goal of Curriculum	• Develop linguistic competence	• Develop communicative competence; effective use of linguistic system	• Technology-enhanced curriculum that facilitates development of both fluency and accuracy
Criteria for Course Content Selection	• Linguistic structures	• Students' personal experiences and communication needs to accomplish goals	• Technology to support real-world needs and experiences

(continued)

TABLE 2.1   *Continued*

	Structural Methods	*Communicative Language Teaching (CLT)*	*Technology Support of CLT*
Types of Activities	• Exercises, text-based, drills, individual work	• Authentic tasks, cooperative activities	• Technology-based tasks and collaborative projects
Types of Materials	• Textbooks; audio tapes	• Authentic writings and literature, computers, videos	• Videos • Computers and software • Authentic, electronic writings and data resources
Assessment	• Tests	• Process and products, portfolios, • Authentic tasks	• Electronic portfolios • Multimedia presentations • Electronic dialogical journals

teaching from the structural methods that preceded it. We will now turn our attention to the role technology can play in three major aspects of CLT: its view of language, the learning environment, and curriculum design.

View of Language

How does technology support language as communication in authentic settings?

Those who follow a communicative language teaching approach view language primarily as communication in real-world settings with a focus on communicative competence. Use of computer-based tools such as email, electronic mail lists, newsgroups, Web discussion boards, and chat rooms in communicative language teaching provides opportunities for students to improve their English skills within a communicative and authentic environment. Email can also be used within the classroom, between the student and teacher, and between students.

Through these Web-based environments, English learners are able to focus on all aspects of communicative competence and participate both productively and receptively in spontaneous contexts. Technology provides many opportunities for real-life communication with authentic audiences. For example, in the process of publishing a school newspaper, students practice all their English skills to word process articles, negotiate the selection of writings and graphics, and desktop publish the final product. In editing their newspaper, students focus on form as a way of expressing meaning and conveying their ideas to the intended readers. To broaden their audience, students taking part in the *Newsday* Project sponsored by Global Schoolhouse (http://www.globalschoolnet.org) write articles to share with students worldwide (see Figure 2.1). Participating classes post articles addressing a

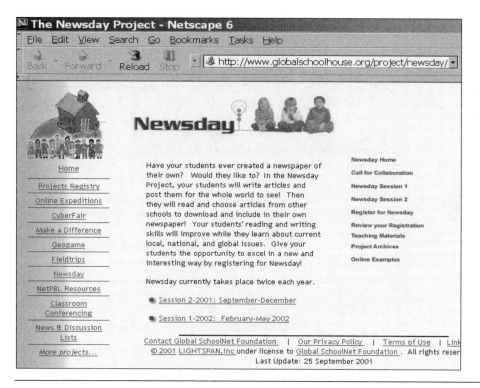

FIGURE 2.1 *Newsday* **Project**

Source: Copyright © Global SchoolNet Foundation. Used with permission.

particular theme on the electronic bulletin board and, in turn, select, download, and edit articles written by students around the world. Teachers might want to supply their students with guidelines to assist them with the editing process. Using articles from the *Newsday* newswire as well as local articles, students then layout and publish their newspaper on the World Wide Web and send printed copies to the participating schools. Samples of previous *Newsday* projects can be accessed to serve as models for first-time users.

Using Email and Electronic Discussion Groups with English Language Learners

Perhaps the simplest starting point for teachers using the Internet in their classrooms is email with its relative ease, accessibility, and numerous lists of would-be key pals in all geographical regions waiting to interact with their students. Numerous websites, including the following, provide email connections and project exchanges specifically for English language learning and intercultural communication:

- Dave's ESL Email Connection (http://www.eslcafe.com)
- Email Projects Home Page (http://www.otan.dni.us/webfarm/emailproject/email.html)
- Global SchoolHouse (http://www.globalschoolnet.org)
- Linguistic Funland (http://www.linguistic-funland.com)
- St.Olaf College's Intercultural E-Mail Classroom Connections (IECC) (http://www.iecc.org) (see Figure 2.2)

Other websites (Robb, 2001) supply articles that give advice on organizing and implementing key pal activities designed to develop language fluency and provide links to pen pal directories.

Students have additional opportunities to discuss specific topics relevant to their needs and interests by selecting and subscribing to electronic listservs, newsgroups, and discussion lists that connect groups of people with similar interests via email. At the college and university level, Latrobe University in Australia maintains

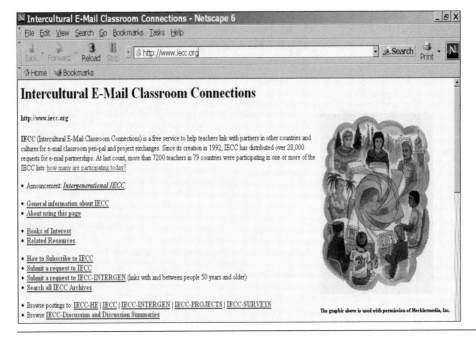

FIGURE 2.2 *Intercultural Email Classroom Connections*

Source: Academic Computing Center, St. Olaf College. Used with permission.

SL-LISTS (www.latrobe.edu.au/www/education/sl/sl.html), one of the most extensive collections of email student discussion lists specifically for ESL and EFL (English as foreign language) learners. Here, English learners join general discussions in subgroups at two levels of difficulty: CHATS-SL (low level) and DISCUSS-SL (advanced level). Special lists also exist for discussion of field-specific topics in business, education, learning English, current events, movies, music, science and technology, and sports. Teachers can register their classes to use the lists and will themselves be placed on a special discussion list for teachers whose classes are participating in the project. Similarly, Dave's *ESL Café Discussion Center* (see Figure 2.3) provides English language learners the opportunity to practice their English skills in natural communication with peers around the world.

Newsgroups such as the USENET Newsgroups, a network of thousands of electronic bulletin board-type discussion groups where students can read and post messages on different themes, also serve as effective sources for authentic communication in English. USENET categories include such topics as culture and current events, science, recreational activities and hobbies, and business. To join newsgroups, students need a special type of program called a *newsreader* that is normally

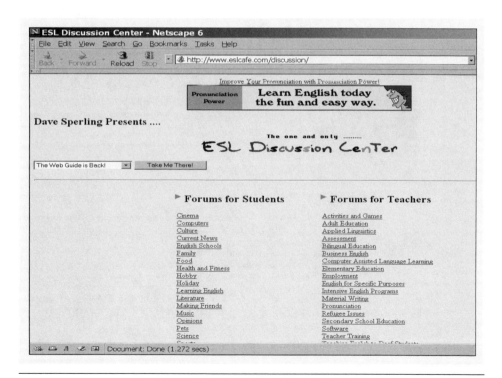

FIGURE 2.3 *Dave's ESL Café*

Source: Dave Sperling, Dave's ESL Café. Used with permission.

packaged with their Web browser (Collabra newsreader with Netscape Communicator, and Outlook Express newsreader with Microsoft Internet Explorer).

Using MOOs and Chat Rooms for "Live" Communication

When using email and discussion forums, students work at their own pace, independent of other participants' schedules and communiqués. For real-time, simultaneous communication, students participate in virtual chat rooms such as *Dave's ESL Café* Chat Central or in MOOs (multiuser domains object-oriented) where students engage in text conversations, simulations, and role-play. A MOO is a primarily text-based environment in which students interact by typing their responses in a variety of interactive simulations. Students visiting MOOs might be asked to assume roles or to help expand a story line or a simulation. One such MOO, schMooze University, created by Julie Falsetti at Hunter College, was designed especially for use by ESL and EFL teachers around the world (see Figure 2.4).

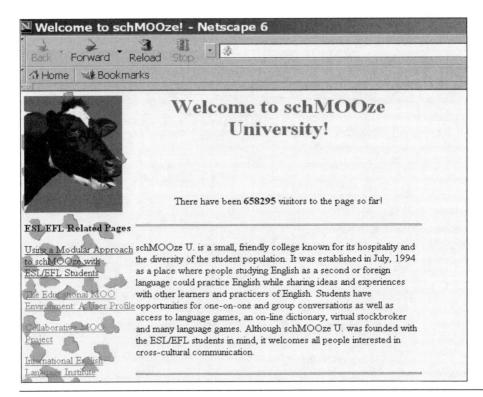

FIGURE 2.4   *schMOOze University*

Source: schMOOze University created by Julie Falsetti. Used with permission.

Whether with asynchronous or real-time tools, students have the autonomy to communicate to an authentic audience on topics of interest to them.

How do electronic teaching environments promote the development of linguistic competency in all language skill areas?

As we have seen, learning environments equipped with Internet and hyper-media capabilities afford students endless opportunities for authentic reading and writing practice to improve both fluency and accuracy. Teachers can use interactive CALL software or Web-based grammar programs in combination with communicative tasks to support the development of grammatical competence. For example, in her adult vocational ESL class, Donna Price-Machado provides her students with computer-based assignments that address the linguistic problems they exhibited in their oral communication or in their writing. For this purpose, she uses a checklist of various types of grammar structures referenced to the appropriate sections of software such as *Azar Interactive* and *Focus on Grammar*. The grammar software programs provide focused practice and feedback on the targeted linguistic structures. For instance, some students were working with software on modals stemming from a role-play of applying for a job. After intensive practice with software exercises, her students applied their knowledge of modals to writing application letters and resumes to send to real-life prospective employers. This instructor also uses software assignments to reinforce explicit grammar instruction of linguistic items that her adult students are "ready" and eager to learn.

In addition to using technology tools to practice their reading and writing skills, students also increase their listening and oral fluency as they discuss computer-based activities with their classmates or engage in other electronic activities that more directly engage them in listening and speaking activities. Through desktop teleconferencing, for example, students speak with peers or subject matter experts around the world on various topics of interest to them and relevant to their studies. In this way, students act as both the speaker and an authentic audience, processing the intended message of the other participants in the conversation and using feedback from them to confirm that their own message was understood. Teleconferencing opportunities that use an interview format allow English learners to practice formulating questions while communicating with peer and expert audiences. Through the use of videoconferencing software such as *CU-SeeMe*, students in schools separated by great distances practice their oral skills as they communicate with each other. The Global SchoolHouse website maintains a directory of K–12 schools that use desktop *CU-SeeMe* videoconferencing and an intensive tutorial on the use of this software. Each year the Global SchoolHouse sponsors an international CyberFair competition in which students from schools around the world create Web projects and in the process frequently videoconference with each other. English learners can benefit from videoconferencing for many of the same reasons cited for its use in all classrooms. It appeals to students' diverse learning styles; facilitates learning about different cultures from original sources; provides practice of presentation and communication skills, and increases student motivation (Jobe, 2000).

In addition to improving their fluency through real-world teleconferencing, students can also work on their oral accuracy with software and Web-based pronunciation programs that allow them to compare their oral speech to that of a native speaker. These programs will be investigated in detail in Chapter 4.

How can technology-enhanced language learning environments encourage the development of discourse, sociolinguistic, and strategic competencies?

Students improve their discourse competence through the use of interactive writing and grammar software and authentic writing practice using email. Grammar programs now available on CDs and the Web require students to apply their grammatical knowledge above the sentence level to, for example, practice transitioning and sequencing by connecting scrambled sentences into logical, meaningful paragraphs. Several computer-based interactive writing programs, such as the *Writing Process Workshop* (Educational Activities), have built-in prompts to guide extensive written discourse in various writing genres. (Chapter 4 examines multiple uses of technology to develop writing skills.)

Through the use of video programs designed for second language teaching, such as *Crossroads Café* (Savage*), New Interchange Series* (Richards), and *Inside America: Scenes of Everyday Life* (Kendall), the language learner can observe the social and cultural rules of the language—for example, different levels of formality in conversations between a student and the teacher and that between the same student and his or her peers. Students learn the connections between the function of polite requests and linguistic modals, such as *would* and *could,* and how to use them in socially acceptable expressions. In these same videos, students can observe the natural speech patterns of native speakers as they use such strategic techniques as the use of fillers, pauses, and body language. (See video resources listed at end of this chapter.)

Learning Environments and Interaction

How does technology support communicative learning environments?

In the previous sections, we focused on the use of technology to support communicative strategies for learning language. In the following section, we focus on the role of technology in restructuring classroom learning environments. One of the most noticeable differences in the shift from structural methods of second language teaching to communicative language teaching is in the roles of the teachers and students. When using CLT, teachers become managers and facilitators of functional learning environments. Classrooms are no longer centered only on the teacher but become learner-centered environments where students collaborate on authentic projects under the guidance of the teacher facilitator. A wide array of technology programs, websites, and communication tools support this type of collaborative learning and provide numerous opportunities for student-student and student-teacher interaction. For example, the Web-based *Global Grocery List Project* (see Figure 2.5) was designed to promote collaboration of students from schools worldwide as they collect and share data on costs of basic food items from their region of the world. Students survey local grocery stores or markets to determine prices for each item and then post their findings through the website for comparison with other entries. Students must indicate which currency and measurement system they used in their pricing and enter the current U.S. dollar exchange rate, which can be determined from the currency conversion engine provided. In this communicative project, the students are engaged in the real-life situations of selecting a grocery store, locating the food items in the store, and accurately recording the prices. The teacher guides students as they use spontaneous speech to negotiate which stores they will visit and what methods they will use for collecting and pooling their data. The teacher can also expand the project to explore mathematical concepts such as averaging, economic issues of poverty and scarcity of resources, and cultural differences that might account for some of the items not

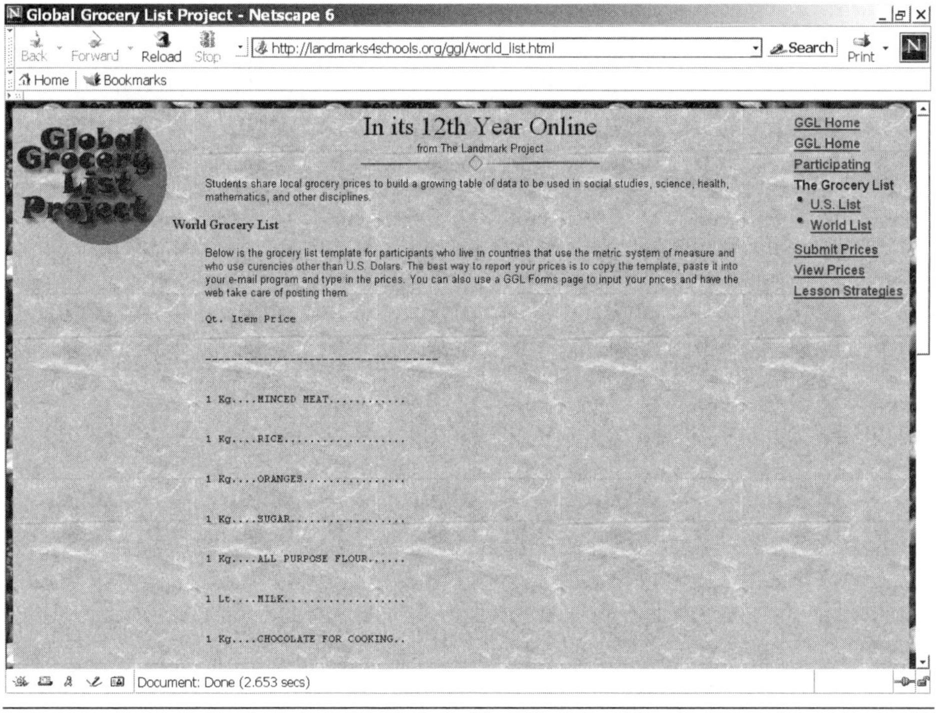

FIGURE 2.5 *Global Grocery List*

Source: Global Grocery List is maintained by David Warlick, an instructuional technology consultant in Raleigh, North Carolina (david@landmark-project.com). Used with permission.

being found in particular countries. Ideally, students could develop on-line dialog with participants from other parts of the world to more fully discuss the issues that arise from the findings.

Another grocery project that is popular with younger students is the *Earth Day Groceries Project* in which students across the United States and Canada decorate and write messages on paper grocery bags provided by their local grocery stores. On Earth Day (April 22) they return the bags to the grocery stores where the bags are filled with groceries of shoppers that day. Students then file a report on the website describing their classes participation in the project.

In technology-rich environments, students have the autonomy to work individually, with partners, or in small groups on authentic tasks while their teacher assists students with individual linguistic needs or facilitates student projects. The teacher frequently begins by introducing materials and modeling learning tasks using a computer and LCD panel or a self-contained projection system. Then, students work at their own levels with software designed to meet their individual needs or in pairs or small groups on collaborative tasks at computer work stations with Internet connections. Students who are more skilled with technology act as tutors or "techno-experts" to help peers accomplish technology-based tasks and projects.

The learning environment is no longer limited to the inside of an isolated classroom but instead is easily expanded via the Web to include the world community of classrooms and organizations, of information resources, and communication opportunities. Student interactions involve sharing information to accomplish common goals or real-world tasks with students in other rooms, states, or countries. Teachers can create communities of language learners on both a local and international level. Cummins and Sayers (1995), in their book *Brave New Schools*, suggest specific strategies and resources for building global electronic communities, which include a respect for diversity. A realization of this concept is the Global Schoolhouse, a virtual schoolhouse that uses Internet tools including live video to link children around the world in collaborative, interactive projects. One such program allows students to electronically travel with an English-speaking guide as he goes from one country to the next, introducing students to the cultural and geographic diversity of our world. Another school-based project allows students to do research on the leaders, special attractions, music, business, and art of their own local communities and then share their findings with students around the globe by publishing their findings on the designated website. Students then read about communities around the world and communicate with each other electronically to ask questions and gather more information.

What will new technology-enhanced language learning environments look like?

The arrangement of desks into learning clusters surrounded by computer work stations in technology-enhanced classes epitomizes the change from traditional teacher-fronted instruction to collaborative learning experiences using technology to meet student needs. Figure 2.6 illustrates three types of learning

Traditional Structural Classes

CLT Classes

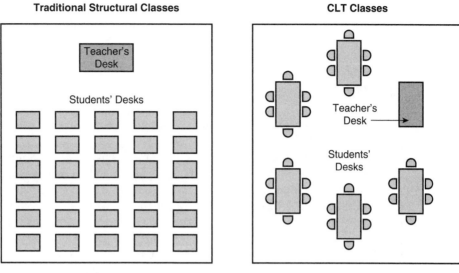

Technology Enhanced Language Learning Environment (TELLE)

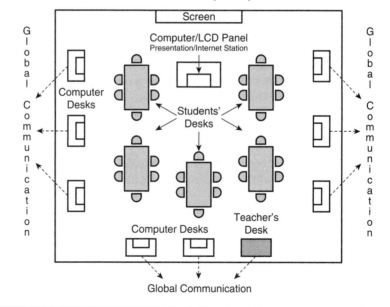

FIGURE 2.6 Language Learning Environments

environments: a traditional structural classroom, a communicative classroom lacking computer capabilities, and a technology-enhanced language learning environment.

Curriculum, Materials, and Activities

How can technology support a restructured CLT curriculum?

The technology-enhanced curriculum of communicative language teaching encourages the development of both language fluency and accuracy with emphasis on students using their linguistic knowledge to accomplish their goals. The communication needs of the students determine the curriculum. Videos and computer-based resources provide authentic writings and data relevant to students' experiences and interests. An effective strategy is for students to keep electronic journals in which they focus on freely expressing their thoughts and opinions. Electronic journals overcome the frequently cited problem of interrupting students' writing production when teachers collect their journals. With electronic journals, students do not have to give up their journals for days while their teacher reads and comments on their entries. Instead, students can email their daily writings to the teacher or print them out on the word processor as frequently as decided on with their teacher. To improve their linguistic accuracy, students can access interactive grammar software or Web-based grammar exercises that provide students practice and feedback on problematic linguistic structures.

The actual content of the CLT curriculum should draw on students' personal experiences and communication needs to accomplish their stated goals. Students' linguistic needs may vary considerably depending on factors such as age, academic objectives, or career plans. For instance, students in Donna Price-Machado's adult vocational ESL class use electronic reading programs from the *Reading in the Workplace* series (Educational Activities) that relate to the jobs they hope to obtain. They practice reading skills, vocabulary development, and job-related tasks in the health, retail, clerical, food, automotive, and electronics professions. In addition to providing students with specific vocabulary and language functions related to the jobs they are seeking, the reading programs also help students prepare for standardized tests that are required for entering into many vocational classes. For example, in automotive and electronics vocational ESL, students are not job-ready at the completion of the class. They must enter job training classes to learn the actual skills of car repair and electronics assembly. To enter these job training programs, students often need to take standardized reading tests and score at the eighth-grade reading level. The *Reading in the Workplace* series reading programs teach specific reading skills, such as looking for details, differentiating fact and opinion, and inferencing—reading skills that help students succeed on the standardized tests required for the vocational classes.

Whereas traditional methods of language teaching relied primarily on tests, technology provides teachers in CLT with a wide assortment of assessment measures, including electronic portfolios and self-reflections, multimedia presentation, and actual accomplishment of authentic tasks using technology resources. At Helix High School in La Mesa, California, seniors (including English language learners) are required to do a multimedia presentation of their senior project as a requirement for graduation. Experts from within and outside the school are invited to evaluate each presentation. Other schools require students to present an electronic portfolio comprised of evidence of their accomplishment and reflections on their progress as a final assessment prior to graduation.

Responding to Issues Raised about the Communicative Approach

How has the communicative language approach been expanded to address pedagogical concerns of its critics?

Communicative language teaching appeared in the 1970s as a counterreaction to earlier methods, flourished in the 1980s, and by the 1990, was itself subject to critical review that largely focused on two areas: (1) the pedagogical neglect of linguistic forms by many who claimed to use CLT and (2) the lack of clear-cut content specifications for the curriculum (Celce-Murcia, Dornyei, and Thurrell, 1997). As discussed earlier in this chapter, many advocates of CLT, including the authors of this book, view the development of grammatical competence as one of the goals of CLT to be addressed. The role of focused grammar instruction in developing communicative competence will be covered in detail in Chapter 5, which looks specifically at technology use in the teaching of writing and grammar.

The lack of guidelines for curriculum content of CLT continues to receive attention from linguists and methodologists. While the early functional-notional approach (Finicchiaro and Brumfit, 1983) of the 1970s and early 1980s provided elaborate content guidelines based on a system of language functions and notions, this purely functional approach did not account for the complexity of the communication process and the nature of discourse (Widdowson, 1978). At that time, theoretical and applied linguistics had not developed a sufficiently coherent description of communicative competence for practical application by methodologists. As CLT evolved in the 1990s, it was this lack of clearly defined linguistic guidelines that resulted in a wide range of communicative approaches that had in common only the rather broad goal of preparing learners to use language in real-life situations rather than focusing on structural accuracy (Celce-Murcia, Dornyei, and Thurrell, 1997).

Linguists such as Nunan (1989, 1991) have addressed the need for curriculum guidelines by promoting approaches such as task-based teaching for determining curriculum content and instructional processes within the CLT framework. We, the authors of this book, extend the definition of communicative language teaching to include task-based instruction.

Task-Based Teaching

What is communicative task-based teaching?

Task-based teaching has been described by some as instruction that is goal focused, but research indicates that the most effective type of task-based instruction for second language learners requires them to negotiate meaning to accomplish a real-world, communicative task (Pica, Kanagy, and Falodun, 1993). Nunan (1989) defined the communicative task as "a piece of classroom work which involves learners in comprehending, manipulating, producing, or interacting in the target language, while their attention is principally focused on meaning rather than form" (p. 10). He further stipulated that a communicative task should contain some form of input (either verbal or nonverbal), an activity resulting from the input that indicates what the learners are expected to do, and a goal—all of which influence the roles of the teacher and learners in a particular setting.

Since the 1970s the communicative, authentic task has evolved as a vital element in second language curriculum planning. In task-based language teaching, the syllabus content is determined by the communicative tasks in which the learners will need to participate outside the classroom. This approach "attempts to link classroom language learning with language activation outside the classroom" (Nunan, 1991, p. 279). Attention is also given to the social and psychological processes that facilitate language acquisition.

Task-based teaching and project-based instruction, in which students frequently engage in collaborative projects, allow students to learn English in an integrative manner, thereby responding to the concern that skills are too compartmentalized in CLT. Task- and project-based teaching mesh with the latest developments in technology. Multimedia and the Internet are pushing computer-assisted language learning toward not only the integration of all language skills but also the integration of meaningful and authentic communication into the curriculum (Warchauer, 1996).

A key characteristic of a communicative language environment is the opportunity for students to use language within a purposeful context. There are many opportunities to participate in meaningful and authentic tasks through the use of the World Wide Web. Using email, students can communicate with each other in projects, such as one conducted by ESL students in adult education programs throughout northern California, where students collected and exchanged information on jobs and housing costs in their respective cities (Gaer, 2001). This project provided an information gap activity relevant to these students' interests and assisted them in developing grammatical structures of comparison in real-life circumstances (see Figure 2.7). This activity and other on-line email and Web-based projects for adult ESL learners are available at the *Email Projects Home Page* maintained by Susan Gaer and sponsored by the Outreach Technical Assistance Network (OTAN).

FIGURE 2.7 *Housing Costs and Job Exchange*

Overview

ESL classes across northern California each collect information on wages for specific jobs and prices of housing and transportation. Classes exchange information for comparison. Each class will collect the following information:

- High and low rent for 2 bedroom, 1 bath apartment
- High and low rent for a three bedroom apartment
- High and low wages for each of these occupations
  - —busser
  - —custodian
  - —security guard
  - —auto mechanic
  - —secretary
  - —plumber
- 1 gallon of the cheapest gas
- bus fare

Source: Susan Gaer, associate professor of ESL, Santa Ana College, School of Continuing Education. Used with permission.

An International Cyberfair Research Project on Endangered Species: A Global Vignette

Many of the communicative language teaching principles and strategies discussed in this chapter are reflected in the following global teaching experience. Each year the Global SchoolHouse conducts the International Schools CyberFair (http://gsh.org/cf/index.html), in which the students of participating schools from around the world draw on local resources to conduct research projects on some aspect of their community and publish their findings on the World Wide Web (see Figure 2.8). Schools may select from one of eight categories, such as local leaders, historical landmarks, music and art, the environment, and so on, as the focus of their research and topic for their website presentation. In addition to their website presentations, participants respond to specific questions about their experiences in implementing the project as part of the "project narrative." Students are provided clear instructions regarding the purpose, expected outcomes, and evaluation criteria of their projects. The Web projects are judged using a peer-review rubric that evaluates both the content and form of the projects.

An example of an entry in the environment category is a joint project submitted by Primary School De Wadden in the Netherlands and Cannelton Elementary School in the state of Indiana. These schools collaborated on The Endangered Species And Nature (TESAN) of the World project, in which they invited other schools worldwide to join them in researching and reporting what was being done to protect endangered animals and plants in different regions of the world (see Figure 2.8).

FIGURE 2.8   International Schools CyberFair

Source: Global SchoolNet Foundation (www.globalschoolnet.org). Used with permission.

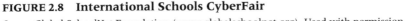

Though these two schools were located over 4,000 miles apart, their students were able to communicate with each other via email, on-line chats, and videoconferencing to develop and maintain the TESAN project. Over 500 students of all grade levels from 29 schools representing 10 countries and 5 different continents contributed to this project. Together, they investigated and shared information on the preservation programs at zoos, nature parks, and wildlife sanctuaries created to protect the species they were researching.

Teachers Joan Goble and Rene de Vries reported that for many of the students taking part in the project, this was the first time that they had been involved with a research project, and for several of the schools it was their first experience with an Internet project. For this reason, the host schools included on their website information to assist students in doing their research, creating websites, and utilizing multimedia tools. The task-based project involved work across the curriculum utilizing collaborative learning and problem-solving strategies. Students used scientific methods to carry out their research and practiced their reading and writing skills as they researched and published their multimedia reports on the Web.

To foster collaboration among the schools and build support from their families and communities, the sponsoring schools held live global chats, sometimes two or three consecutively, to accommodate all the different time zones. Perhaps one of the most rewarding aspects of the project was the impact the participating schools actually had in their local communities. For instance, at Alta Elementary School in California, students collected over $500 in their Coins for Cats drive to provide assistance to the Sierra Endangered Cat Haven in their efforts to protect endangered wild cats.

The culminating activity of the CyberFair is the Internet videoconferencing of the awards ceremony at which the winning schools and projects are announced. The prize-winning TESAN project encouraged global collaboration and telecommunication among students and promoted greater awareness of the environment and steps students could take to protect various endangered species. In the process, students from all parts of the world, including English language learners in the United States, practiced their English skills in a rich and motivating project that required them to communicate high-level concepts and ideas to real-life audiences for a specified purpose.

Conclusion

Technology, with its interactive software, Web-based projects, and rich resources and materials, has proven to be a motivating tool for communicative language teaching. Technology extends the communicative classroom to provide authentic tasks and audiences for English language learners locally and globally. Students use technology to engage in collaborative learning experiences that require them to communicate in order to accomplish meaningful tasks. As we learn more about the language acquisition process and continue to expand our concept of communicative competence, other teaching strategies and approaches within the CLT framework will emerge. It is our hope that the convergence of improvements in technology and greater insights into second language acquisition will continue with future technological advances facilitating classroom application of the most promising new SLA theories.

Summary of Key Ideas

1. Communicative competence is the primary theoretical construct underlying the communicative language teaching approach. *Communicative competence* is defined as the language learner's ability to (1) draw on his or her knowledge of linguistic structures; (2) engage in oral and written discourse; (3) utilize the language appropriately based on an understanding of the social and cultural rules of the L2 environment; and (4) employ body language and other strategic competencies to compensate for any breakdowns in communication.

2. Technology enhances all aspects of communicative language teaching by providing collaborative functional learning environments and interactive skill-based programs.

3. Developments in second language teaching have mirrored those in technology, with models of teaching moving from behavioral to constructivist theory and from structural to communicative practices that focus on language performance.

4. Technology provides communicative language teaching channels for students to use the acquired language in unrehearsed communication with authentic audiences, to have the autonomy to make choices about what they will say, and to receive feedback from those audiences.

5. The transformation of classrooms from a traditional teacher-fronted format to student-centered learning environments has been assisted by technology tools. Through email, Web discussion boards, teleconferencing, and electronic databases, technology-enhanced language learning environments take students beyond the walls of the classroom and allow them to access authentic resources and communicate with students around the world.

6. Technology promotes collaborative teaching strategies of CLT as students research topics using electronic databases and work together on multimedia presentations and Web-based projects.

7. Task-based learning within the CLT approach utilizes technology to link classroom learning with language use outside the classroom to accomplish real-world goals of the students.

8. Through the use of authentic assessment tools, such as electronic portfolios, multimedia projects, and electronic dialogical journals, teachers can more accurately monitor the achievement of English language learners.

Learning Activities _____

1. Learn more about internet projects by visiting the Global Schoolhouse site (www.gsh.org.). Click on the Projects Registry on the opening page. Next, click on the "sort by age" button to access projects appropriate to your grade levels. Explore these sites and come up with three or four sites that offer Internet projects that you think are most useful. Design an activity for your own classroom or future classrooms and explain how you could use a key pal project in the classroom.

2. Design a problem-solving project that will address a current local school issue, such as the amount of trash generated on a high school campus or the problem of lack of parking spaces on a college campus. Utilize the following components in the project: on-line research techniques, use of email to communicate with local or distant experts, word processing, and Web-based presentation of findings and conclusions.

3. Write a short skit or play revolving around language interactions in a social situation, such as waiting for a bus, meeting for a meal and ordering food, buying tickets and snacks, attending a dinner party or tea, asking a person out on a date, visiting someone in a hospital, and so on. Then videotape the scene, watch and critique your tape, and improve it until it is ready to be used in your own language learning classroom.

4. In addition to using email to connect students to another classroom, email can also be used within the classroom to encourage communication of student to teacher

and student to student. Sometimes students will be able to let the teacher know how they feel and think when they have time to communicate privately via email. Students can also email each other between classes and practice using the target language. Write about how you think you could use email in a classroom to provide language practice and also reinforce the learning of content being studied.

5. Participate in one of the professional discussion groups (listed later in the section called Teacher Professional Development Resources) and then write about and share your experiences using electronic discussions. Describe how you might use a discussion group if you were teaching other teachers about technology-based communication.

Technology Resources

Software

Azar Interactive (1998). By H. Smith and B. S. Azar. New York: Merrill Prentice-Hall.
Focus on Grammar (1996–1998). By M. Fuchs and M. Bonner. Reading, MA: Addison Wesley Longman.
Reading in the Workplace Series (1992). Freeport NY: Educational Activities.
Scholastic's Process Writer, Scholastic, Inc.

Websites

Dave's ESL Email Connection for Students (http://www.eslcafe.com) developed by Dave Sperling.
Earth Day Groceries Project, 2000 (http://www.earthdaybags.org).
Education World (http://www.education-world.com).
Email Projects Home Page (http://www.otan.dni.us/webfarm/emailproject/email.html) developed and maintained by Susan Gaer and sponsored the Outreach Technical Assistance Network (OTAN) of the California Department of Education.
Global SchoolHouse (http://www.gsh.org).
Intercultural E-Mail Classroom Connections (http://www.iecc.org).
Latrobe University SL-LISTS www.latrobe.edu.au/www/education/sl/sl.html. Co-owners of lists: Lloyd Holliday, La Trobe University, Australia (L.Holliday@latrobe.edu.au) and Thomas Robb, Kyoto Sangyo University, Japan (trobb@cc.kyoto-su.ac.jp).
Linguistic Funland (http://www.linguistic-funland.com).
National Geographic's Pen Pal Network (http://www.nationalgeographic.com).
SchMOOze University (http://schmooze.hunter.cuny.edu:8888/).

Videos

Crossroads Café by L. Savage et al., Heinle and Heinle Publishers.
Inside America: Scenes of Everyday Life by Martha E. Kendall.
New Interchange Series by Jack C. Richards, Cambridge Publishers.

Other Technology Resources for Communicative Activities

CNN Newsroom (http://www.halcyon.com)
GlobalLearn (http://www.globalearn.org)
Kidpoj:Kidlink (http://www.kidlink.org)

Virtual Galapagos (http://www.terraquest.com)
Buddy Project (http://www.org/less/collab)
NickNack's Tellecollaboration (http://home.talkcity.com/academydr/nicknacks/
NickProjects.html)

Teacher Professional Development Resources

TESOL teachers and graduate students will find TESLCA-L, the computer-assisted
language learning subgroup of the TESL-L (listserv@cunyvm.cuny.edu) electronic
discussion list, an excellent resource for discussion of technology and second language teaching issues. A similar list, TESLK-12 (listserv@uga.cc.uga.edu), is dedicated to elementary and secondary school issues, including those related to
technology in K–12 instruction of English learners. One major USENET group
looks at topics specifically related to K–12 educational issues and includes subcat-
egories on teaching literacy and language arts.

References

Bonk, C., and King, K. (1998) *Electronic Collaborators: Learner-Centered Technologies for Literacy, Apprenticeship, and Discourse.* Mahwah, NJ: Erlbaum.

Buell, J. (1999). CALL Issues: Resources for CALL. In J. Egbert and E. Hanson-Smith (Eds.), *CALL Environments: Research, Practice and Critical Issues* (pp. 216–238). Alexandria, VA: Teachers of English to Speakers of Other Languages.

Brown, H. D. (2000). *Principles of Learning and Teaching.* Englewood Cliffs, NJ: Prentice-Hall Regents.

Brown, H. D. (1994). *Teaching by Principles: An Interactive Approach to Language Teaching.* Englewood Cliffs, NJ: Prentice-Hall Regents.

Canale, M., and Swain, M. (1980). Theoretical bases of communicative approaches to second language teaching and testing. *Applied Linguistics* 1 (1):1–47.

Candlin, C. N. (1976). Communicative language teaching and the debt to pragmatics. In C. Rameh (Ed.), *Georgetown University Roundtable 1976.* Washington DC: Georgetown University Press.

Cummins, J., and Sayers, D. (1995). *Brave New Schools: Challenging Cultural Illiteracy through Global Learning Networks.* New York: St. Martin's Press.

Celce-Murcia, M., Dornyei, Z., and Thurrell, S. (1997). Direct approaches in L2 instruction: A turning point in communicative language teaching. *TESOL Quarterly* 31 (1): 141–152.

Egbert, J., and Hanson-Smith, E. (1999). *CALL Environments: Research, Practice and Critical Issues.* Alexandria, VA: Teachers of English to Speakers of Other Languages.

Finocchiaro, M., and Brumfit, C. (1983). *The Functional-Notional Approach: From Theory to Practice.* New York: Oxford University Press.

Gaer, S. (2001). *Cost of Living Data Project.* Retrieved from http://www.otan.dni.us/webfarm/emailproject/over.htm on September 17, 2001.

Halliday, M. A. (1973). *Explorations in the Functions of Language.* London: Edward Arnold.

Hymes, D. (1971). Competence and performance in linguistic theory. In R. Huxley and E. Ingram (Eds.), *Language Acquisition: Models and Methods.* London: Academic Press.

Hymes, D. (1972). On communicative competence. In J. B. Pride and J. Holmes (Eds.), *Sociolin-
guistics* (pp. 269–93). Harmondsworth: Penguin.

Jobe, H. (2000). Desktop videoconferencing: Novelty or legitimate teaching tool? *Education World.* Available: http://www.education-world.com/a_curr/curr120.shtml. Visited September 4, 2000.

Johnson, K., and Morrow, K. (1981). *Communication in the Classroom: Applications and Methods for a Communicative Approach.* Burnt Mill, England: Longman Group Limited.

Littlewood, W. (1981). *Communicative Language Teaching: An Introduction.* Cambridge: Cambridge University Press.

Nunan, D. (1988). *The Learner-Centered Curriculum.* Cambridge: Cambridge University Press.

Nunan, D. (1989). *Designing Tasks for the Communicative Classroom.* Cambridge: Cambridge University Press.

Nunan, D. (1991). Communicative tasks and the language curriculum. *TESOL Quarterly* 25 (2): 279–295.

Pica, T., Kanagy, R., and Falodun, J. (1993). Choosing and using communication tasks for second language instruction. In G. Crookes and S. Gass (Eds.), *Tasks and Language Learning: Integrating Theory and Practice* (pp. 9–34). Clevedon, England: Multilingual Matters.

Quinn, T. (1984). Functional approaches in language pedagogy. *Annual Review of Applied Linguistics.* Cambridge: Cambridge University Press.

Robb, T. (2001). *Email Keypals for Language Fluency.* Available: http://www.Kyoto-su.ac.jp/~trobb/keypals.html. Visited October 26, 2001.

Savignon, S. J. (1972). *Communicative Competence: An Experiment in Foreign Language Teaching.* Philadelphia: Center for Curriculum Development.

Savignon, S. J. (1983). *Communicative Competence: Theory and Classroom Practice.* Reading, MA: Addison-Wesley.

Savignon, S. J. (1991). Communicative language teaching: State of the art. *TESOL Quarterly* 25 (2): 26–277.

Seedman, P. (1995). Communicative call: Focus on the interaction produced by CALL software. *ReCALL* 7 (2): 20–28.

Warschauer, M. (1996). Computer-assisted language learning: An introduction. In S. Fotos (Ed.), *Multimedia Language Teaching* (pp. 3–20). Tokyo: Logos International.

Widdowson, H. G. (1978). *Teaching Language as Communication.* Oxford: Oxford University Press.

Widdowson, H. G. (1979). The communicative approach and its applications. In H. G. Widdowson (Ed.), *Explorations in Applied Linguistics.* Oxford: Oxford University Press.

Wilkins, D. A. (1976). *Notional Syllabuses.* Oxford: Oxford University Press.

3

Content-Based Instruction for English Language Learners

Chapter Overview

This chapter describes four different types of content-based instruction for English language learners (ELLs), their underlying principles, and the use of technology to strengthen these approaches. Examples of content-based instruction as it is utilized in ESL, sheltered instruction, adjunct model, and mainstream classrooms are presented. The chapter focuses on sheltered instruction as a means of making subject matter content accessible to English language learners. Technology-enhanced sheltered instruction (TESI) is presented in detail and organized around the use of technology for instruction, classroom discourse and interaction, and assessment. A case study of a fourth-grade social studies class is included as an illustration of how a technology-enriched sheltered curriculum can promote language development and subject matter success. The chapter concludes with a summary of key points and suggested activities to prepare teachers to utilize technology in the design and delivery of content-based instruction for English language learners in various settings.

Content-Based Instruction

Content-based instruction for ELLs is the broad umbrella term to indicate that the instruction draws on subject matter material. The degree of focus on content in relationship to English language skill development varies according to the particular type of content-based instruction. This may include rigorous grade-level sheltered instruction in math, science, social studies, and language arts, in which language development occurs as a result of its use while studying the subject matter. Conversely, content-based instruction can also include content ESL classes that utilize subject matter material primarily as resources for instruction in English language skills development. The particular form of content-based instruction depends on the students' needs, the educational setting, and the resources available. This chapter will consider different types of content-based classes for English language learners, the research that demonstrates the need for this type of instruction, and the ways in which technology can support it.

What is the rationale for using content-based instruction for English language learners?

Frequently, second language learners quickly learn the English needed to survive and interact in social settings with which they are very familiar, but when faced with the demands of a subject area classroom, they find it impossible to succeed. This has been the experience of countless students who have found themselves in classrooms where they were expected to keep pace in the subject matter with their native English-speaking peers while still trying to acquire the linguistic skills required for this level of academic work. Such situations ignore two key findings about second language development. The first involves a distinction in types of language proficiency of second language learners and the other addresses the length of time needed to acquire these proficiencies.

In his research with second language learners, Cummins (1984) made a distinction between (1) basic interpersonal communication skills (BICS) needed for social interaction and (2) cognitive academic language proficiency (CALP) required for success with the more abstract concepts and cognitively demanding tasks required in subject matter courses in academic settings. He later expanded this theory, conceptualizing language proficiency along two continuums. The first continuum ranges from cognitively undemanding tasks that are largely automatized and therefore require minimum active cognitive involvement to those that are cognitively very demanding. The second spans from context-embedded language that is in an environment rich with visual and situational cues to context-reduced language that relies on the surface features of language without context to convey meaning. While BICS will suffice for communication in context-embedded, cognitively undemanding social settings, advanced CALP is required in academic environments exemplified by the context-reduced, cognitively demanding combination (see Figure 3.1).

Though these two types of proficiencies often overlap, it is important to understand the distinctions between them and to recognize that students who have highly developed BICS need additional time and support to acquire the academic linguistic skills required in most subject-area classrooms. Research has shown that while learning language skills for social purposes can be accomplished in 1 to 2 years, the language proficiency needed for academic purposes typically requires 5 to 7 years of study for students who have had 2 to 3 years schooling in their native language before coming to the United States and 7 to 10 years of study for those who have had no education in their native language (Cummins, 1981, 1984; Collier, 1995). Recognizing the time lag between acquisition of conversation skills and academic English skills, it is important that instruction for English language learners offers maximum exposure to subject matter vocabulary, schema, and concepts in a manner that is comprehensible to these students.

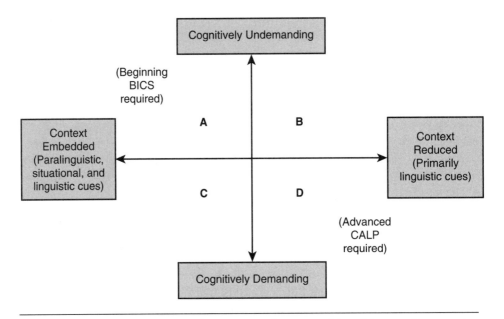

FIGURE 3.1   Range of Contextual Support and Degree of Cognitive Involvement in Communicative Activities
Source: Adapted from Cummins (1981a).

How can technology support content-based instruction?

With the development of software that provides scaffolding in the form of audio, video, and kinesthetic support for concept learning, the time it takes for ELL students to move from BICS to CALP can be reduced. Papert (1980) designed a robotic turtle that children could direct by typing commands into a computer. They could manipulate this object to explore mathematical ideas. Papert and his research group at MIT found that when children are given control of objects to think with, they are soon comfortable exploring such advanced mathematical ideas as variables and geometric principles. When ELL students are provided with simulation programs for learning about geographic and historical ideas, language becomes less of a barrier to thinking about abstract disciplinary concepts, such as how and why people travel, and what are the effects of a science experiment. Examples of computer programs that support high levels of thinking while reducing the need for extensive language will be examined later in this chapter.

What are the theories behind content-based instruction?

Content-based instruction draws on the constructivist theories of Bruner (1986) and Vygotsky (1978), which hold that learning depends on how students structure knowledge about themselves and their environment. Vygotsky focused on the important influence of the environment on facilitating socially constructed learning. He argued that learning preceded maturation as students moved between two levels of development: actual and potential. He termed the difference between these two levels the *zone of proximal development (ZPD),* an area of growth in which students under adult guidance or through collaborative work with more capable peers could move from their current ability level to a higher one where they would become capable of independent work. Bruner (1986) proposed that students' ability to interact with their environment is influenced by the organization of that environment. Bruner advocated for educators to provide instructional supports by scaffolding their teaching in ways that assist students' mental organization and development of schema.

Constructivist applications in content-based instruction are grounded not only in cognitive constructivism, but also in social constructivism. Willis, Stephens, and Matthew (1996) suggest the difference between these two theoretical perspectives: "Social constructivism spotlights the role of language as a tool used to spur forward intellectual growth; cognitive constructivism explores how language is processed at different stages of natural human development" (p.46). Constructivist theory has also evolved to include the notion of *situated cognition,* which occurs when students work on authentic tasks in real-world settings (Brown, Collins, and Duguid, 1989). Designing opportunities for students to learn deeply depends on a recognition of the interconnectedness of tools, authentic activity, and the culture of practice (Norton and Wiburg, 1998).

In her conceptual model for acquiring a second language for school, Collier (1995) draws attention to the interconnections in the students' cognitive, academic, and language development within the context of surrounding social and cultural processes. All components are interdependent with the students' success, depending on their simultaneous development in a socioculturally supportive environment. She points out that, until the past decade, the cognitive dimension had been largely neglected by second language educators in the United States, resulting in the highly structured and sequenced language curricula of the 1970s and the watered-down academic content of language lessons in the 1980s. Research supports Collier's call for strong support for language development in the primary and second languages and uninterrupted academic development in subject matter content (Berko Gleason, 1993; Collier, 1992a; Cummins, 1981a; Hakuta, 1986).

What are the different types of content-based instruction for English language learners?

Names for various types of content-based instruction have evolved over the years, with some degree of overlap and confusion in definitions. One method of categorizing the various types of content-based classes for ELLs is in terms of two key distinctions: (1) the language proficiency of the students ranging from non-English to native-English proficiency and (2) the primary focus or purpose of the instruction on either the development of English language skills or the mastery of subject-area content.

In this chapter, we will look at the following four main categories of content-based instruction with some variations within each group.

1. Content-based English as a second language (ESL), also called English language development (ELD) instruction
2. Sheltered instruction (SI) or specially designed academic instruction delivered in English (SDAIE) as it is referred to in some states
3. Adjunct ESL/sheltered subject matter combination
4. Mainstream classes employing sheltering techniques and strategies

TABLE 3.1   *Types of Content-Based Instruction for English Language Learners*

	Content-Based English as a Second Language (ESL)	Sheltered Instruction (SI)	Adjunct Model	Mainstream
Also Known as	English language development (ELD, EAP, ESP, VESL)	Specially designed academic instruction in English (SDAIE)	Cooperative model	Regular
Student Populations	English language learners (ELLs), adult professional and vocational students, English learners (EL), limited English proficient (LEP)	English language learners (ELLs) or English learners (ELs) or limited English proficient (LEP)	Native English speakers and English language learners (ELLs)	Native English speakers and transitioned and nontransitioned ELLs
Preferred English Language Proficiency Prerequisite	None	Intermediate	Advanced-Intermediate	Advanced
Primary Focus of Curriculum	English language skills	Subject area material	English language skills and subject area material	Subject area material
Primary Expertise of Teacher(s)	English as a second language (ESL)	Subject area	One teacher—subject area, or one teacher—English as a second language	Subject area

Content-Based ESL or ELD Classes

Content-based ESL classes focus on the development of English reading, writing, listening, and speaking skills through the use of academic subject matter materials. This is in contrast to other ESL approaches that use materials centered on situations, notions, functions, or grammar structures. The curriculum in content-based ESL is often theme-based around academic topics such as global warming, inventions, or world peace, or specific fields such as business, engineering, or vocational trades.

The term *English language development (ELD)* is a more recent name used by some state boards of education for K–12 instruction designed to promote the acquisition of English by students for whom English is not their primary language. The ELD instruction might be offered as a component of a bilingual program or of a program in which English is the primary language of instruction. Regardless of the type of program, the focus of content-based ELD is on developing the basic communication skills in English needed for students to successfully transition into sheltered and mainstream subject matter classes. Students frequently continue advanced ELD instruction while in sheltered courses.

Content-based English classes are offered at all levels ranging from elementary ESL/ELD to college-level English for academic purposes (EAP) designed to meet academic language needs of students entering undergraduate and graduate degree programs. An increasing amount of Web-based support is now available in many content classes, providing students with visual scaffolds for content learning. In recent years there has been a growing number of Internet-based courses designed to help college students learning new content. Many of these on-line courses provide visual examples, charts, and expanded explanations of words and concepts that can assist second language learners with their academic work. The university EAP courses frequently utilize authentic materials, including syllabi, readings, research assignments, and videotaped lectures from degree courses, while focusing on the development of English language skills required for success in these courses. Universities such as Brigham Young University in Hawaii offer advanced content-based English as an international language (EIL) courses in which students receive credit toward an undergraduate degree for linguistic accomplishments similar to those of native English speakers taking a foreign language.

Also included in the content ESL for adults are English for specific purposes (ESP), in which ESL instruction is applied to particular fields such as engineering, business, hotel management and tourism, and vocational English as a second language (VESL). In ESP classes, students study vocabulary, reading and writing genres, and processes characteristic of a particular field. In general, VESL courses, like those offered through the continuing education centers of the San Diego Community College district, are designed to create bridges between ESL classes and vocational programs. In these programs, technology is used to support English language and cognitive development to prepare students to enter the job force at their highest potential level.

Sheltered Instruction (SI)

Based on extensive research that suggested that English classes alone could not provide sufficient comprehensible input to prepare students for subject matter classes, Krashen (1981, 1985) advocated that students with intermediate-level English proficiency be provided sheltered instruction that would serve as a bridge between their ESL/ELD and mainstream classes. Utilizing techniques and strategies that foster cognitive and academic development, sheltered content-area courses provide English learners access to the core curriculum at the same academic level as that provided their native English-speaking peers. More recently, the term *specially designed academic instruction in English (SDAIE)* has largely replaced *sheltered instruction* in some states, such as California, where state guidelines clearly define the content and delivery of SDAIE. Called by either name, sheltered instruction or SDAIE includes strategies that draw on students' prior knowledge and cultural background, present material in a comprehensible manner, tailor the complexity of discourse to the students' proficiency level, provide ample opportunities for students to process the material, utilize a variety of interaction groupings, and assess student progress using multiple measures. This chapter describes how the use of technology can strengthen these strategies even further.

Several states with large English language learner student populations offer sheltered subject-area instruction in various types of programs, including structured immersion and bilingual programs. In structured immersion programs, non-native English learners receive sheltered subject matter instruction in English while gradually transitioning into mainstream classes. Bilingual programs offer beginning-level English learners subject matter instruction in their primary language prior to and concurrent with sheltered core courses in English before they transition into mainstream classes.

The use of sheltered instruction is not limited to elementary and secondary schools. Recognizing its advantages for non-native English-speaking college students just completing ESL programs and facing the rigorous demands of undergraduate and graduate degree programs, several colleges and universities now offer selected academic courses as sheltered courses for non-native speakers only. Finally, sheltered instruction can be helpful to anyone, regardless of language ability, if they are being introduced to a new and complex topic. Some of our graduate students often ask us to please *shelter* a new idea for them.

Mainstream Classes Employing Sheltering
Techniques and Strategies

When sheltered content-area classes and/or bilingual programs are not available, non-native English-speaking students whose English proficiency is not at grade level are frequently submersed in mainstream classes with native English speakers. Teachers of these classes need special instruction in how to apply sheltering techniques to best meet the needs of their non-native English-speaking students who are struggling with the demands of the core curriculum while still acquiring

English skills, sometimes at low levels of proficiency. Students who have transitioned from bilingual, immersion, or sheltered classes also benefit from appropriate use of these sheltering techniques. Several states now require that all teachers in schools with culturally diverse student populations have training in sheltered instruction in order to meet the special needs of English language learners. Similarly, colleges and universities with large minority and international English language learner populations provide faculty development training in language-sensitive curriculum development and instructional practices. Teachers should remember that these sheltering techniques might also provide additional help to students who are struggling with the academic concepts regardless of their language ability.

Access to technology can be of special benefit to teachers in the mainstream classroom where teachers must serve students with a wide variety of instructional needs. Computer software provides a variety of skill-development programs that students can use for individualized tutorials and practice. Content simulations are available in which students can travel the Oregon Trail, explore Mayan ruins, or build civilizations. Through the use of pictures, charts, and game playing, these programs allow students still learning English to explore social studies concepts.

Early technologies such as tape recorders and video cameras can also be of great benefit. Students learning English may benefit from listening to a tape or watching a videotape of a teacher demonstration or lecture. They can also video their presentations and explanations of concepts in a content area and then view the video repeatedly as they work on improving their communication of ideas. One elementary teacher saw an improvement of students' mathematical language when she allowed them to create and video skits presenting different mathematical ideas such as fractions, numeration, and operations.

At the college and university level, it is often suggested that ESL students take one of the introductory technology courses when entering the regular college program. Learning to use a technology tool is scaffolded by the tool itself. For example, a student learning to use a spreadsheet or a word processing program is provided with natural feedback on what works and does not work, continuous help options within the program, and unlimited opportunities to continue to learn by trying without extensive language demands. At the same time, learning a technology tool does provide students with opportunities to learn English through the technical language involved. One of the authors recently taught PowerPoint (Microsoft, 1996) in Spanish in Mexico and learned many Spanish words as she taught the students how to make presentations.

Adjunct Models

In recent years, there has been increased attention to various types of adjunct models that combine some aspects of ESL teaching with mainstream instruction that features sheltering strategies (Teemant, Bernhardt, and Rodriguez-Munoz, 1997). In these models, ESL instructors observe subject matter classes in which their ESL students are enrolled and work collaboratively with subject matter teachers or professors to design an ESL curriculum that supports concepts and assignments of the academic curriculum. Both the ESL and subject matter teachers are well versed in all aspects of sheltered instruction. Teachers in the elementary and secondary classes are typically required to meet state certification requirements for teachers of English language learners. At the post-secondary level, subject matter faculty in adjunct programs receive training in strategies for teaching linguistically and culturally diverse students. A few programs such as the University Academic Program at St. Michael's College (Richard-Amato, 1996) combine adjunct, sheltered, and mainstream courses. Here students with intermediate skills take two credit-bearing courses: an adjunct course co-taught by a faculty member from the undergraduate program and a language teacher from the Center for International Programs, and a sheltered class in college writing. At the next level, students with advanced skills take sheltered courses in introduction to literature and advanced college writing, as well as two undergraduate mainstream courses.

Chapters 4 and 5 of this book will look at content-based ESL instruction that focuses on the development of reading, writing, listening, and speaking skills of English language learners as well as the utilization of technology for learning English. The remainder of this chapter looks at technology-enhanced sheltering strategies designed to support ELLs in sheltered, adjunct, and mainstream classes.

Technology-Enhanced Sheltered Instruction (TESI)

How can technology support sheltered instruction in facilitating English language acquisition?

Technology can support the major components of sheltered instruction in a variety of ways to assist English language learners to master grade-level subject matter while acquiring academic English proficiency. Features of computer-based technology serve to strengthen specially designed instructional scaffolds or supports that aid students in processing content material. For example, having well-organized templates and examples of content-area work on a computer can be of great assistance to the ELLs. The computer also serves as a tool for collaborative learning, facilitates comprehensible discourse, and encourages a variety of classroom groupings and interactions. Finally, technology supports the use of both traditional and alternative assessment, allowing students to demonstrate competencies in multiple ways. In this section we discuss these three components of technology enhanced sheltered instruction (TESI): instructional strategies, classroom discourse and interactions, and assessment (see Table 3.1).

Instructional Strategies

What are instructional scaffolds and how can technology strengthen them?

Over the last two decades English language teachers (Walqui-van Lier, 1992; Becijos, 1997) have refined a number of specific scaffolding strategies designed to help ELL students learn content material, including modeling, bridging, schema-building, contextualizing with visuals and realia, text re-presentation, and metacognitive development. In addition, we suggest the inclusion of a seventh instructional scaffold: computer-based representational manipulatives. Such representational manipulatives provide a bridge to help students move from BICS to CALP language proficiency. We will look at how these scaffolds operate to support second language acquisition and in what ways the use of technology increases their effectiveness.

1. *Modeling*—providing examples of products or processes expected of students
2. *Bridging*—connecting the subject matter to students' prior knowledge, personal experiences, and culture
3. *Schema building*—organizing subject matter into interconnected clusters of meaning
4. *Contextualization*—using realia and visuals in ways that make abstract concepts and academic subject matter more comprehensible
5. *Text re-presentation*—changing the text from the original version to a different format, such as from a poem to a narrative or from text to a multimedia presentation
6. *Metacognitive development*—students reflecting on their own learning
7. *Representational manipulatives*—using computer-based manipulatives to make connections between concrete objects and their representation as abstract concepts.

Actual classroom examples of teachers using these strategies will follow and help clarify their use in the reality of a dynamic classroom.

Modeling

Modeling provides students with clear examples and templates of what is expected of them. It is helpful for ELL students to see what the final product they are being asked to make is supposed to look like. Such modeling can eliminate many problems in the sheltered classroom. A clear example of the type of writing being requested, whether a simple letter or an imaginary story, will help the students understand what they are expected to do. For example, computer-based writing process programs, such as Writing Process Workshop, model various types of expository writing and provide prompted answers and guided writing.

A teacher using a presentation station, which hooks the teacher's computer to an overhead projector, can model the type of product she or he would like the student to produce. The teacher can also demonstrate the steps students might need to take to complete a specific assignment, such as a research report or a personal autobiography. Once demonstrated, the templates for different assignments can then be stored on the computer and be accessible at any time the student has questions about how to do the assigned work. Using a simple word processing program, a teacher can develop, store, and have available at any time instructions, templates, and examples of student work. When classroom computers are then connected to other classrooms or schools through Intranet or Internet systems, a large collection of resources and examples can then become available to a growing community of ELL students and teachers.

Ms. Lujan-Pincomb was teaching her students about the planets and had decided to use a multimedia authoring tool, *HyperStudio,* for her students to create their planet reports. She created a blank template using the program and then filled in one example while her Spanish and English-speaking students watched her on the overhead. Figure 3.2 shows what the template and class generated example looked like.

However, a word of caution about the extensive use of templates is needed. Students also need to be encouraged to develop their own way of representing their ideas. Time spent in class discussing and demonstrating different ways to meet the assignment will allow students to try new things. Once students have gained an understanding of how to do a basic illustrated card or a book report, the teacher should then help them expand their examples in new ways.

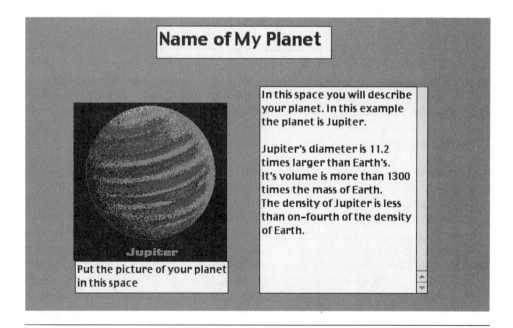

FIGURE 3.2   *HyperStudio*

Source: Image courtesy of Knowledge Adventure, Inc. and is used under license. HyperStudio® and all its screen images is a registered trademark of Knowledge Adventure, Inc. and is used under license. Used with permission.

Bridging

Bridging activities build links between the student's prior knowledge and/or personal experiences and the subject matter. This helps make the new material relevant to the student's life and in the case of newcomers, serves to validate their native cultures. An example of this practice would be utilizing an interactive map program, such as that provided with a multimedia encyclopedia and/or available on the Web, to teach social studies to second language learners (see Figure 3.3). In the process of demonstrating the program, the teacher could ask the students to talk about where they came from, places they have lived, and/or where their relatives or friends came from. Internet map programs are especially interesting, since many allow access to worldwide locations to which diverse students can relate. The teacher could also model this activity by sharing where members of her family had been born and moved during their lifetimes.

The student can click on the interactive world map shown in Figure 3.3, and zoom in on an areas such as Europe to explore these countries in more detail.

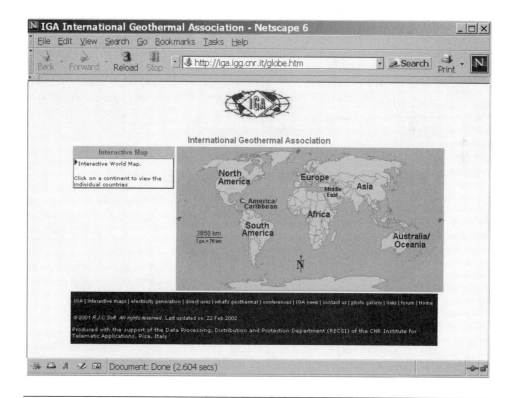

FIGURE 3.3 Location of Geothermal Power Sites

Source: Courtesy of the International Geothermal Association. Used with permission.

When you click on a country, the interactive website provides extensive data about that country's use of geothermal energy.

A large variety of maps are now available on the Web and in CD-ROM encyclopedias. These electronic maps are often tied to pictures and articles that relate to the map. ELL students might enjoy showing places in which they have lived or traveled using pictures and maps from the Web or a CD. Experiences in classrooms with second language learners have convinced the authors that while students may be reluctant to read a textbook in English, they will spend many hours reading on the net. The contextual cues such as pictures and sounds may be one of the reasons for this. This use of an interactive maps is one example where it is possible to provide a kind of learning with technology that is not possible with only paper and pencil. As access to technology increases in these classrooms, additional research is needed in this area.

Schema Building

Teachers can help students develop clusters of meaning that are interconnected through schema building. Computer-generated prompts, outlines, and other graphical organizers can be used for brainstorming and clustering activities. Using computer-based drawing and idea development programs such as *Inspiration,* students can develop and complete hierarchical concept and language charts, vocabulary trees, matrix diagrams and tables, and outlines of main ideas. Using the draw feature of a word processor, students can begin to understand levels of language by visually constructing a class and specific example tree like the one shown in Figure 3.4. For example, transportation is a class, land is a mode of transportation, and grandpa's blue car is a specific example of land transportation.

Contextualization with Visuals and Realia

Contextualizing information is another important scaffolding strategy that makes textbook and formal academic language more understandable by providing meaningful contexts. Traditionally, teachers have relied on pictures, charts, realia, and manipulatives to create a context that gives clues to the meaning of the material. Interactive computer-based vocabulary programs such as *Learning English* and *Community Exploration* (see Figure 3.5) allow students to chose environments and community facilities they wish to explore—a park, the library, a school, or the hospital. Through this type of theme-based program, students are able to learn vocabulary in a meaningful context.

Clarifying the meaning of textbook language with pictures, videos, and sound is easily accomplished in computer-based environments and involves the addition of graphics, movies, and even sounds to print. Commercially prepared interactive CD-ROM books range from elementary books to classic tales of literature, such as Edgar Allen Poe's writings. Story writing programs such as *Storybook Weaver* provide students with vocabulary within a multimedia context. One example is a mul-

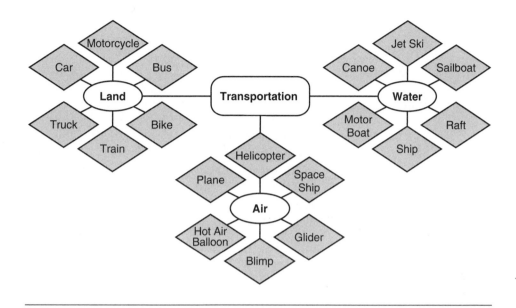

Figure 3.4   Clustering Graphical Organizer

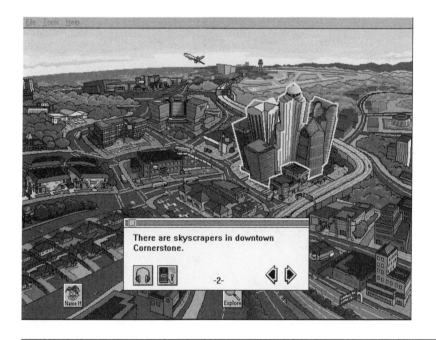

FIGURE 3.5   *Community Exploration*

Source: Courtesy of CompassLearning, Inc. Used with permission.

timedia storybook in which students can click on objects and be provided with sounds, actions, and additional explanations related to that object (see Figure 3.6).

Other programs provide a rich context in unique ways across the curriculum. For example, the software *Body Works* (Learning Company and Princeton Review Publishing) utilizes rotating, multimedia three-dimensional models to demostrate anatomical parts of the human body. Another program, *Operation Neptune* (Learning Company), uses a problem-solving game format to teach students mathematical concepts. As part of a deep-sea rescue mission of an unmanned space capsule, students must use fractions, decimals, and ratios to solve real situational problems. Students interpret data from electronic charts, maps, and tables to solve word problems requiring measurement of area, volume, and distance. Geography and history of countries throughout the world are brought alive through sound and video clips of electronic encyclopedias and atlases and software such as *Africa Trail* (Learning Company) and *Postcards* (Curriculum Associates, Inc.), which takes students to Turkey, Ghana, Japan, and Mexico.

Re-Presentation

It is beneficial for ELLs to read, write about, and otherwise represent content material in alternative forms such as drama, poetry, and songs. Text re-presentation is

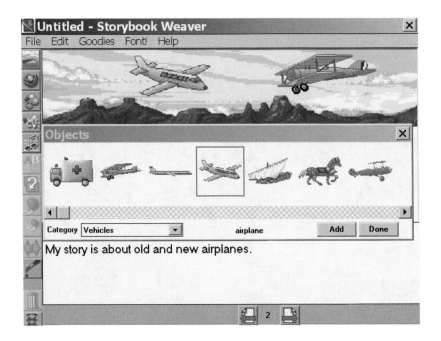

Figure 3.6 Story in the City, from *Storybook Weaver*

Source: © 1994 Riverdeep Interactive Learning Limited. Used with permission.

a common technique for helping students to gain an understanding of content material by their processing and presenting a text in some form other than the original version. Students might change a poem into a narrative, act out parts of a story, or write a dialog after watching a short skit. In addition to the traditional arts, there are now a variety of creative technology tools that can be used for the re-presentation of textual materials.

A simple paint or draw program that is probably available with all computers can be used to help students draw images that represent ideas discussed in a text or during a class discussion. Tom Sears, an instructional technology professor at New Mexico State University teaches his college students to create word pictures. The idea is to take an important concept and write a few sentences about this concept and then answer the following questions: What are the key words in their writing? How do these key words relate to each other? Are there some pictures that help illustrate these words? What pictures or images can be used to represent these ideas? Figure 3.7 is an example from a teacher education class.

A technology presentation tool such as *PowerPoint* provides an excellent way to help students re-present, reorganize, and review content. Working alone or in

FIGURE 3.7 *Word Picture*

Old Versus New Models of Learning	
Old	*New*
People learn by listening, memorizing, and giving back information.	People learn by constructing knowledge from many sources.
Learning is individual and competitive.	Learning occurs in social and cultural contexts.
The teacher is the sole source of information.	There are multiple sources of information.
Education is assign and assess.	Education is learning.

small groups students can be asked to take assigned reading and re-present the main ideas in the text in an attractive format using pictures, sound and animation. Such tools also make it easy to add scanned images, videos, and even provide links to websites when connectivity is available in the classroom.

Metacognitve Development

When students take the material they are learning and transform it into a presentation using a tool such as *PowerPoint,* they are required to think about the concepts they will be presenting. Metacognitive skills are developed as they consider what are the most important aspects of a concept, what should be presented first, in what order ideas should be presented, and how to make the ideas as clear as possible.

Encouraging metacognitive development is included in this section as a technology-enhanced sheltering strategy; it will also be discussed in other sections of the book. Students need to be encouraged to reflect on their own thinking and learning processes as they learn academic content. They do this by planning strategies to accomplish a task, monitoring their own performance, and evaluating their accomplishment of a task.

Ironically, learning to use technology itself supports metacognition. When a student writes an essay on a computer, the student must also plan and accomplish a variety of complex tasks, such as opening a program; creating a new document; manipulating, reformatting, and moving text within the document; and saving and printing correctly. Learning to search for appropriate Internet resources, or to use a spreadsheet to communicate mathematical information, or even to use a presentation program requires extensive planning, reflection, and self-evaluation.

Technology can also help students to reflect on their learning by providing electronic portfolios or word-processed learning logs in which students can periodically reflect on their progress using the documents they developed to help them measure their growth. Sometimes using a simple tool, such as the notepad that comes with the computers, is effective. As students are working on an academic assignment at the computer they can be asked to stop for a minute and write down a question they have about the material. The instructor can then circulate among the students and see what kinds of questions they have. These questions can be used as a stimulus for self-reflection, as well as feedback on the instruction or instructional materials.

More advanced students can develop guided lessons on how to use software or work on the Web by studying their own learning and then writing directions for other students. The advanced students might want to work with partners who would then read and follow their directions and provide feedback on how clearly they had explained how to use a specific program. Students can also practice selective attention by scanning for particular grammar structures or vocabulary in authentic writing in Internet listservs (Bickel and Truscello, 1996).

Computer-Based Representational Manipulatives

The computer provides opportunities for students to manipulate representational objects that help students move from concrete to abstract understanding of academic content. The manipulatives may range from pictures of rods or squares that can be manipulated to solve mathematical problems to visual databases that can be reorganized to support the making of sentences and stories. For example, students can construct multiplication solutions by manipulating representational rods or create fraction or percentage pictures using draw objects. Some programs, such as *Inspiration,* allow students to manipulate text and ideas. They can easily move words and phrases on the screen in order to group them in new ways.

Classroom Discourse and Interaction

How can technology support appropriate discourse and interaction?

As teachers work to increase content learning for their ELL students, they need to modify a number of variables in their presentation style, use of language, pacing, grouping strategies, and assignments. English language learners benefit from repetition, comprehension checks, and frequent opportunities for discussion, questions, and review of the material (Richard-Amato, 1996). Technology can greatly facilitate providing all of these. For example, one helpful presentation strategy is using the computer with an LCD panel and monitor to introduce and discuss different academic concepts with the class. The ELL students can pause and revisit visually interesting representations of ideas appropriate to the subject being taught. Teachers can also record on tape their explanations and comments of key concepts using vocabulary and pacing appropriate to the students' comprehension levels. ELL students can then listen to the teacher's lecture as many times as needed. The tapes can also include questions for comprehension checks interspersed throughout the talk to give students an opportunity to reflect on and assess how well they have understood the content.

Technology can assist teachers in tailoring the oral and written discourse in sheltered classes by creating their own materials. For instance, software programs, as well as websites, permit teachers to create materials geared to the reading levels of their students. Targeted vocabulary can be presented in many different formats, such as games, crossword puzzles, and cloze exercises. These exercises can also be individualized for different skill levels in the classroom. Kathy Schrock's educational website, which has now paired up with that of Discovery School (http://puzzlemaker.school.discovery.com/), provides multiple educational resources, lesson plans, and tools for teachers, including a variety of puzzle generators (see Figure 3.8).

Teachers can also utilize commercial software that is designed to present subject matter concepts utilizing language appropriate to the students' English profi-

FIGURE 3.8 *Puzzlemaker*

Source: This information is copyrighted by and provided courtesy of Discovery Channel Education. For more information and resources related to education, kids, and school, visit www.discoveryschool.com. Used with permission.

ciency levels. Students are then able to work with content-based software that tirelessly repeats any material they wish to review.

ELL students require longer wait time before answering questions in class than do their native English-speaking peers. Computer programs give students the autonomy to determine the amount of time they need in which to respond to questions or complete tasks. Record-keeping components of these programs facilitate comprehension checks by monitoring student progress and identifying key areas that need further clarification and reinforcement.

Web-based environments such as email and electronic bulletin board systems respond to the need of ELLs for additional time to reflect on material before participating in class discussions. The teacher can ask specific questions and the students can answer in a variety of ways. Using such a bulletin board system, whether available via a school Intranet or the Internet, allows students to continually revisit the instructional conversations that have been set up and to see the variety of answers their peers have entered. In such computer-mediated instructional spaces, students can discuss their understanding of the subject matter with other students or even call on experts in the field to clarify key concepts and expand on the topics they are studying or to explain linguistic problems. For example, at *Dave's ESL Café* (Sperling), students visit the discussion center where they can participate in electronic student forums to pose and respond to questions on various topics (see Figure 3.9). At the help center of this site, students seek assistance with their language problems from ESL/EFL teachers who respond electronically to their questions.

How can technology support different kinds of classroom groupings?

Teachers can use a variety of strategies for grouping ELL students that are conducive to discussion and comprehension of subject matter materials. These might range from collaborative learning projects, to paired activities, to peer tutoring. Technology simulations are powerful tools for supporting such group work.

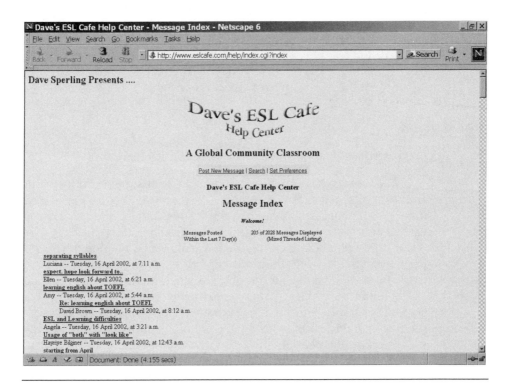

FIGURE 3.9 *Dave's ESL Café Website*

Source: Dave Sperling/Dave's ESL Café. Used with permission.

Students can work together as they utilize the audio, visual, and text features of simulation CD-ROMs, such as *SimCity* and *Wagon Trail,* to plan modern communities or participate in historical expeditions across the United States. They can also use multimedia tools, as discussed earlier, to create products that demonstrate their understanding of academic content.

Sheltered instruction also utilizes collaborative learning techniques that encourage students to learn from their more advanced peers. As can be seen in Mr. Cortez's class (a case study following this section), inviting in "techno-wizards" from another classroom is very helpful in providing needed guidance to for students new to technology. At the same time teaching others to use technology builds the self-esteem of the peer tutors. Technology can support a wide range of instructional groupings. The computer is a powerful tool for pair work, small group research, and a large variety of computer-based projects. Students might search through teacher-provided Internet addresses to find information on a subject such as whales and then write and illustrate a report together at the computer. One student who is strong in English can be paired with another who is good at operating the computer or illustrating concepts using a paint program. In such cases, the students are not only interfacing with the computer but are also using their English skills to communicate and negotiate with each other.

In summary, technology can be used to enhance teacher and student discourse by tailoring it to students' proficiency levels; it can provide repetition, reinforcement, extended discussion, and opportunities for students to review content material; and technology use naturally supports a wide variety of grouping strategies helpful in the ELL classroom. These three types of technology use to enhance discourse in the ELL classroom are summarized in Table 3.2.

Assessment

How can technology facilitate effective assessment?

Technology has unique characteristics that support both traditional testing and authentic measures. For example, the extensive record keeping capabilities of tutorial programs monitor student test results and provide specific feedback to the teacher and/or student on skill development. Computers can also provide space for storing authentic examples of student learning such as student work, journals, and presentations. Electronic portfolios can be used to store samples of not only written work but also oral language, graphical designs, pictures, and even video.

Computer-based activities lend themselves to authentic assessment since both performance and product assessment are so easily supported. Students in sheltered content courses need to be able to demonstrate their knowledge of the subject matter in a variety of ways suited to different learning styles. Word-processed reports, self-reflective journals, multimedia projects, and *PowerPoint* research presentations are representative of multiple computer-based assessment measures that can be used effectively with ELLs. Chapter 9 will discuss in detail the multitude of ways in which technology can be utilized to assess the academic progress of English language learners.

TABLE 3.2 *Technology-Enhanced Sheltered Instruction (TESI)*

Classroom Practice	*Technology Enhancements*
Instructional Strategies	
• Modeling	• Display of hypermedia stacks and Hyperstudio presentations from previous classes
• Bridging to students' prior knowledge and cultures	• Interactive map or family tree programs
• Schema building	• Hierarchical concept and language charts, vocabulary trees, matrix diagram, and outlines
• Contextualizing with visuals and realia	• Multimedia pictures, video, and sound to clarify meaning of text, Web-based charts, pictures, graphs, and numerical data
• Text re-presentation	• Presentation and authoring programs to transform information from one form to another
• Metacognitive development	• Electronic portfolio programs and word-processed learning logs
• Use of representational manipulatives	• Computer-generated rods and other representational objects
Classroom Discourse and Interactions	
• Discourse tailored to students' proficiency levels	• Software that allow a choice of proficiency levels—word games, authoring programs; computer presentations, and tape recordings of teacher lessons/lectures
• Repetition and reinforcement; frequent comprehension checks; and opportunities for discussion, questions, and review of material	• Electronic bulletin boards and discussion forums; content-based software that reinforces key concepts and allows student control of timed interactions; electronic record-keeping programs
• Collaborative learning techniques; peer or cross-age tutoring	• Computer-based group research and projects; "student techno-wizards"
• Variety of classroom groupings: whole class, individual work, pairs, small groups	• Collaborative computer-based projects; LCD focused whole-class discussions; individualized programs
Assessment	
• Variety of measures suited to multiple learning styles; performance and product assessment	• Word-processed papers; multimedia projects; research presentations; self-reflective journals
• Electronic monitoring of student progress	• Electronic portfolios; software with test recording capability; feedback from tutorials

In addition to their use in subject matter classes, these sheltering applications of technology can be employed by mainstream teachers to meet the challenge of offering specific strategies for ELLs while concurrently providing challenging material for all students. Most are also applicable to teaching content-based ESL or a combination of sheltered content and academic courses in an adjunct model. We will now take a close look at how one teacher at Juarez-Lincoln Accelerated Elementary School incorporated Technology Enhanced Sheltered Instruction into his fourth grade classrooms.

A Fourth-Grade Sheltered Class: A Classroom Vignette

Mr. Cortez's fourth-grade transitional class of English language learners is part of the bilingual program at Juarez-Lincoln Accelerated Elementary School in San Diego, California. Here, students receive two hours of language arts instruction in their primary language of Spanish and the remainder of the day in sheltered math and social science/health instruction taught in English and ELD instruction. The students are taught art, music, and PE in mainstream classes throughout the week. As they move into the fifth and sixth grades, they will also be in mainstream math and language arts classes. (Table 3.3 illustrates the school-wide program for English Language Learners in which this fourth-grade class operates.)

As part of the fourth-grade social science curriculum, Mr. Cortez's class is studying the Spanish missions of California and their impact on

TABLE 3.3 *Juarez-Lincoln Accelerated School Program for English Language Learners*

	K	1	2	3	4	5	6
ELD	ELD	ELD	ELD	ELD	ELD	ELD	ELD
Sheltered Content (SDAIE)	Math* Soc. Sci. Sci/Health	Math* Soc. Sci. Sci/Health	Math* Soc. Sci. Sci/Health	Math* Soc. Sci. Sci/Health	Math* Soc. Sci. Sci/Health	*Math*	*Math*
Primary Language Instruction	Lang. Arts Math	Lang. Arts Math	Lang. Arts Math	Lang. Arts Math	Lang. Arts Math	Lang. Arts	Lang. Arts
Mainstream Content	Art Music PE	Art Music PE	Art Music PE	Art Music PE	Art Music PE	Art Music PE Soc. Sci./ Health Lang. Arts Math	Art Music PE Soc. Sci./ Health Lang. Arts Math

Italicized = Instruction for newcomers

*Initial concepts taught in primary language and reinforced through SDAIE.

the state's development. The students are busily completing a project that has brought together their parents, teachers, school administrators, and both native and non-native English-speaking peers. Some students are seated around five computers in the classroom putting together the final pieces of their multimedia presentations on California missions, while others are attending to details of the models of the missions that they built at home with their parents. Recognizing the importance of bridging to his students' prior knowledge, experiences, and cultures, and wishing to further involve his students' parents in their children's education, Mr. Cortez selected California missions, a topic with which the parents were familiar, for a project-based thematic unit that incorporated science, math, language arts, and social studies. He had previously discovered that the project-based curriculum offered a variety of learning modalities that appealed to students with various learning styles. Next week, the school administrators, teachers, students, their families, and friends from the community will gather in the large cafeteria for the Missions Fiesta Night. This is the culminating activity of the missions project when students display their models and give *Hyperstudio* presentations on their missions. With their computers and their models next to each of them, the students will stand proudly with their parents to give their *PowerPoint* presentations and answer any questions guests might have about their missions.

If we look back on the steps in this quarter-long project, we see several examples of how Mr. Cortez utilized technology as a primary tool to provide the instructional supports needed to accomplish this undertaking.

Mr. Cortez explained that he and his students engaged in several activities in preparation of the actual missions project. He knew how important it would be that his students understood exactly what would be expected of them and that they have the knowledge and skills to be successful. With this in mind, Mr. Cortez designed learning experiences that served as models for various components of the missions project and for using computers for research, academic writing, and presentations.

One of the key objectives of the missions project was to give students an understanding of the research process and have them appreciate the wide range of resources available to them. As part of their assignments, students were required to have two book resources, one from the school library and another from a local library. Mr. Cortez recognized that encouraging students to use the local libraries would further involve the parents in their children's work, since they would likely be providing transportation to the library. First, Mr. Cortez took his class to a local library to demonstrate the steps involved in acquiring a library card, researching a topic, and checking out books. He notified other neighborhood libraries as to when his students would be visiting, described the class project and assignments, and requested their assistance with his students. Having developed schema for conducting research with hard copy materials, the students were now ready to begin to do research on the Internet.

Other mini-projects involved students communicating via email with two California missions, composing personal profiles using the Bilingual Writing Center program, and creating multimedia presentations of their family trees with *Hyperstudio*. With all of these projects, Mr. Cortez used the computer and LCD monitor to model each step that the students would be expected to perform. For example, students were shown how to cut and paste from their word processed personal profile to their *Hyperstudio* presentations and how to scan pictures for their family trees. These preliminary projects gave them the knowledge, skills, and confidence to take on the more extensive missions project. They also gained an understanding of the roles of the teacher, the student, and the Internet in the research process. The teacher would serve as a facilitator while the students used an exciting new tool to conduct the research.

Mr. Cortez clearly explained the components of the project to his students and to their parents in a letter requesting their support. The project would consist of a word processed booklet about a chosen mission, a model of the mission, and a multimedia presentation—all to be exhibited at the Missions Fiesta Night at their school. Since Mr. Cortez was doing the missions project for the first time, there were no models from previous classes to use, so it was imperative that he utilize other aids to make the material and expectations clear. Adhering to his practice of doing shared activities followed by guided structured lessons, Mr. Cortez introduced the topic of California missions with photographs, books, and videos of the missions. To make the topic more personal and meaningful to his students, he had visited and photographed himself at the nearby San Juan Capistrano Mission prior to his introduction to the subject. Next, using the Internet, he and his students took a virtual walk through the San Juan Capistrano Mission and interviewed employees there about its history and interesting characteristics. Now they were ready to see how to write their reports.

In addition to having computers in their classroom, students at Juarez-Lincoln have access to a networked computer lab where they can share their work as a whole class, with each other, or individually with their teacher. Here, Mr. Cortez projected a template of questions about the mission as a guide for students composing their reports on their computers. Equipment linking their answers to the LCD panel allowed the teacher and students to see and discuss their responses. As the class worked as a group to create a model report, they utilized the Internet to answer the basic questions about the mission. Mr. Cortez provided a list of helpful sites that he had previewed prior to the lesson and assisted the class in studying computer terminology they would need to know. This increased the self-esteem of the students who were excited that they knew how to use the same technical terms as the English-only students who shared the lab with them.

Another unique feature of this class was the use of cross-age tutoring in the class and computer lab. Fifth- and sixth-grade students, called *tech wizards,* who were expert at using technology, were released from class to assist the fourth-grade ELLs with the development of their language and technology skills. Later some of these fourth-graders became tech wizards themselves with one at each table empowered to assist and train their peers to use the computer to accomplish the assigned tasks. The tech wizards also assisted students with the math/science component of this cross-curriculum project in which the students received dimensions for the construction of their mission models and a timeline for their completion. After studying the missions on the Internet, the students' parents accompanied them and their teachers on a field trip to the San Juan Capistrano Mission. With a multitude of sheltering strategies, parental support, and peer tutoring, Mr. Cortez's fourth-graders were able to perform at grade level in academic subjects while still acquiring English proficiency.

Conclusion

Once again we see that the fields of technology and the teaching of English language learners share the same underlying constructivist learning theories. It is not surprising, then, that technology supports content-based instruction in a multitude of ways. It strengthens each instructional strategy that teachers find successful in linguistically sheltered classes and provides a rich environment for individual work and increased discourse and interaction. Through adult support, peer assistance, and collaborative projects using technology, students with below grade-level language proficiency are able to perform and demonstrate success in content-area subjects.

Summary of Key Ideas

1. Technology is an effective tool for the content-based approach of English language learners in ELD, sheltered instruction, adjunct models, and mainstream classes.

2. While basic interpersonal communication skills (BICS) can be acquired in one to two years of language study, the language skills needed for academic study requires five to ten years of schooling depending on the number of years of prior study in the student's native language. Technology can assist a student's progression from BICS to the acquisition of the more advanced cognitive academic language proficiency (CALP).

3. Technology-enriched, content-based instruction is based on the constructivist theories of Bruner and Vygotsky, who proposed that learning depends on how students structure knowledge about themselves and their environment.

4. Through instructional supports, adult assistance, and collaboration with more capable peers, students can move from their current level of development to a higher one where they are capable of working independently. Technology can play an important role in giving this assistance.

5. Technology can assist in providing instructional support, or scaffolding, that promotes the cognitive and academic development of English language learners. This chapter presented several technology-enhanced scaffolds, including modeling, bridging, schema building, conceptualization, text re-presentation, metacognitive development, and representational manipulatives.

6. Effective use of technology greatly enhances both teacher and student discourse and interaction in a sheltered learning environment.

7. A variety of technology-based assessment tools, such as word-processed reports, electronic journals, multimedia projects, and *PowerPoint* presentations, provide additional ways in which to monitor and assess the progress and achievement of English language learners.

8. Within a technology-rich collaborative environment, such as that of Mr.Cortez's fourth-grade class, English language learners are able to successfully do grade-level academic work.

Learning Activities

1. Scaffolding strategies can be a great benefit to English language learners struggling with both language acquisition and subject matter content concurrently. In small groups, identify a complicated subject matter concept and decide on four or five technology-based scaffolding techniques that could assist ELLs in comprehending and applying this concept. Explain the rationale for your choices.

2. We have seen how a number of modifications and variations in discourse and interaction can promote language acquisition in a sheltered class. In small groups, select a particular sheltered setting for ELLs and discuss how technology could be used to enhance both student-student and student-teacher discourse and interaction. Give specific choices of technology tools that you would recommend for this class and explain the rationale for their selection and the manner in which you would use them.

3. We know that multiple assessment measures give the most accurate picture of students' achievement. Discuss the current assessment procedures used to evaluate ELLs in a school in your region and identify alternative technology-based assessment measures that could be used to improve both formative and summative assessment of these students.

4. Visit Kathy Shrock and Discovery Schools Site for Making Puzzles. Working in small groups, make up puzzles that will be useful to other members of your class and then

invite them to solve the puzzles. Talk about how the puzzle-making activity could be useful when teaching in an ELL or bilingual classroom.

5. In pairs or triads, examine a successful lesson you or your colleagues currently use with ELLs that does not utilize technology tools. Redesign the lesson using technology to strengthen the lesson's content, instructional activities and assessment measures. Role-play presenting your new lesson to an ELL class with your classmates acting as the students

Technology Resources

Body Works (1999). Cambridge, MA: The Learning Co. and Princeton Review Publishing.
Community Exploration (1994). San Diego: Jostens Learning Corporation.
HyperStudio (Version 3.1) [Computer software]. (1997). San Diego, CA: Roger Wagner.
Inspiration (1998). Lake Oswego, OR: Ceres Software.
Learning English: Neighborhood Life (1994). San Diego: Conter/Jostens Learning Corporation.
Microsoft PowerPoint 97 (1996). Redmond, WA: Microsoft.
Microsoft Word (Version 6.0). (1995). Redmond, WA: Microsoft.
Operation Neptune (1996). The Learning Company Postcards. North Billerica, MA: Curriculum Associates, Inc.
Oregon Trail II. (1997). Minneapolis, MN: The Learning Company.
SimCity (1995). Walnut Creek, CA: Maxis.
Storybook Weaver (1992). Minneapolis, MN: The Learning Company.
Wagon Trial 1848 (1997). Minneapolis, MN: The Learning Company.
Writing Process Workshop (1992). Educational Activities.

Websites

European Geothermal Information(http://www.demon.co.uk.geosci/world.html)
Geothermal Power Sites (http://www.demon.co.uk.geosci/world.html)
Puzzlemaker (http://puzzlemaker.school.discovery.com).Kathy Schrock's Guide for Educators.

References

Becijos, J. (1997). *SDAIE Strategies for Teachers and English Learners.* Bonita, CA: Torch Publications.
Berko Gleason, J. (1993) *The Development of Language* (3rd ed.). New York: Macmillan.
Bickel, B., and Truscello, D. (1996). New opportunities for learning: Styles and strategies with computers. *TESOl Journal* 6 (1): 15–19.
Brown, J., Collins, A., and Duguid, P. (1989). Situated cognition and the culture of learning. *Educational Researcher* 18(1): 32–42.
Bruner, J. (1986). *Actual Minds, Possible Worlds.* Cambridge, MA: Harvard University Press.
Collier, V. P. (1987). Age and rate of acquisition of second language for academic purposes. *TESOL Quarterly* 21: 617–641.
Collier, V. P. (1992). The Canadian bilingual immersion debate: A synthesis of research findings. *Studies in Second Language Acquisition* 14: 87–97.
Collier, V. P. (1995, Fall). Acquiring a second language for school: Directions in language and education. *National Clearinghouse for Bilingual Eduacation* 1 (4).
Collier, V.P., and Thomas, W.P. (1989). How quickly can immigrants become proficient in school English? *Journal of Educational Issues of Language Minority Students* 5: 26–38.
Cummins, J. (1981a). The role of primary language development in promoting educational success for language minority students. In California State Department of Education (Ed.),

Schooling and Language Minority Students: A Theoretical Framework (pp. 3–49). Los Angeles: National Dissemination and Assessment Center.

Cummins, J. (1981b). Age on arrival and immigrant second language learning in Canada: A reassessment. *Applied Linguistics* 2: 132–149.

Cummins, J. (1984). *Bilingualism and Special Education: Issues in Assessment and Assessment and Pedagogy.* San Diego, CA: College-Hill Press.

Ellis, R. (1985). *Understanding Second Language Acquisition.* Oxford: Oxford University Press.

Goodman, Y. M., and Wilde, S. (Eds.). (1992). *Literacy Events in a Community of Young Writers.* New York: Teachers College Press.

Hakuta, K. (1986). *Mirror of Language: The Debate on Bilingualism.* New York: Basic Books.

Krashen, S. (1981). *Second Language Acquisition and Second Language Learning.* New York: Pergamon.

Krashen, S. (1985). *The Input Hypothesis: Issues and Implications.* New York: Longman.

Norton, P., and Wiburg, K. M. (1998). *Teaching with Technology.* Fort Worth, TX: Harcourt Brace.

O'Malley, J. M., and Chamot, A. U. (1990*). Learning Strategies in Second Language Acquisition.* Cambridge: Cambridge University Press.

Papert, S. (1980). *Mindstorms: Children, Computers and Powerful Ideas.* New York: Basic Books.

Reid, J. (1995*). Learning Styles in the ESL/EFL Classroom.* Boston: Heinle & Heinle.

Richard-Amato, P. (1996). *Making It Happen.* White Plains, NY: Longman.

Swain, M. (1985). Communicative competence: Some roles of comprehensible input and comprehensible output in its development. In S. Gass and C. Madden (Eds.), *Input in Second Language Acquisition* (pp. 235–253). Cambridge, MA: Newbury House.

Teemant, A., Bernhardt, E., and Rodriguez-Muñoz, M. Collaborating with content-area teachers: What we need to share. In M. A. Snow and D. M. Brinton (Eds.), *The Content-Based Classroom: Perspectives on Integrating Language and Content* (pp. 311–318). White Plains, NY: Longman.

Thomas, W. P., and Collier, V. P. (1995). *Language Minority Student Achievement and Program Effectiveness.* Manuscript in preparation.

Vygotsky, L. S. (1978). *Mind in Society.* Cambridge, MA: Harvard University Press.

Walqui-van Lier, (1992). *Sheltered Instruction: Doing It Right.* San Diego, CA: San Diego County Office of Education Sheltered Instruction Teacher Training.

Willis J., Stephens, E., and Matthew, K. (1996). *Technology, Reading, and Language Arts.* Boston: Allyn and Bacon.

Wiburg, K., Montoya, N., and Sandin, J. (1998). *Nuestra Tierra: A University/Public PowerPoint School Technology Integration Project.* A paper presented at the annual American Educational Research Association (AERA) Conference, San Diego, CA.

Wong Fillmore, L. (1991). Second language learning in children: A model of language learning in social context. In E. Bialystok (Ed.), *Language Processing in Bilingual Children* (pp. 49–69). Cambridge: Cambridge University Press.

4

Using Technology to Teach Oral Communication Skills

Chapter Overview

Chapters 4 and 5 focus on the use of technology to facilitate the acquisition of language skills, beginning with the oral communication skills—listening, speaking, and pronunciation—in Chapter 4. Though we advocate an integrated approach to teaching a second language, we also recognize the need for focused practice of individual skills at various stages of a student's linguistic development. The purpose of this chapter is to examine the processes involved in the development of listening and speaking skills and to investigate how technology can assist the learner in acquiring these skills.

The first part of the chapter focuses on listening with attention directed to two approaches to second language teaching that place a strong emphasis on listening, the natural approach and the total physical response (TPR), and the theories that support these approaches. It concludes with an examination of the processes involved in listening and the learner's purpose for listening plays. Numerous examples of computer uses to support the development of listening skills are presented.

The second section looks at speaking skills, beginning with a brief historical overview of the treatment of speaking in various methods and approaches over the past 50 years, and culminates with current views on learning to speak in a second language and ways in which technology can facilitate the process. The last section focuses on pronunciation, a subskill of listening and speaking. Basic learner goals for pronunciation are presented with discussion and several illustrations of computer-based programs designed specifically to assist learners to improve their pronunciation skills. The chapter concludes with a classroom vignette of an intermediate level ESL listening and speaking class at a large, urban university, a summary of the key ideas presented in the chapter, and suggested learning activities.

Developing Listening Skills

Listening was first recognized as a major component of language learning and teaching in the late 1970s. At that time, foreign language teaching research suggested that language instruction should focus on the learner's listening comprehension in the early stages of acquisition, while delaying oral production until the student was more familiar with the new language (Winitz, 1981). This school of thought manifested itself in the form of the comprehension approach (Richards and Rogers, 1986) which proposed the following:

1. Comprehension abilities precede productive skills in learning a language.
2. The teaching of speaking should be delayed until comprehension skills are established.
3. Skills acquired through listening transfer to other skills.
4. Teaching should emphasize meaning rather than form.
5. Teaching should minimize learner stress. (p. 88)

Two approaches to second language teaching, TPR and the natural approach, shared many of these views and are frequently grouped within the broader comprehension approach umbrella (Larsen-Freeman, 2000). The *monitor model* of second language acquisition proposed by Krashen (1981, 1982, 1985) provided the theoretical underpinnings for the natural approach and to some extent for TPR. Because of the strong emphasis both these approaches and Krashen's model place on the development of listening skills prior to other language skills, we begin this chapter with a look at their principles and practices. A third method, the lexical approach proposed by Michael Lewis (1993, 1997), was also conceived in the tradition of the communicative approach. It stresses the communication of meaning by focusing on the acquisition of fixed or semi-fixed lexical items present in the English language. This approach is discussed in Chapter 5, where we examine vocabulary development.

Krashen's Monitor Model of Second Language Acquisition

What are the five hypotheses that form Krashen's monitor model of second language acquisition?

The language acquisition theory developed by Krashen (1981, 1982, 1985) and implemented in the classroom as the natural approach (Terrell, 1977) has received wide attention in the SLA (second language acquisition) literature and has had a strong influence on ESL methodology. This model consists of five hypotheses relating to second language learning:

1. Acquisition/learning hypothesis
2. Monitor hypothesis
3. Natural order hypothesis
4. Input hypothesis
5. Affective filter hypothesis

The *acquisition/learning hypothesis* states that language skills can be developed through two means: (1) acquisition, the process used by children to acquire their native language; and (2) learning, the conscious and explicit knowing about the language. Acquisition is subconscious, whereas learning is consciously developed by instruction and aided by error correction.

The *monitor hypothesis* claims the primary responsibility for language fluency belongs to acquisition. Conscious learning is limited to use as a monitor that can edit and make corrections in the learner's output before the learner writes or speaks. Krashen (1987) stipulates three conditions that are necessary for effective use of the monitor: (1) sufficient time to consult and use conscious rules, (2) a focus on form, and (3) knowledge of the applicable rule.

The *natural order hypothesis* asserts that language learners acquire linguistic structures in a predictable order in their native language and that a similar order is present in second language acquisition. This theory is supported by first language research of Corder (1967) and Brown (1973) and similar findings by Dulay and Burt (1977) in second language acquisition studies. Students, for instance, acquire the negative verb formation in English beginning with the no + verb form, as in *He no like tomatoes,* and proceed through a predictable progression of ungrammatical forms until they correctly produce *He doesn't like tomatoes.*

In his *input hypothesis,* Krashen (1985) asserts that learners move from one level (i) of comprehension to the next (i + 1) by means of comprehensible input (that which contains i + 1). Learning is first focused on meaning, and structure is learned as a consequence of understanding the message. According to Krashen, speaking will emerge from this comprehensible input without instruction. The best input is not grammatically sequenced; rather, structures will be automatically acquired if sufficient i + 1 input is presented. Though many linguists have questioned the "speech emergence" claim and have argued that other variables such as the learner's level of engagement in the learning process are equally important to understanding, comprehensible input is recognized as a crucial factor in the language learning process (Brown, 1994; Mitchell and Myles, 1998).

The fifth component of Krashen's monitor model is the *affective filter hypothesis* proposed by Dulay and Burt (1977), which addresses the affective variables of second language acquisition. They hypothesized the presence of an affective filter that could act as a mental block if a poor affective state existed. Anxiety, lack of motivation, or low self-esteem could prevent the input from being processed even though the learner understood the input.

The Natural Approach

What are the principles of the natural approach and how are they applied to classroom practice?

The *natural approach* as practiced by Terrell (1977) in Spanish foreign language teaching and supported by Krashen's (1982) model of second language acquisition theory was founded on four key principles. First, according to the natural approach (Krashen and Terrell, 1983), comprehension precedes production; that is, listening and reading skills will be acquired before speaking and writing. The primary goal of language instruction is to facilitate language acquisition by making the messages understandable to the learner. This approach has several pedagogical implications: Teachers speak in the target language only, subject matter is selected according to its relevance to student interests, and careful attention is given by the instructor to consistently provide comprehensible input.

The second principle calls for allowing language production to emerge in particular stages moving from nonverbal responses, single words, and combinations of two or three words to phrases, sentences, and ultimately to complex discourse. Accordingly, in this "silent period" (Krashen and Terrell, 1983, p. 20), students are never forced to speak before they are comfortable doing so and error correction is kept to a minimum limited primarily to global errors that interfere with communication. The third principle holds that the syllabus and course content be organized around topics with communicative goals rather than linguistic structures. The focus is on communicating ideas with little or no attention to grammatical accuracy in the early comprehension and production stages. Lastly, the classroom environment must be conducive to learning. Activities should ensure that students can practice the language in a nonthreatening setting that reduces student anxiety, promotes motivation, and builds self-esteem (Krashen and Terrell, 1983).

It should be noted that the natural approach is different in fundamental ways from the natural method of the nineteenth century which laid the foundation for what became known as the direct method in the early part of the twentieth century. While both methods held to the naturalistic principles of language learning, the natural approach relied far less on the predetermined teacher monologues, repetition, and highly structured question and answer practice that the natural method had earlier advocated. The natural approach, instead, focused on comprehensible input and the optimum affective state of the learner (Richards and Rogers, 1986).

Largely because of the theoretical support it received from Krashen's theory of second language teaching and its appeal to classroom teachers, the natural approach had a strong impact on second language teaching in the last quarter of the twentieth century. It has not been, however, without critics who questioned its advocacy for delay in students' oral production (Gibbons, 1985; Brown, 2000) and its neglect of comprehensible *output* (Swain, 1985).

How does technology provide comprehensible input?

Technology assists students in acquiring language skills indirectly by acting as a major motivator and stimulus for language development. It provides students with incentives to communicate orally as they work collaboratively on tasks and communicative projects such as those discussed in Chapter 2. Two other major benefits of technology for second language learners are the exposure to large amounts of comprehensible speech and access to low-anxiety learning environments. A key role of the second language teacher is to act as a facilitator in providing comprehensible input. Traditionally, teachers have relied heavily on the use of pictures, realia, and gestures to convey meaning to beginning learners. The computer, with its multimedia and hypermedia features, is a powerful addition to the second language teacher's repertoire. Computers allow teachers to add multisensory elements, text, sound, pictures, video, and animation, which provide meaningful contexts to facilitate comprehension. Picture what we've come to call three-dimensional text. Take an ordinary text passage related to what students will learn. Add to the text a link or button so that when students link on that word, they can call up a video about the concept, or a spoken explanation or an expanded definition with examples of the word.

Software programs for beginning-level students let them connect words and sentences to pictures or animations in context of a particular setting to assist in comprehension. Computer programs are also helpful in demonstrating more complex vocabulary and concepts. Working with her fourth-grade English language learners on sequencing and the use of the conjunctions *before* and *after*, Mrs. Kaneko encouraged her students to practice with the *New Dynamic English* program that provides pictures to illustrate the order of the events described by the narrator (see Figure 4.1). Listeners are able to hear the sentences as many times as needed and record their own voices using *before* and *after* to retell the events. They then arrange the pictures in the correct order as the events occurred.

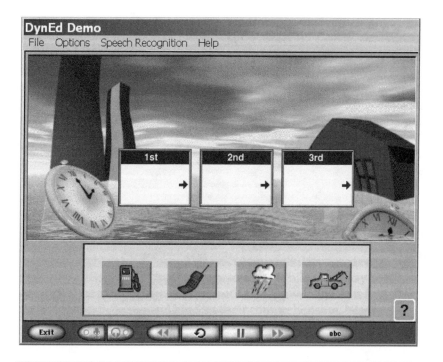

FIGURE 4.1 *New Dynamic English*

Source: New Dynamic English, © 1998 DynEd International, Inc. Used with permission.

In what ways can technology assist in creating a nonthreatening language learning environment?

Technology can aid teachers in creating a supportive, nonthreatening learning environment in which second language learners feel secure enough to practice the target language and to make and correct their own errors without embarrassment or anxiety. The computer can be programmed to present material at different difficulty levels with adjustments in speed of delivery according to individual learner needs. The untiring, nonjudgmental nature of the computer gives students the autonomy to review any part of the lesson as many times as they wish and receive immediate feedback and additional assistance as needed. By reducing stress and anxiety, learners are able to negotiate meaning and convert the raw message they hear into comprehensible input. Listening programs, such as *Let's Go*, use animation and songs to provide young learners motivating and comprehensible input (see Figure 4.2). Students are asked to listen to the speaker and click on the picture that describes the word or sentence they hear.

Teachers can capitalize on students' interest in songs by using websites such as *Listening Room* (http://www.manythings.org/el/at) developed by Charles I. Kelly, where students listen to songs and then fill in missing words of a cloze ver-

FIGURE 4.2   Let's Go

Source: Let's Go © 1995 DynEd International, Inc. and Oxford University Press. Used with Permission.

sion of the song (see Figure 4.3). Students may listen to a song they are working with as many times as they wish and, after completing the cloze exercise, request that their answers be checked and/or that all correct answers be given.

Listening programs for older or more advanced students require them to listen to a narrator and choose the scene on the screen that illustrates what they are hearing, or they might be given a set of instructions that require them to manipulate objects on the screen. For instance, in Mrs. Aguillar's life skills class, her students use the *Learning English: Home and Family* program to do a simulation of using an ATM machine (see Figure 4.4). They listen to step-by-step directions and through a click-and-drag action, respond to each command, starting with placing the credit card in the correct slot of the machine.

Total Physical Response (TPR)

What are the principles and practices of the TPR?

The theoretical foundation of TPR, developed by Asher (1977), consists of an interesting combination of principles and insights. Students are exposed to large amounts of language input before they are encouraged to speak. Total physical response recognizes the natural order of first language acquisition in which chil-

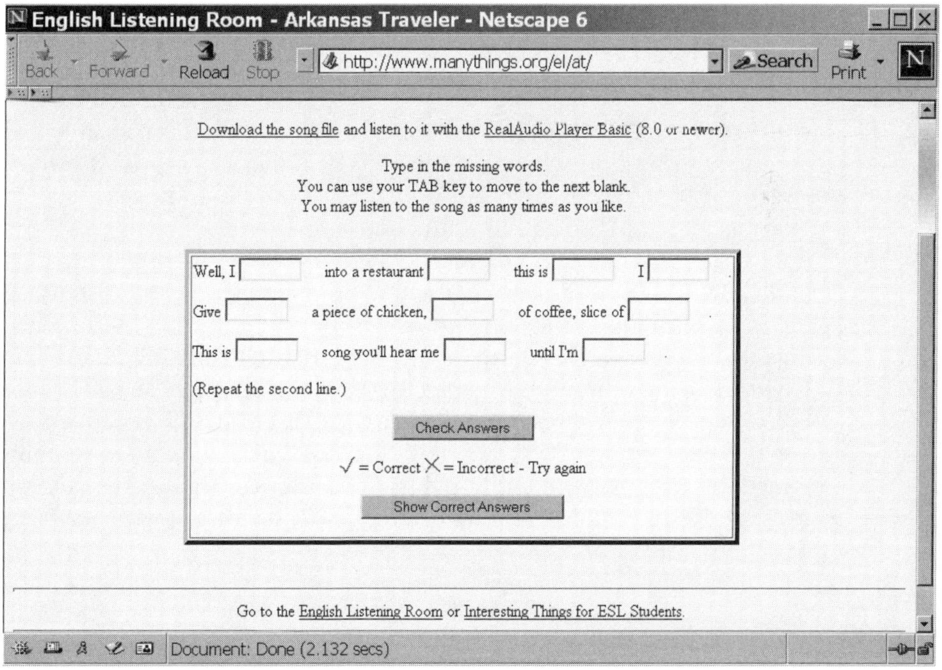

FIGURE 4.3 *Listening Room*

Source: Charles I. Kelly. Used with permission.

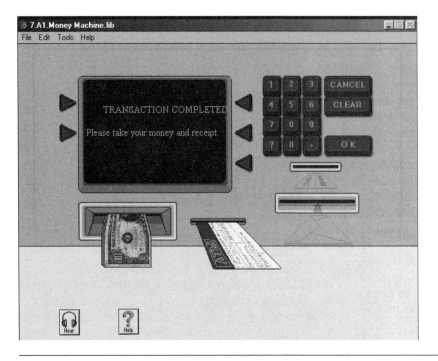

FIGURE 4.4 *Learning English: Home and Family*
Source: Courtesy of Contér Software. Used with permission.

dren listen extensively before speaking. Coupled with this principle of delayed oral production is the principle of psychomotor associations, which claims memory is enhanced through the association of language with motor activity. According to TPR theory, motor activity is a function of the right hemisphere of the brain, and right-brain activities should precede the language processing functions of the left-brain (Brown, 2000). Accordingly, practitioners of TPR rely heavily on command forms such as "Open the door" to which the student responds by physically opening the door. In this way, both hemispheres of the brain are utilized to reinforce the language being taught. In the affective domain, by concentrating on listening and not requiring an oral response, TPR lowers the student's affective filter and stress level. While this approach can be utilized to teach more advanced linguistic constructions such as the conditional in the sentence, "If you would like to listen to music, raise your hand," it has most frequently been used with beginning-level students.

Total physical response is frequently used as a technique within a variety of teaching approaches and methods rather than strictly as an approach unto itself. Some recent software programs use the same imperative format as TPR and attempt to simulate command responses on the screen. For instance, with the *Live Action English Interactive: TPR on a Computer*, the student responds to a command by clicking on the correct object and dragging it to a person on the screen (see Figure 4.5). A short video clip then illustrates the command with the actor on the screen

FIGURE 4.5   *Live Action English Interactive: TPR on the Computer*

Source: Software screen from *Live Action English Interactive: TPR on a Computer;* copyright Command Performance Language Institute, 1755 Hopkins St., Berkeley, CA 94707; tel/fax: (510) 524-1191; based on the book *Live Action Englis*h by Elizabeth Kuizenga Romijn and Contee Seely.

performing the correct action. In the *Time to Clean the House* clip, students see the actor perform commands such as "Sweep the floor" or "Empty the trash can" when they provide him with a broom or basket with which to perform the task.

Listening Processes

In order to most effectively use technology to support the development of listening skills of English language learners (ELLs), it is important to understand the processes involved in listening comprehension and to recognize the impact the learner's purpose for listening has on the ways in which he or she engages in the listening process. The next sections look at both processes and purpose as major components of listening comprehension.

What kinds of processing strategies are involved in listening?

Two types of processes, bottom-up and top-down, have been identified as central to listening comprehension (Chaudron and Richards, 1986; Richards, 1990). In *bottom-up processing,* focus is placed on individual components of oral discourse. Comprehension is viewed as a process of decoding messages proceeding from phonemes to words, to phrases and clauses and other grammatical elements, to sentences. Richards (1990) gives the following examples of bottom-up processes the listener experiences in order to comprehend a message:

1. Scanning the input to identify lexical items
2. Segmenting the stream of speech into constituents—for example, in order to recognize that "abookofmine" consists of four words
3. Using phonological cues to identify the information focus in an utterance
4. Using grammatical cues to organize the input into constituents—for example, in order to recognize that in "the book which I lent you" [the book] and [which I lent you] are the major constituents rather than [the book which I] and [lent you]. (pp. 50–51)

Bottom-up activities might ask a student to identify sounds or parts of a sentence according to their function as subject, verb, object, and so on, or to distinguish between positive and negative sentences or statements and questions. Several computer programs provide students listening practice with bottom-up processing skills in which they develop their lexical, phonological, and grammatical knowledge. Several software programs offer phonics practice as part of more extensive programs for young learners in which they identify the sound they hear in a word by clicking onto the correct letters representing that sound (see Figure 4.6).

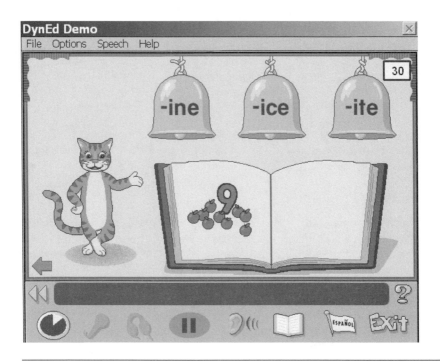

FIGURE 4.6 *Let's Go*

Source: Let's Go, © 1995 DynEd International, Inc. and Oxford University Press. Used with permission.

Phonics programs designed for adults frequently concentrate on practicing similar-sounding words that are problematic to non-native speakers. Students practice both listening and producing the sounds at their own speed and for however long they wish, thus avoiding anxiety and embarrassment that adult learners frequently experience when attempting to speak in a second language. The TESL/TEFL/TESOL/ESL/EFL/ESOL Links website, maintained by the *Internet TESL Journal*, links to numerous self-study listening and pronunciation exercises for adults that have been developed by TESOL professionals worldwide (see Figure 4.7).

Top-down processing strategies take into account the macro-features of discourse such as the speaker's purpose and the discourse topic. Comprehension is seen as a process of activating the listener's background information and schemata for a global understanding of the message. If, for instance, a friend tells you "I forgot to buy candles at the grocery store," your prior knowledge will determine the type of candle you assign to that statement. If you already know that today is the birthday of your friend's daughter, you will probably assume your friend needs to buy small, birthday candles. If, however, you only know that you had a power outage last night and the weather report predicted more storms, the candles you

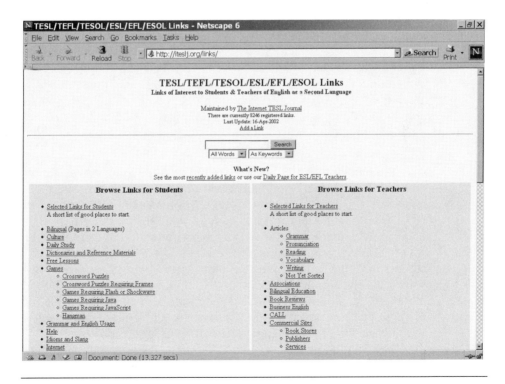

FIGURE 4.7   TESL/TEFL/TESOL/ESL/EFL/ESOL Links

Source: Charles I. Kelly. Used with permission.

would envision would be quite different. In addition to this type of contextual and situational knowledge, listeners also draw on their knowledge about the topic of the discourse, scripts, and schemata. *Scripts* include formulaic speech patterns, such as greetings and introduction, whereas *schemata* refer to what Richards (1990) defines as "plans about the overall structure of events and the relationships between them" that are stored in the listener's long-term memory. These schemata relate to our real-world experiences and how we expect people to behave and events to occur. If I order a sandwich at a fast food restaurant and the cashier hands me a receipt and says, "Your number is 146," I know that there are not 145 people to be served before me and that someone will give me the food I ordered in a few minutes.

A segment from the video *Cold Water* (Ogami, 1988) provides a good example of what happens when someone is missing an important schema for a particular situation as well as some crucial bottom-up processing information. A college student just arriving for study in the United States described the experience he had in placing an order at a fast food restaurant. When the cashier asked whether he wanted his order "forhereortogo," the student did not understand her message. The cashier repeated the words slowly, which as the student explained, "I understood but I didn't get the meaning." It wasn't until the man in line behind the student asked him, "Do you want your food here or do you want to take it home?" that he finally understood the cashier's question. With the new schema of taking food "to go," this student, through bottom-up processing, was able to apply his linguistic knowledge to figure out the message. This and similar videos have been especially beneficial to ESL students in helping them to understand the language and cultural challenges that they predictably will encounter.

How can technology assist students in demonstrating their background and linguistic knowledge?

Students frequently draw on both their previous knowledge of a topic and linguistic knowledge. Computers allow students to demonstrate their knowledge and competencies in a variety of ways. For instance, in Mrs. Temores's sheltered sixth-grade social sciences class, students were to work in groups to research and do a timeline on the life of great American inventors. One group that had selected Albert Einstein was working with the *New Dynamic English* program, which featured a listening unit on Einstein (see Figure 4.8). As the students listened to a short narration about Einstein's life, pictures would appear on the screen to visually represent what was being said about different events in his life. With the help of these picture cues and guided questions, the students were able to place the major events of Einstein's life in the correct order on a timeline.

In still other programs, such as *Firsthand Access,* students listen to a dictation and fill in a cloze exercise by clicking and dragging the words they hear to their correct position within the sentences (see Figure 4.9). With many similar software programs, teachers can use a text they select or the writing of their students to create their own oral dictations and generate cloze exercises.

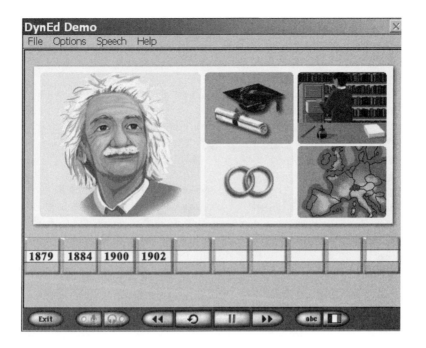

FIGURE 4.8 *New Dynamic English*

Source: Firsthand Access, © 1994 DynEd International, Inc. and Longman Asia Ltd. Used with permission.

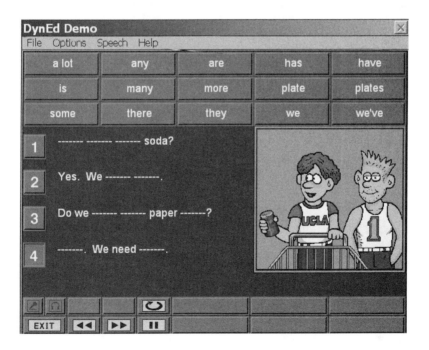

FIGURE 4.9 *Firsthand Access*

Source: Firsthand Access, © 1994 DynEd International, Inc. and Longman Asia Ltd. Used with permission.

How do different purposes for listening affect the way learners listen?

Although there are several models for classifying purposes for listening, Brown and Yule (1983) proposed a system that has been widely used that distinguishes between *interactional* and *transactional* functions of language. When language is used for interactional purposes, the focus is on harmonious communication in social contexts. As such, interactional language most typically includes greetings and small talk that center on noncontroversial topics that illicit agreement among the participants. These "listener-oriented" (Richards, 1990:56) interactional uses of language do not require careful attention to detail and facts.

In contrast, *transactional* uses of language focus on conveying information and are "message oriented." As such, they should be explicit, clear, and coherent in order for the listener to comprehend the meaning of the message, as is required for example, when students listen to lectures and take notes or practice dictations and cloze exercises.

Tikunoff (1985) and Richards (1990) proposed that both transactional and interactional language functions are needed for effective classroom participation. Students use interactional language to socially interact with each other and their teacher and engage in transactional uses to develop new skills and construct new knowledge. Use of both types of language functions is especially important to second language learners as they move into mainstream classrooms where they must acquire new knowledge and interact with their peers in appropriate ways. Research by Fillmore (1979) indicated that second language learners in mainstream classrooms had less frequent contact with native English speaking peers and were called on to respond less frequently than first language children. Technology can afford ELLs additional opportunities to use English for both interactional and transactional functions.

How can technology assist students in interactional communication?

The *Learning Oral English Online* website, created by Rong-Chang Li, is an online conversation book designed for intermediate-level ELLs. This website offers interactional speaking practice through dialogs centered on topics such as making friends, going to a party, and dating. In these exercises, students can elect to listen to the entire dialog or access individual sentences. Brief introductions to the dialogs and explanatory notes on slang and idioms used in the dialogs are provided. Students also practice different aspects of social conversation. For example, in "Making Friends," students are guided to recognize three parts of casual conversations: the greeting, small talk, and leave taking. This site also practices another type of interactional listening that focuses on simple service-oriented tasks such as ordering lunch and shopping in America.

How can technology assist students in transactional communication?

Use of technology to support transformational communication was demonstrated in Mr. Lee's high school health class. Here, students were assigned various issues related to smoking to investigate for an upcoming debate on the topic. As a prompt for discussion and a source of information on the topic, his students listened to a lecture on smoking presented in a video clip from the *Issues in English* program. While listening to the speaker, Mr. Lee's students typed in the main points they heard on the computer screen. If they had any difficulty understanding the lecture, they would stop the lecture and replay it or ask the computer program for vocabulary assistance. In this exercise, students were listening intently to the lecture for transactional purposes as they attempted to determine the key points of the talk for later use in their debate on the topic.

Other programs give more guided practice in listening for transactional purpose. Working with the software program *Engage* (see Figure 4.10), students first listen to a dialog for the key words. They then identify these words and place them on their computer notepad. Later they are required to answer comprehension questions from their key words and notes.

Websites such as *Randall's ESL Cyber Listening Lab* use streaming audio and video to offer listening quizzes for both interactional and transactional communication at varying levels of linguistic competencies (see Figure 4.11). One section of this website that provides transactional language practice presents mini-lectures that are designed to promote English development for academic purposes. Each listening exercise consists of a mini-lecture that students would be likely to hear in

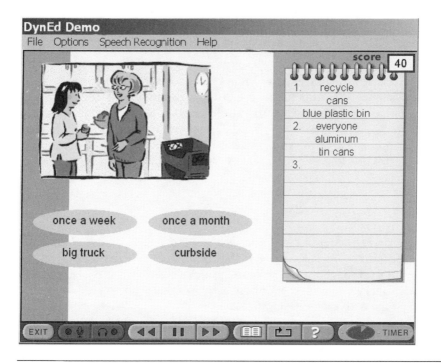

FIGURE 4.10 *Engage*

Source: Engage, © 1997 DynEd International, Inc. and Kirihara Uni. Used with permission.

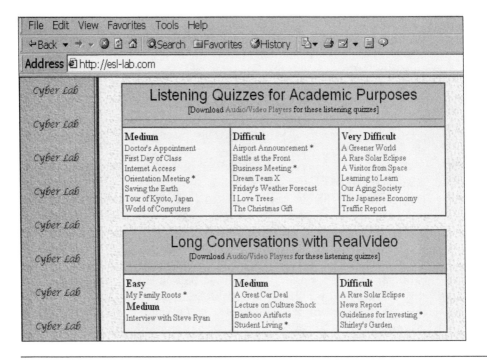

FIGURE 4.11   *Randall's ESL Cyber Listening Lab* (**http://www.esl-lab.com**)
Source: Randall S. Davis. Used with permission.

the classroom. After playing the lecture as many times as they wish and taking notes as needed, students take a quiz that evaluates their comprehension of the material covered in the lecture. Students are provided their scores and the correct answers with explanations of the correct choices. Transcripts of all the mini-lectures are available for students to print out. In this way, technology becomes a powerful tool for the simulation of classroom listening experiences.

Developing Speaking Skills

The primary benefit of a technology-enhanced environment for the development of speaking skills is the speech that occurs as students talk to each other while working on collaborative tasks and projects or while just chatting around the computer. It is while engaged in these activities that students call on their oral skills to negotiate with each other and take risks to use new language in order to get across their meaning. As we saw in Chapter 2, technology also allows students to communicate via teleconferencing software such as *CU-See Me* with authentic audiences around the world and facilitates global technology-based projects that serve as incentives for this communication.

In addition to creating a motivating speaking environment, technology can provide focused practice of listening skills through software programs and websites for student interaction. Several websites have recording capabilities to allow students to practice speaking. For example, as part of the post-listening exercises of *Randall's ESL Cyber Listening Lab,* on-line students utilize a dual-track audio/video player to record their reading of the listening conversations and compare their recordings to the audio files. Similarly, its audio active comparative corrections (AACC) exercises allow students to listen to statements or questions recorded on the program track and record their answers on a separate student track. In this way, students can compare their oral responses to those provided on the program track.

In utilizing technology to assist in developing speaking skills it is informative to first look at how the teaching of this skill has been viewed in the past and to examine the current thought and practice in this area. Additionally, practitioners need to be aware of the different types of verbal interactions the speaker engages in to communicate in various circumstances.

How have the different methods of second language teaching treated the teaching of speaking skills?

We begin this section with an examination of the varied ways in which speaking skills have been addressed in different methods and approaches of second language teaching (Murphy, 1991; Larsen-Freeman, 2000). Various perspectives on speaking have ranged from total neglect of listening or speaking in the grammar translation method to extended communication in the communicative and task-based approaches (see Chapter 2). Murphy points out that some of the methods and approaches most widely discussed in the literature—such as total physical response (TPR), the natural approach, the silent way, and suggestopedia—are more appropriate for the beginning levels of instruction. He reminds practitioners that varying treatments of speaking are based on a broad range of theories whose merits each teacher will have to evaluate for his or her own particular teaching situation. Frequently, teachers of English language learners need to draw on more than one approach and use a variety of instructional tools, including the computer and other forms of technology, to meet the needs of all their students. Approaches to second language teaching are described in Table 4.1.

Current Views on Speaking in a Second Language

In today's world with easy access to travel, globalization of business and industry, and the desire of non-native English speakers to communicate with native English-speaking peers, English learners of all ages and purposes value the ability to orally communicate in the second or foreign language. Speaking is viewed in the larger context of communication with the focus on the speaker's ability to take in messages, negotiate meaning, and produce comprehensible output. This view recog-

TABLE 4.1 *Overview of Treatment of Speaking in Second Language Teaching Methods*

Method/Approach	Treatment of Speaking
Grammar Translation	No speaking or listening is required of students
Audio-Lingual Method (ALM)	Focus on speech with heavy reliance on repetition and oral drills
Direct Method and Situational Language Teaching	Teacher does much of the talking; students engage in many controlled speaking activities centered on specific topics or situations
Silent Way	Teacher rarely speaks while students engage in speaking activities centered around grammatically sequenced forms
Suggestopedia	Students listen to reading of dialogs or "concerts" by the teacher and later engage in controlled engage in controlled or guided speaking activities such as role-plays
Community Language Learning	Teacher acts as "human computer" to translate what the learner wishes to say in the target language
Comprehension Approach	Emphasize development of listening and reading skills; little attention to speaking and writing
Natural Approach	Early emphasis on listening comprehension with delayed guided speaking activities
Total Physical Response (TPR)	Students rarely speak but use physical actions to demonstrate listening comprehension
Communicative Language Teaching (CLT)	Focus on speech for communication; use of variety of authentic speaking activities
Task Based	Speech centers around authentic tasks needed to accomplish real-world tasks

Source: Adapted from Murphy (1991: 52–53).

nizes the interactive nature of listening and the crucial role of negotiating meaning in order to produce comprehensible speech.

How does the learner's negotiating meaning assist in comprehensible output?

While acknowledging the significance of comprehensible input in second language acquisition (SLA), linguists such as Swain (1985) have argued for the importance of comprehensible output that requires the learners to negotiate meaning and formulate and test hypotheses about the structures and functions of the language they produce. In this way, when non-native speakers receive feedback from their interlocutors that their message is not clear, they revise their speech to clarify their meaning. Through this process of adjusting their language output in order to make their messages more comprehensible to native speakers, language learners improve the accuracy of their language production.

What are the different types of oral interactions?

Just as listening tasks can be classified in functional terms according to specific situations, so can speaking tasks, the difference being that the latter reflect the perspective of the speaker rather than that of the listener (Nunan, 1991). Bygate (1987) proposes a model of oral interactions based on routines, which Nunan (1991) defines as "conventional (and therefore predictable) ways of presenting information which can either focus on information or interaction" (p. 40). In the first category, information routines consist of both information genres such as expository (which include description, instruction, and comparison) and evaluative routines (which include explanation, justification, prediction, and decision routines).

In the second category, interaction routines are viewed as either being primarily service (for example, speech used in a job interview) or social (for instance, the small talk you would engage in at a dinner party). All of the participants in these routines constantly negotiate meaning of the oral messages and manage the interactions in terms of who says what, to whom, and so on (Nunan, 1991). Figure 4.12 illustrates Bygate's model of oral interactions. Bygate's information and interaction

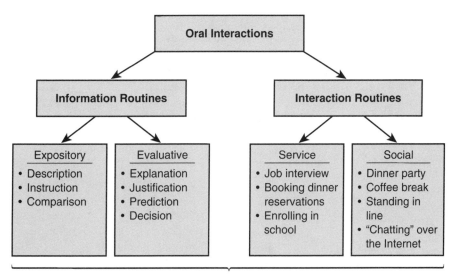

FIGURE 4.12   Model of Oral Interaction
Source: Adapted from Bygate (1987).

routines correspond respectively to the transformational and interactional purposes of listening proposed by Brown and Yule (1983) and discussed earlier in this chapter.

How can technology provide focused practice for the development of English language learners' speaking skills?

In selecting appropriate technology uses to enhance speech opportunities for language learners, one has to consider what type of interaction needs to be facilitated. For instance, video is a natural way to teach *information routines* requiring *prediction.* One illustration of an effective prediction strategy suggests that the teacher show the beginnings and ends of movie scenes and then ask students to make predictions about what happened in between. Another activity using predicting asks half the class to watch the video without sound while the other half listens to the sound without seeing the picture. The students who watched the video without sound write a script, while the students who heard only the sound describe what the context or scene might look like. Then they compare their scripts and scenes. Finally, they watch the video with sound and picture and discuss how the movie fits with their predictions (Gebhard, 1996; Huerta-Macias, 1997). Oral language ability as well as conceptual understanding will improve as students work together to produce or interpret videos. Once again, technology's key role was to create an environment that encouraged communication and provided increased and more varied communicative opportunities for students to utilize their oral skills.

Websites such as *FocusEnglish: ESL Conversation On-Line* offer opportunities for students to listen to dialogs on various conversational topics and respond to real-life situations. The Conversation Starters section of this website describes everyday situations and then poses questions that require the listener to identify an appropriate response to the circumstances presented. For example, one type of starter requires students to give instructions. Students are shown a map of the various buildings and sites of a town and asked a question requiring them to give directions to a particular location. By clicking on the response buttons, students can hear possible correct answers to which they can compare their own responses (see Figure 4.13).

Several software programs utilize audio and video clips of everyday scenes in which people are engaged in *interaction routines.* The software program *English Your Way,* for example, covers topics such as social engagements, dining out, travel, and around town. In this highly interactive software, the student becomes one of the characters in the dialog. She or he can respond either in the listening mode using a mouse or the speaking mode utilizing a microphone. Depending on which answer the student selects, the conversation is "branched" to a particular panel where the conversation continues. In this manner, different conversations are constantly generated (see Figure 4.14).

Websites such as the *Virtual Language Centre* of Hong Kong Polytechnic University are also a rich resource for listening and speaking practice using dialogs

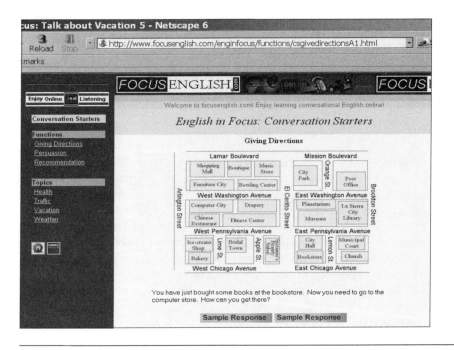

FIGURE 4.13   Conversation Starters

Source: John Liang. Used with permission.

FIGURE 4.14   *English Your Way*

Source: English Your Way is a trademark of Vivendi Universal Games, Inc. Used with permission.

from everyday situations involving greetings, weather, telephone calls, restaurants, and travel.

Developing Pronunciation Skills

Perspectives on the role and value of pronunciation instruction changed dramatically over the last half of the twentieth century. From the 1940s into the 1960s, the behavioristic audio-lingual method stressed the importance of pronunciation in the form of imitation drills, pattern practice, memorization of dialogs, and articulatory explanations. The 1970s saw a revolution in thought that questioned whether these practices were effective, that suggested a need for expanded strategies, and in some cases that advocated for the elimination of formal pronunciation instruction from the second language curriculum altogether. Though not abandoned entirely, during the 1970s the teaching of pronunciation was largely ignored. This was in keeping with the other trends of this period that focused more on fluency than form. By the 1980s and 1990s, it was evident to many second language teaching professionals that pronunciation was a key ingredient to the development of communicative competence and successful communication. There was a gradual return to a more balanced approach that valued both accuracy and fluency.

Reflecting on the history of teaching of pronunciation, Celce-Murcia, Brinton, and Goodwin (1996) note that pronunciation instruction has followed two basic approaches, intuitive-imitative and analytic-linguistic. In the intuitive-imitative approach, the learner listens to and imitates the sounds and rhythms of the target language without the assistance of explicit instruction. While a possible drawback to this approach in earlier years was a lack of good models, this has been largely overcome by technology with audiotapes, videos, and now computer-based programs and websites offering rich resources of native speech. The analytic-linguistic approach depends on structured teaching utilizing articulatory descriptions and charts of speech apparatus, phonetic alphabet and vowel charts, and, most recently, a variety of interactive speech analysis software and websites. Both of these approaches are needed as the learner moves between explicit instruction of speech features and their practice in communicative situations. We know that learners can perform in controlled exercises much sooner than they can integrate new features into spontaneous speech; however, as Grant (1999) points out, even partial integration of newly acquired features can have a positive impact on speech intelligibility.

Current theory advocates a prominent place once again for the teaching of pronunciation, but it does so with very different premises and practices than those of earlier years. Morely (1991) discusses several principles that guide current practices in the treatment of pronunciation in the second language curriculum, beginning with it being an integral component of communication as opposed to an isolated drill and practice subskill. Pronunciation is viewed as an important aspect of communication and is practiced within meaningful task-based activities. There is a renewed interest in the connection between listening and speaking/pronouncing resulting in increased use of pronunciation-focused listening activities. Though substantial attention is placed on important segmentals such as sound-spelling relationships, within the sound system there is more focus on the suprasegmentals of stress, rhythm, and intonation as practiced in extended discourse beyond the phoneme and word level (Yule, 1989; Morely, 1991). Emphasis has moved from the teaching to the learning of pronunciation with the focus on engaging the learners more in their own progress to meet their particular needs. The role of teacher has shifted to that of a "facilitator-coach and organizer of instructional activities" (Morely, 1991, p. 493).

Based on these principles, Morely (1994) suggests a dual-focus oral communication program that addresses both micro and macro levels. The micro level instruction is focused on linguistic, and more specifically, phonetic-phonological competence through practice of segmentals and the suprasegmentals. The macro level attends to more global elements of communicability with the goal of developing discourse, sociolinguistic, and strategic competencies by using the language for communicative purposes.

What are realistic goals of pronunciation instruction?

The primary goals of pronunciation teaching are for the learner to develop intelligible speech and to be able to effectively communicate in the target language (Miller, 2000). It is not the role of pronunciation training to hide all signs of the learner's original language, but there are specific pronunciation goals that are obtainable. Morely (1991) identified four basic learner goals that are realistic aspirations:

Goal 1: Functional intelligibility
The intent is to help learners develop spoken English that is (at least) reasonably easy to understand and not distracting to listeners.

Goal 2: Functional communicability
The intent is to help the learner develop spoken English that serves his or her individual communicative needs effectively for a feeling of communicative competence.

Goal 3: Increased self-confidence
The intent here is to help learners become more comfortable and confident in using spoken English, and to help them develop a positive self-image as a competent non-native speaker of English and a growing feeling of empowerment in oral communication.

Goal 4: Speech monitoring abilities and speech modification strategies for use beyond the classroom
The intent here is to help learners develop speech awareness, personal speech monitoring skills, and speech adjustment strategies that will enable them to continue to develop intelligibility, communicability, and confidence out side class as well as inside. (p. 500)

How can technology support the current goals of pronunciation learning?

Technology-enhanced speech instruction can be instrumental in advancing the learner's communication goals identified by Morley. Websites designed explicitly for the purpose of assisting students with their pronunciation as well as CDs that also focus on segmental and prosodic features, such as pitch and intensity, have made technology a prominent tool in pronunciation instruction. These sources typically feature a combination of different types of lessons and exercises that present sounds orally and visually and provide students practice in identifying and producing these sounds. Several also include practice at the suprasegmental level, where students engage in speech at the sentence or longer discourse level. Sources include the following:

1. *Articulatory charts* that show front and side views of the mouth as the speaker is producing a targeted sound.
2. *Sample words* utilizing the targeted sound.
3. *Minimal pairs/comparison words*—a presentation of two similar sounding words usually with only one (minimal) phoneme difference (see Figure 4.15).
4. Listening discrimination of *minimal pairs within a sentence*—students listen to a sentence and identify which one of the two minimal-pair words (for example, lake or rake) the speaker is saying.
5. *Sample sentences* with several words utilizing the targeted sound.
6. *Dictations*—students listen and repeat or write what the speaker is saying.
7. *Cloze exercises*—students listen to sentences and select/produce correct missing words.
8. *Suprasegmental exercises* that practice intonation, rhythm, stress, and timing.

Individual teachers and many universities and schools worldwide now maintain extensive websites for students to independently practice pronunciation. The *Virtual Language Centre* of Hong Kong Polytechnic University features collections of articulatory charts, audio files, and text-to-speech capability to provide practice in pronunciation, conversation, and listening. The *Interesting Things for ESL Students* website offers an extensive list of minimal pair exercises that provide listening practice, self-quizzes, and immediate feedback. Students can request that their answers be checked and scored and/or that all correct answers be displayed. Similarly, Okanagan University College's *ESL Pronunciation Online* website consists of ten units of intensive pronunciation practice on difficult sounds utilizing minimal pairs, tongue twisters, and dictations.

Students can practice discriminating minimal pairs at the sentence level at the *Internet TESOL Journal's* website which offers an extensive compilation of ESL quizzes. Dave's *ESL Café Idea Cookbook* has a collection of highly motivating games and other creative activities such as Pronunciation Baseball, Poetry Writing to Teach Pronunciation, and Murphy's Laws and Linking.

Various visualization devices to allow speakers to compare some aspect of their pronunciation to that of a native speaker are utilized by dedicated computer

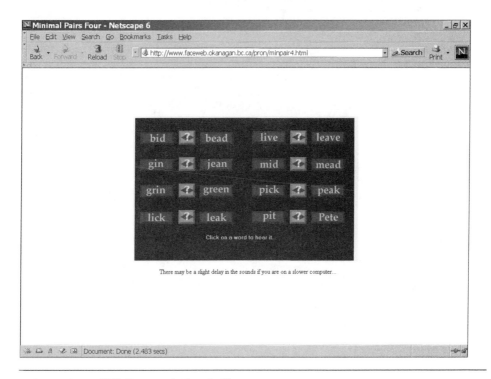

FIGURE 4.15 *ESL Pronunciation Online*

Source: Okanagan University College. Used with permission.

systems such as Visi-Pitch or CD-ROM programs including *BetterAccent Tutor, Accent Lab, Connected Speech,* and *Pronunciation Power.* For example, working with English sounds, *Pronunciation Power* (http://www.englishlearning.com) uses waveforms to compare the student's pronunciation of a particular sound to that of the computer instructor. Prior to this, another activity displayed an animated representation of the human speech apparatus to assist students in understanding how each phoneme they selected was produced (see Figures 4.16 and 4.17).

At the sentence level, the *BetterAccent Tutor* software asks the learner to select a sentence and identify which suprasegmental features he or she wishes to address—intonation or intensity and rhythm. A native-English voice says the sentence accompanied by a visual display to illustrate the native English pronunciation of this sentence. The process is then repeated with the non-native speaker recording the sentence and seeing the visual illustration of his or her speech on the same screen. A visual description is also provided to explain the differences between the two utterances. In this manner, non-native speakers can readily practice and monitor their pronunciation as they attempt to modify their speech production to more closely resemble that of native speakers (see Figure 4.18).

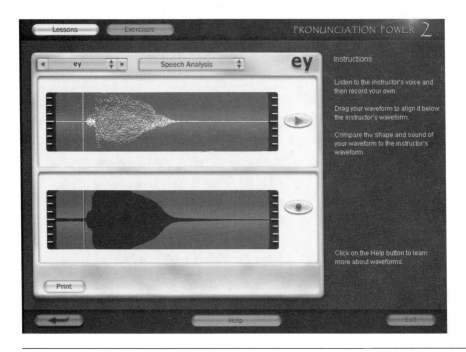

FIGURE 4.16 *Pronunciation Power*

Source: Pronunciation Power, Inc. Used with permission.

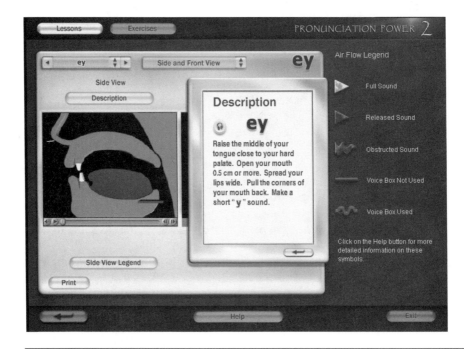

FIGURE 4.17 *Pronunciation Power*

Source: Pronunciation Power, Inc. Used with permission.

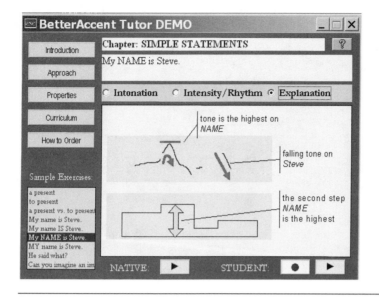

FIGURE 4.18 *BetterAccent Tutor*

Source: © BetterAccent, LLC www.betteraccent.com. Used with permission.

Programs such as *Connected Speech* utilize video tapes to provide content-rich listening and pronunciation practice. Students engage in a wide assortment of activities including ones working with syllables, linking of sounds and pitch changes. Students are also able to save recordings of their own production and see, hear, and print out feedback on their spoken production (see Figure 4.19).

With the use of screen visualization to compare their speech patterns with those of native speakers and other articulatory aids, such as vowel charts and animated presentations of speech apparatus and functions, English language learners have powerful tools with which to improve their communication skills. However, this type of structured practice at the micro level must be balanced with macro-level practice, in which pronunciation is an integral part of the communication process. Students need to practice pronunciation within a curriculum that provides activities that require the use of extended discourse in a variety of settings. Using teleconferencing programs to accomplish communicative tasks such as those discussed in Chapter 2 is one way students can develop macro-level skills.

Classroom Vignette: A University ESL Listening and Speaking Class

As you walk into Mr. Campbell's ESL listening and speaking class at a large urban university, you observe immediately that the students are enthusiastically engaged in some type of small group task. The students are not grouped heterogeneously, as is usually the case in ESL classes, but instead by countries of origin. The reason for this, we later learned,

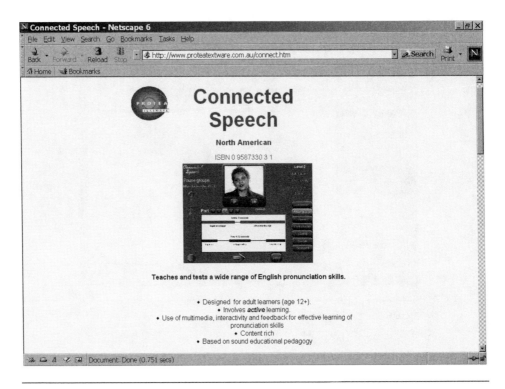

FIGURE 4.19   *Connected Speech*

Source: Protea Textware Pty Ltd. Used with permission.

is because each group is preparing a short presentation to American high school students on organizations in their native countries or regions of the world that contribute to solving global problems. The students have been working for days preparing their talks and are now ready for their videotaped rehearsals, which will be observed and critiqued by their teacher and peers in class. The first group consists of students from Ethiopia and Somalia who are giving a presentation on the Organization of African Unity (OAU) located in Addis Ababa, Ethiopia. The video camera rolls as they introduce themselves, the countries they represent, and the institution that is the subject of their talk. To help illustrate various aspects of their presentation, they had previously set the stage with maps, pictures, and documents they obtained from the OAU website. After a few nervous false starts, the group gives its presentation, using visual props where appropriate as they talk. Two other groups also give their presentations during this class session. At the end of each presentation, classmates have the opportunity to ask questions to obtain further information or to clarify any points that were not clear to them.

In class the following day, classmates share their observations on various aspects of the previous day's presentations, including organization, overall clarity, pronunciation, and use of body language and visuals. Having given this initial feedback to the speakers, the class then watches videotapes of each presentation with classmates paying special attention to strengths and weaknesses that they had observed and commented on previously. This gives a focused purpose for watching the videotapes. After viewing the video presentations, the whole class again discusses ways of making each one more comprehensible and engaging to its intended audience.

In cases where the videotapes reveal that students have specific pronunciation problems with certain sounds or words or with stress and intonation patterns, Mr. Campbell assigns structured practice using software programs that focus on the problematic speech items. His students then work independently in the computer lab with pronunciation software that concentrate on their particular needs.

With this preparation behind them, the students are ready to give their presentations to audiences beyond their classroom and university. Using *CU-See Me* software, these ESL students will be giving talks to a social studies class in a high school located over one hundred miles from them in a rural area of their state. They have already been introduced to the high school students through email and are anxious to actually see them via video conferencing. Utilizing this medium, the students from both schools will be able to see and hear each other as the ESL students give their presentations and respond to questions posed by the high school students afterward.

As we reflect on Mr. Campbell's teaching strategies, it is clear that he uses a dual approach to teaching speaking and pronunciation, with students engaging in both micro- and macro-level activities. At the macro level, the students communicated in the form of oral presentations on a topic they had thoroughly researched and with which they were familiar. They practiced organizing and presenting their talks in a comprehensible manner to an authentic audience for a real purpose. When appropriate, they used body language and visual props to clarify their message. At the micro level, students worked individually as needed on discrete points of pronunciation using computer software designed for that purpose.

In this class, Mr. Campbell's students engaged in three types of speech practice. One was *imitative practice* of problematic sounds using computer programs to compare their speech with that of a native speaker. They also utilized *rehearsed speech* in their presentations to the high school class. Finally, they practiced *extemporaneous speech* as they answered unrehearsed questions from their high school audience.

With the combination of activities that Mr. Campbell incorporated into his teaching, his students were able to practice their speech within a communicative approach that spanned the *structured-to-free practice* continuum.

Conclusion

This chapter focused on ways in which technology can be used to assist in the development of oral communication skills of English language learners. To this end, technology provides both focused practice of oral skills and opportunities to utilize those skills in authentic communication. The chapter discussed theories of learning listening, speaking, and pronunciation skills in a second language and examined a variety of computer programs and websites designed to assist in the teaching and learning of these skills.

Summary of Key Ideas

1. Technology supports two approaches to second language teaching, the natural approach and total physical response (TPR), which stress the importance of developing listening comprehension prior to other skills and of providing a low-stress environment. Technology fosters a low-anxiety learning environment in which beginning learners can practice listening by allowing students to work at their own proficiency level and pace and to receive immediate feedback without embarrassment.

2. One of technology's strongest attributes is its ability to provide additional sources of comprehensible input. Using sound, pictures, video, and animation, multimedia programs help provide a meaningful context that aids comprehension.

3. Technology can assist students in developing top-down and bottom-up listening comprehension processes. Through videos and CDs, students can develop new schemata on information foreign to their backgrounds, and with the use of specialized software, they are able to develop their bottom-up lexical, phonological, and grammatical knowledge.

4. Second language learners can use technology to practice transactional functions, such as note taking while listening to a lecture and engage in interactional purposes, in which they use the language to socialize with peers.

5. Through the use of technology, students engage in both focused practice of oral skills and authentic oral communication. Many software programs and websites provide exercises for listening and speaking practice and serve as a stimulus for peer interactions and oral communication.

6. The various methods and approaches of second language teaching have, over the last few decades, treated the teaching of speaking skills in very different manners. Technology can be used to support a variety of approaches, such as the natural approach or TPR, and is well matched with communicative and task-based teaching approaches.

7. Listeners engage in two types of oral routines. One focuses on information; the other on interactions that are generally social in nature or related to accomplishing some specific task such as making an airline reservation. Technology programs and websites can be used to model these speech routines and provide practice using them.

8. Technology is an important tool that gives learners increased autonomy in developing their pronunciation skills. They can employ sound visualization devices such

as wave forms, intonation and intensity graphs, and interactive representations of the human speech apparatus to compare their speech with that of native speakers.

Learning Activities

1. Brainstorm the different approaches you use or plan to use with English language learners to improve their oral skills and consider ways in which technology can assist you with this. Which theories, techniques, and strategies do you feel are the most appropriate for your students and in what ways would you use technology to enhance their oral communication skills?

2. Discuss the numerous ways in which technology can provide comprehensible input. Describe how technology use impacts both the affective and cognitive factors that impact comprehension. What role can multimultimedia programs play? What features would your ideal multimedia program have? Explain why you feel these features would contribute to comprehensible input. How would you incorporate the use of this program into your curriculum? What websites would you use to broaden the sources of input?

3. Identify top-down and bottom-up processes and activities that you feel are important to listening and speaking development and brainstorm ways in which technology can assist in this development.

4. Select one of the software programs or websites presented in this chapter and incorporate it into a lesson that provides both focused practice and also communicative use of listening and speaking skills. (You might want to review Chapter 2 for ideas on communicative applications.)

5. Discuss the advantages and disadvantages of the various types of pronunciation practice presented in this chapter. Considering factors of age, language proficiency level, and purpose of study, what types of English learners do you think would benefit the most from the various types of software and Web-based activities presented?

6. Look back at the four basic learner goals Morely proposed for pronunciation and reflect on Mr. Campbell's listening and speaking class. In what ways do you think the activities of this class foster the goals identified by Morely?

Technology Resources

Software

Accent Lab (Version 2). (1995). Los Angeles, CA: Accent Technologies. (http://www.accentlab.com)

Better Accent Tutor. San Carlos, CA: BetterAccent, LLC. (http://www.betteraccent.com)

Connected Speech. (1997). Protea Textware Pty. Ltd.

CU-SeeMe (Version 3.0.0). (1997). Nashua, NH: White Pine Software.

Engage (Version 6.0). (1999). Burlingame, CA: DynEd International, Inc.

English Your Way. Syracuse Language Systems.

Firsthand Access. (Version 6.0). (1999). Burlingame, CA: DynEd International, Inc.

Learning English: Home and Family. (1994). San Diego, CA: Contér, A division of Jostens Learning Corporation.

Live Action English: TPR on a Computer. (2000). Berkeley, CA: Command Performance Language Institute. Based on the book *Live Action English*, by Elizabeth Kuizenga and Conty Seely.
New Dyanmic English (Version 6.0). (1999). Burlingame, CA: DynEd International, Inc.
Pronunciation Power and Pronunciation Power 2. (1996). English Computerized Learning Inc., Blackstone Multimedia Corporation. (http://www.englishlearning.com)
Visi-Pitch CSL.(http://www.kayelemetrics.com)

Websites

Dave's ESL Café Idea Cookbook (http://www.eslcafe.com)
The English Listening Lounge (http://www.englishlistening.com/)
ESL Pronunciation On Line. Okanangan University (http://www.faceweb.okanagan.bc.ca/pron)
Focus English: ESL Conversation on Line (http://www.focusenglish.com/conversationstarters.html)
Internet TESOL Journal TESL/TEFL/TESOL/ESL/EFL/ESOL Links http://iteslj.org/links/
   ESL: Speaking, Learning Oral English Online Collection (http://iteslj.org/links/ESL/Speaking)
   ESL: Listening (http://iteslj.org/links/ESL/listening)
   ESL: Pronunciation (http://iteslj.org/links/ESL/Pronunciation/)
   ESL: Quizzes, Self Study (http://www.aitech.ac.jp/~iteslj/quizzes/)
Interesting Things for ESL Students (http://:www.manythings.org), Kelly, C. and Kelly, L. E.
   English Listening Room (http://www.manythings.org/el/at)
   American English Pronunciation Practice (http://www.manythings.org/pp/)
Learning Oral English Online (http://rong-chang.com/book/index/html)
Organization of African Unity (http://www.oau-oua.org/)
Randall's ESL Cyber Listening Lab (http://www.esl-lab.com/)
Virtual Language Centre of Hong Kong Polytechnic University (http://vlc.polyu.edu.hk/)

References

Asher, J. (1969). The total physical response approach to second language learning. *Modern Language Journal* 53: 79–84.
Asher, J. (1972). Children's first language as a model of second language learning. *Modern Language Journal* 56: 133–139.
Asher, J. (1977). *Learning Another Language Through Actions: The Complete Teacher's Guide Book.* Los Gatos, CA: Sky Oaks Productions. (2nd ed.: 1982)
Asher, J. (1981). The extinction of second language learning in American schools: An intervention model. In H. Winitz (Ed.), *The Comprehension Approach to Foreign Language Instruction* (pp. 49–68). Rowley, MA: Newbury House.
Asher, J. (1996). *Learning Another Language Through Actions: The Complete Teacher's Guidebook* (5th ed.). Los Gatos, CA: Sky Oaks Productions.
Brown, H. D. (1994). *Teaching by Principles: An Interactive Approach to Language Pedagogy.* Englewood Cliffs, NJ: Prentice Hall Regents.
Brown, H. D. (2000). *Principles of Language Learning and Teaching.* White Plains, NY: Addison Wesley Longman, Inc.
Brown, R. (1973). *A First Language: The Early Stages.* Cambridge, MA: Harvard University Press.
Brown, G., and Yule, G. (1983). *Teaching the Spoken Language.* Cambridge: Cambridge University Press.
Bygate, M. (1987). *Speaking.* Oxford: Oxford University Press.
Celce-Mucia, M., Brinton, D., and Goodwin, J. (1996). *Teaching Pronunciation: A Reference for Teachers of English to Speakers of Other Languages.* New York: Cambridge University Press.
Chaudron, C., and Richards, J. C. (1986). The effect of discourse markers on comprehension of lectures. *Applied Linguistics* 7(2): 113–127.

Corder, S. P. (1967). The significance of learner's errors. *International Review of Applied Linguisitics* 5 (4): 161–170.

Dulay, H., and Burt, M. (1977). Remarks on creativity in language acquisition. In H. Dulay, M. Burt, and M. Finnocchiaro (Eds.), *Viewpoints on English as a Second Language* (pp. 95–126). New York: Regents Publishers.

Fillmore, C. J. (1979). On fluency. In C. Fillmore (Ed.), *Individual Differences in Language Ability and Language Behavior.* New York: Academic Press.

Gebhard, J. (1996). *Teaching English as a Foreign or Second Language.* Ann Arbor: University of Michigan Press.

Gibbons, J. (1985). The Silent Period: An Examination. *Language Learning* 35: 255–267.

Grant, L. (1999). Form to meaning: Bridges in pronunciation teaching. *TESOL Matters* 9 (6): 18.

Huerta-Macias (1997). *Conversations and Observations.* Las Cruces: New Mexico State University.

Krashen, S. D. (1981). *Second Language Acquisition and Second Language Learning.* Oxford: Pergamon.

Krashen, S. (1982). *Principles and Practices in Second Language Acquisition.* Oxford: Pergamon.

Krashen, S. (1985). *The Input Hypothesis: Issues and Implications.* Torrance, CA: Laredo Publishing.

Krashen, S. (1987). Applications of psycholinguistic research to the classroom. In M. Long and J. Richards (Eds.), *Methodology in TESOL: A Book of Readings.* New York: Newbury House Publishers.

Krashen, S. D., and Terrell, T. D. (1983). *The Natural Approach: Language Acquisition in the Classroom.* Oxford: Pergamon.

Larsen-Freeman, D. (2000). *Techniques and Principles in Language Teaching.* Oxford: Oxford Press.

Lewis, M. (1993). *The Lexical Approach.* Hove, UK: Language Teaching Publications.

Lewis, M. (1997). *Implementing the Lexical Approach.* Hove, UK: Language Teaching Publications.

Miller, S. (2000, June/July). Looking at progress in a pronunciation class. *TESOL Matters* 10 (2).

Mitchell, R., and Myles, F. (1998). *Second Language Learning Theories.* London: Arnold Publishers. New York: Oxford Press.

Morely, J. (1991). The pronunciation component in teaching English to speakers of other languges. *TESOL Quarterly* 25 (3): 481–520.

Morely, J. (1994). A multidimentional curriculum design for speech-pronunciation instruction. In J. Morely (Ed.), *Pronunciation Pedagogy and Theory: New Views, New Directions* (pp. 64–91). Alexander, VA: TESOL.

Murphy, J. (1991). Oral communication in TESOL: Integrating speaking, listening, and pronunciation. *TESOL Quarterly* 25 (1): 51–75.

Nunan, D. (1991). *Language Teaching Methodology.* London: Prentice Hall International.

Ogami, N. (1988). *Cold Water: Intercultural Adjustments and Values of Foreign Students and Scholars at an American University.* Yarmouth, ME: Intercultural Press.

Richards, J. C. (1990). *The Language Teaching Matrix.* Cambridge: Cambridge University Press.

Richards, J. C., and Rodgers, T. S. (1986). *Approaches and Methods in Language Teaching.* Cambridge: Cambridge University Press.

Rost, M. (1989). *Listening.* London: Longman.

Swain, M. (1985). Communicative competence: Some rules for comprehensible input and comprehensible output in its development. In S. Gass and C. Madden (Eds.), *Input in Second Language Acquisition.* Rowley, MA: Newbury House.

Terrell, T. D. (1977). A natural approach to second language acquisition and learning. *Modern Language Journal* 61: 325–336.

Terrell, T. D. (1982). The natural approach to language teaching: An update. *Modern Language Journal* 66: 121–132.

Tikunoff, W. J. (1985). *Applying Significant Bilingual Instructional Features in the Classroom.* Rosslyn, VA: National Clearinghouse for Bilingual Education.

Wennerstrom, A. (1999). Why suprasegmentals? *TESOL Matters* 9 (5): 20.

Winitz, H. (Ed.). (1981). *The Comprehension Approach to Foreign Language Instruction.* Rowley, MA: Newbury House.

Yule, G. (1989). The spoken language. In R. Kaplan (Ed.), *Annual Review of Applied Linguistics* 10: 163–173.

5

Using Technology to Teach Reading and Writing

Chapter Overview

This chapter looks at issues involved in teaching reading and writing to English language learners and examines the ways in which technology can facilitate this process. The first section presents models of the reading process and then discusses the use of technology to promote characteristics associated with fluent reading. The chapter then identifies component skills and knowledge areas related to fluent reading and examines the role technology can play in assisting English language learners (ELLs) to acquire these skills and knowledge. The second part of the chapter discusses four major focuses of second language writing instruction over the last few decades that impact writing instruction today and looks at the support technology offers to each of these areas. Next, a classroom vignette of a fifth-grade sheltered ESL class engaged in a science WebQuest is presented. The chapter concludes with a summary of the key ideas, suggested learning activities, a list of technology resources, and references.

Developing Reading Skills

What is reading?

The reading process involves the reader, the text, and the interaction between the two. As Aebersold and Field (1997) explain,

> In a general sense, reading is what happens when people look at a text and assign meaning to the written symbol in the text. The text and the reader are the two physical entities necessary for the reading process to begin. It is, however, the interaction between the text and the reader that constitutes actual reading. (p. 15)

Theorists have proposed three basic models of how reading occurs: bottom-up, top-down, and interactive (Barnett, 1989; Aebersold and Field, 1997; Carrell, Devine, and Eskey, 1988).

In the audio-lingual era of the 1960s reading was viewed primarily as a vehicle for practicing oral skills and focusing on grammar and vocabulary development (Silberstein, 1987; Grabe, 1991). Through the 1970s several researchers and practitioners (Yorkey, 1970; Eskey, 1973; Saville-Troike, 1973) argued for a more prominent role for reading in second language instruction. Various perspectives on the reading process and second language reading that emerged in the 1970s and 1980s and that continue to have an impact on current reading instruction can be grouped into three broad categories for describing the reading process. These processes are (as mentioned earlier): bottom-up models, top-down models, and interactive models.

Bottom-Up Models

In bottom-up models, reading is primarily a decoding process in which the reader matches written symbols with their aural equivalents (Nunan, 1991). Readers first identify the written letters (graphemes) with the matching sounds (phonemes) and then blend the sounds and letters together to identify words (Cambourne, 1979). Assisted by an understanding of grammar rules and syntax, students can then read sentences, paragraphs, and eventually longer discourse. Nunan (1991) warns that such a decoding system makes assumptions that might not necessarily be true in the case of second language learners. For instance, the phonics approach assumes that when the reader blends the sounds orally to form a word that the reader will then be able to identify that word. With the limited oral vocabulary of many second language readers, this may not be an accurate supposition. Research on human memory (Kolers and Katzman, 1966) and reading miscues (Goodman and Burke, 1972) led to the postulation of the existence of processes other than this serial decoding process. In the 1970s, the focus of attention shifted from the text to the reader in what has become known as the psycholinguistic or top-down approach to reading.

Top-Down Models

While reading was once considered a passive skill, the work of scholars such as Goodman (1967, 1985) and Smith (1971) espoused a psycholinguistic perspective that recognized the active role the reader's cognitive processes play in reading. According to Goodman's (1967) top-down, psycholinguistic model, reading is a "psycholinguistic guessing game" in which the reader receives input from the text, makes predictions, tests and confirms or revises those predictions, and so forth as he or she reads. According to this perspective, efficient readers read quickly, test their hypotheses as they read, and reread material only when they are unable to confirm their predictions.

It was against this psycholinguistic backdrop that the "whole language" movement began in the 1970s and gained popularity in the 1980s. Research on literacy development of second language learners such as that by Elley and Mangughai (1983) supported the use of a holistic activities for ELLs that merged all four skill areas—listening, speaking, reading, and writing. Inspired by a holistic approach to reading and writing that advocated the use of children's literature and authentic reading materials in lieu of contrived stories based on sound-symbol connections, proponents like Goodman (1988) and Cambourne (1988) advocated for an integrated approach to the teaching of reading. While phonics was not eliminated from the curriculum, it was deemphasized as a method of teaching reading and instead was incorporated into literature-based instruction (Savage, 2001). Coady (1979) expanded on Goodman's psycholinguistic model, suggesting that second language readers draw on their conceptual or intellectual abilities, processing skills (including language processing skills that utilize phonological, syntactic, lexical and contextual information), and background knowledge to comprehend the text.

Interactive Models

According to interactive theorists, reading is a process of constructing meaning from text through the use of both bottom-up and top-down processes, strategies and skills. In the *bottom-up* processing, the input is text based or data driven as the reader relates his or her background knowledge to the linguistic information found in the text. In the top-down processing, the input is based on more general concepts and schemata, and interrelated patterns of background knowledge that the reader uses to make predictions and test against incoming bottom-up content and structure data. Both types of processing from the specific bottom-level schemata to the more general schemata at the top must occur simultaneously for the reader to comprehend the meaning of the text (Carrell and Eisterhold, 1988; Silberstein, 1994).

Interactive approaches to reading focus on two different concepts of interaction. The first is the interaction between the reader and the text. The reader draws on both his or her background knowledge and information from the printed text in order to create meaning. The text cannot just be decoded but rather requires the reader to comprehen that there is interaction with the experiences and knowledge he or she brings to that text.

The second interaction is between two sets of different kinds of cognitive skills that Grabe (1991) terms *indentification* and *interpretation*. The identification skills are lower-level skills that allow the reader to quickly and unconsciously identify letters, words, and grammatical structures. With fluent readers this automaticity occurs simultaneously with the higher-level skills that account for the reader being able to comprehend and interpret the reading.

The interactive model is widely supported by most theorists and researchers today and is practiced in the form of variations of the *balanced approach* to teaching reading. This approach incorporates the study of phonics into a literature or content-based curriculum and draws on the student's background knowledge in the form of schemata. Later in this chapter, we will see how technology assists students to interact with printed materials and develop cognitive skills required in the reading process.

What are schemata and schema theory?

Though Goodman's and Coady's models of ESL reading included the reader's background knowledge, several theorists have argued that the psycholinguistic model of reading did not adequately emphasize the pivotal role that background knowledge plays in ESL/EFL reading (Carrell and Eisterhold, 1988). Further attention to reader background knowledge and experience was embodied in what has become known as *schema theory.*

The function of background knowledge in the reading process is formalized in schema theory, a term first used by Bartlett (1932) and since widely recognized by second language theorists and practitioners (Carrell, 1983a, 1983b; Carrell, Devine, and Eskey, 1988; Widdowson, 1979). According to schema theory, the reader brings previously acquired background knowledge organized into interrelated patterns, or schemata, to the reading process. The reader creates meaning by relating the text to this background knowledge, including knowledge of customs and beliefs from his or her own experiences. As Carrell and Eisterhold (1988) explained, "According to schema theory, the process of interpretation is guided by the principle that every input is mapped against some existing schema and that all aspects of that schema must be compatible with the input information" (p. 76).

Carrell (1987) identified two types of background knowledge that have an impact on reading comprehension: formal schemata and content schemata. *Formal schemata* would include prior knowledge of rhetorical structures and conventions such as the different types of expository organizational patterns—cause and effect, comparison and contrast, and chronological order, and so on. *Content schemata* refer to background knowledge of the subject of the text, an area that frequently is problematic for second language readers who often lack the culturally based content schemata of the English text. A third type, *linguistic schemata,* refers to decoding knowledge used to recognize words and determine their syntax in a sentence (Aebersold and Field, 1997). Both L1 (native language) and L2 (target language) readers who have not learned a particular vocabulary word or a grammar rule lack this information when they attempt to read. While they may be able to eventually guess the meaning of the text without this knowledge, it is initially missing from their linguistic schema and hinders their comprehension. We turn now to the characteristics of fluent reading and the subskills required in that process and then consider the ways in which technology can have a positive impact on the acquisition of these reading skills.

Fluent Reading

What are the characteristics of fluent reading and what skills and knowledge do second language learners need in order to successfully read in the target language?

In the 1980s and 1990s, attention turned to research on first language readers as a source of insight that could be applied to second language readers as well. Research on the development of reading skills of second language learners draws heavily on first language reading research. Rather than attempt a definition of a process as complicated as reading, Grabe (1991) identified and described six key characteristics of fluent reading—rapid, interactive, flexible, purposeful, comprehending, and gradual—and proposed that this general perspective of the reading process was equally fitting for ESL students who had not attained fluency, but aspired to do so for academic purposes. He cited research that suggested that fluent reading needed to be at a sufficient pace to avoid distracting the reader from making the connections and inferences required for comprehension. Findings demonstrated that fluent reading is an interactive process in which the reader draws on both his own background knowledge and data from the printed page while utilizing several skills simultaneously in the process. The typical skilled reader uses a variety of strategies, including adjusting reading speed, scanning, skimming ahead, predicting, and gathering information to comprehend the text. The fluent reader possesses confidence in his or her reading ability and has a definite purpose for reading, thereby providing motivation for the reading activity. Also, research demonstrates that developing reading fluency is a long-term process that results from continuous effort and gradual improvement.

Following other researchers (Carr and Levy, 1990; Haynes and Carr, 1990) who have attempted to analyze fluent reading in terms of component skills, Grabe identified at least six component skills and knowledge areas essential for reading fluency (1991).

1. Automatic recognition skills
2. Vocabulary and structural knowledge
3. Formal discourse structure knowledge
4. Content/ world background
5. Synthesis and evaluation skills
6. Metacognitive knowledge and skills (p. 379)

Several features of technology make it uniquely suitable to assist English language learners in acquiring these skills and knowledge. We will look at each of these skill areas and investigate the role technology can play in their development.

Automatic Perceptual/ Identification Skills

Automatic recognition skills allow the reader to identify letters and words without being consciously aware of the process. Grabe (1991) sites research that indicates that automatic access to lexical items is crucial to the reading process. Such automaticity requires very little use of the reader's processing capacity, allowing the mind to then attend to other matters (Adams, 1990; Stanovich, 1990). Good readers are able to read rapidly because they can recognize most words automatically, and therefore process this information very efficiently. Furthermore, research on word recognition suggests that fluent readers take in and recognize all the letters in a word (Grabe, 1991). This combination of rapid and precise word recognition has proven to be an effective predictor of reading ability, particularly of young readers.

How does technology facilitate developing recognition skills and increasing reading speed?

Several software programs assist students in developing phonemic awareness and alphabet knowledge. Through phonemic awareness, learners begin to recognize and manipulate the basic sounds that constitute spoken words. Early literacy also involves knowing the letters of the alphabet and phonics, making connections between the sounds and the written symbols as readers decode the written language. Programs such as Leap Into Phonics concentrate specifically on developing phonemic awareness as learners match objects whose names rhyme or begin with the same sound (see Figure 5.1). These programs are especially helpful to second

FIGURE 5.1 *Leap Into Phonics*

Source: Leap Into Phonics®, Leap Into Learning, Inc.® and Omaha Public Schools, Omaha, NE. Used with permission.

language learners dealing with recognizing sounds that are not in their primary language.

Another software program for young readers, *Kids Phonics II,* gives students practice in connecting sounds to clusters of letters. Through digitized speech, graphics, and animations, learners unscramble words and practice with prefixes, suffixes, and compound words. Several programs are based on a balanced approach to beginning literacy, offering phonics practice and whole language literature activities. Programs such as the *Reader Rabbit's Learn to Read* program supports a balanced approach to beginning reading instruction through practice with letter-sound relationships, phonemic awareness, sight words, and highly interactive electronic storybooks. For adults, *The Alphabet* is an interactive multimedia program that uses graphics, photographs, sound, and keyboarding exercises to teach alphabet skills. This program is specifically designed for adult literacy, as well as ESL, and allows the learner to select American, Australian, or British accents as they use recorder and play back options.

While processes involving sound, letter, and word recognition skills are often associated with beginning-level reading instruction, these bottom-up processes have also been identified as the source of problems for students in more advanced reading classes. Birch (1998, p. 20) suggests ways for nurturing bottom-up reading strategies of this group to assist them in understanding the alphabetic principle that each letter represents a sound and that these sounds form words. Teaching strategies include reading out loud, reading numerous books that are very simple in meaning, listening and following along as someone else reads aloud, and reading the same book as many times as desired. Interactive multimedia books such as *Discis Books* and *Scholastic Literacy Place* offer a wide selection of storybooks that learners can listen to as they read the story. Using the *Scholastic Literacy Place* series, which includes the *Wiggleworks* program for K–2 learners, students can record themselves reading electronic storybooks aloud and compose, illustrate, and print out their own versions of the stories.

For adult readers, software programs such as *Issues in English* present readings on high-interest topics such as quitting smoking or environmental concerns for the adult learner. Learners can watch and listen to video clips of a speaker giving a lecture while viewing the printed text on the screen.

To foster increase in reading speed, several reading software programs give the reader control to pre-set the speed of readings. By gradually increasing the pace of the readings, students are challenged to increase and monitor their own reading rates. Exercises such as timed phrase readings give students perceptual practice chunking words into meaningful groups and serve as an incentive to develop greater reading speed (see Figure 5.2).

Structural Skills and Knowledge

Research (Grabe, 1991) indicates that knowledge of grammatical structure has an important effect on second language reading development (Devine, 1988, Eskey, 1988; Swaffar, Arens, and Byrnes, 1991). Grammatical structures provide readers

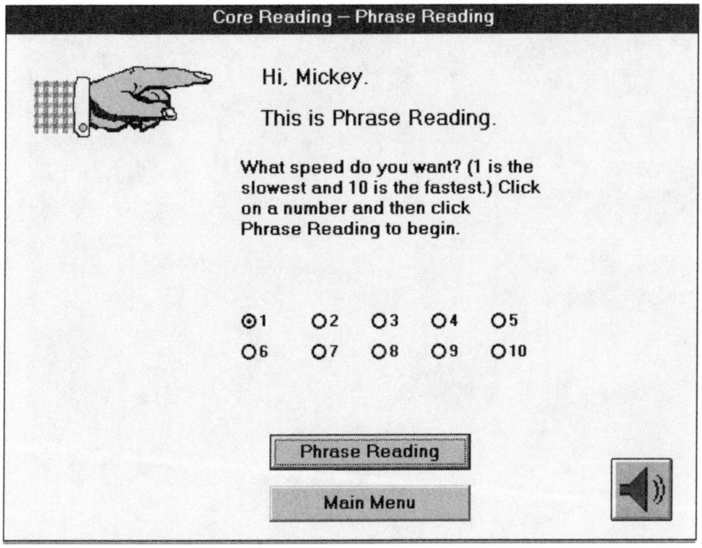

FIGURE 5.2   Core Reading and Vocabulary Development

Source: Core Reading & Vocabulary Development Program, by Priscilla Hamilton and Barbara Hombs.© 1996 Activities Records, Inc. Used by permission of Educational Activities Software, Baldwin NY.

significant information about the content of the reading passage. For instance, an apostrophe followed by an *s* ('s) after a proper noun as in *Mary's new hat* signals to readers that someone owns something. In the sentence, *He gave Skiggle the book,* readers understand that *Skiggle* is probably a person, even though they have never heard that word before. In this case, readers rely on their structural knowledge of capital letters and direct and indirect objects and their lexical knowledge of "read" to correctly comprehend the sentence.

How can technology assist in developing structural skills?

Several multimedia software programs include a grammar component as part of their more comprehensive programs that focus on other skills. The *English Your Way* program, for example, presents grammar usage exercises within a comprehension approach that features practical English in everyday situations. The *Rosetta Stone,* one of the earliest multimedia English programs, presents words, phrases, and sentences in a structurally sequenced manner so that students receive intensive practice with different grammatical forms, but it does so without the benefit of expanded discourse or social context. Despite this limitation, it remains a popular program particularly with adults who appreciate the autonomy it gives them to practice at their own rate and skill level (see Figure 5.3).

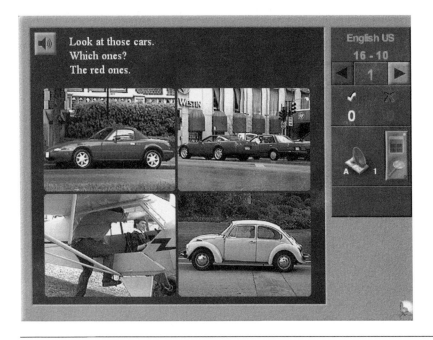

FIGURE 5.3 *Rosetta Stone*
Source: Fairfield Language Technologies. Used with permission.

Several adventure and subject matter programs provide sentence level reading and grammar practice. *WorldWalker: Destination Australia* is one in a series of interactive explorations that uses video, sound, graphics, and text to take the learner to scenic spots around the world. With this program, students work with life science and social studies content as well as practice syntax and grammatical structures. Games require them to recognize animals indigenous to Australia, to classify them as herbivores, carnivores, or omnivores, and to determine where they belong in the food chain. In the Language Exploration mode, students are presented with a cartoon-type scene and a scrambled sentence describing some aspect of the scene. Their task is to arrange the sentence in the correct order. Students may click on any object in the picture to hear its name, and a sound option allows them to hear the scrambled words and completed sentence (see Figure 5.4).

In addition to software, the Internet offers a wealth of tools for manipulating and analyzing linguistic structures in reading passages. The *Hot Potatoes* collection of authoring tools (University of Victoria) allows users to enter their own text, questions, and answers to create different types of Web-based interactive exercises, including multiple choice, gap-fill, crossword, jumbled sentence, matching, and ordering (see Figure 5.5). This program is free of charge to all educators in a non-profit-making educational institution who are willing to share their exercises on a publicly accessible Web server.

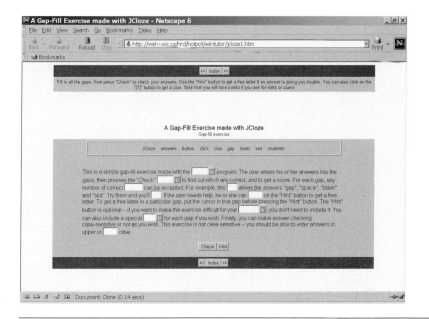

FIGURE 5.4 *WorldWalker Destination Australia*

Source: WorldWalker® Destination: Australia is a product of Soleil® Software, Inc., 3853 Grove Court, Palo Alto, CA 94303, telephone 650-494-0024. Used with permission.

FIGURE 5.5 *Hot Potatoes,* **University of Victoria Humanities Computing and Media Centre**

Source: Half-Baked Software, Inc. Used with permission.

Another excellent Web-based source of grammar practice within authentic readings is provided by a joint project between the CNN Newsroom and Brigham Young University of Hawaii. The language center at BYU maintains weekly grammar completion exercises based on the CNN Worldwide News reports that are aired daily around the world via cable or satellite. The current and previous exercises are categorized by grammatical structures with the name and date of the news story provided. Students may request that their answers be corrected and, if they wish, emailed to their teacher. Any school or educational institution has permission to make copies of the news broadcasts, which typically feature three to four current international stories. Membership is required and can be obtained from the CNN Newsroom enrollment website at http://learning.turner.com/newsroom/index. html. In addition to these types of reading- and listening-based grammar practice, technology provides multiple sources of explicit grammar instruction and focused practice that we will examine later in this chapter as we look at teaching writing skills.

Vocabulary Development

There are several reasons why vocabulary study is so vital to reading comprehension. First, Grabe (1991) notes that estimates for the number of words required of fluent reading in a first language range from 10,000 to 100,000 (Chall, 1987; Nagy and Herman, 1987) whereas the number typically cited for second language reading is usually much lower at 2,000 to 7,000 (Coady, 1988; Nation, 1990). Grabe argues that readers in a second language need to have a vocabulary more similar in number to that of native speakers, if they are expected to read with a fluency approaching that of first language readers.

Second, readers need to know a large percentage of the words in any given text in order to comprehend the meaning of the reading or to guess the meaning of words unfamiliar to them. While the number might differ somewhat depending on the reader's background knowledge of the topic and purpose for reading, recognition of approximately 95 percent of the words in a passage is needed. Language teachers clearly cannot explicitly teach this number of words in the classroom, so most of these words need to be learned by exposure of some type outside the classroom (Schmitt and Carter, 2000).

The third point is that vocabulary is not acquired in quick doses, but rather is a process of incremental learning and constant reinforcement. Additionally, it is not sufficient to know just one meaning of the word in a particular context; instead, the reader needs to know other aspects of the word such as its grammatical properties and alternative meanings in different contexts (Schmitt and Carter 2000; Nation, 1990). Reading assists in vocabulary development by providing sufficient repetition of new words in multiple contexts. Zimmerman (1997, p. 125) argued for direct interactive vocabulary lessons for college level ESL/EFL students that included the following:

1. Multiple exposure to words;
2. Exposure to words in meaningful contexts;
3. Rich and varied information about each word;

4. Establishment of ties between instructed words, student experience, and prior knowledge; and

5. Active participation by students in the learning process. (Adapted from Nagy and Herman, 1987, p. 33)

How does technology assist in vocabulary development?

Many features of the computer enhance the type of direct vocabulary study suggested by Zimmerman and supported by other researchers (Coady, 1997). English language learners benefit from reading for fluency, whereby they are encouraged to guess the meaning of unknown words from the context of the reading. The many pictures, animation, and other contextual cues provided by interactive CD-ROM books assist in this strategy. *Just Grandma and Me* and *Arthur's Teacher Trouble* from the *Broderbund Living Books Series*, for example, are excellent reading materials for young ELLs, because of the scaffolding provided by their well-organized scenes that correspond to the story plot. Students have access to special features such as "stickers" of objects that match the outlines of objects missing from the picture on the screen. The names of the objects are written below each sticker to build word/object recognition. Using a click-and-drag maneuver, students "fill in" the missing objects with the matching stickers.

How did one use technology to support students' reading development?

Maria Lopez was teaching a bilingual third through fifth grade multiage classroom when she decided to use the power of technology to help her students gain reading and writing skills. She gathered a collection of interactive CD-ROM stories and built her reading lessons around the stories for several weeks. Then she introduced the *HyperStudio* program and had her children learn *HyperStudio* while practicing a variety of reading skills, including vocabulary development. The students drew trees on each card and then added connected words to the branches. They then learned how to make a button on each word that would go to another card with more information related to that word.

Later, they learned to create their own "Read-your-own adventure stories." They would put an introductory scenario on the first card with two choices. For example, a scenario might read, "One day Leah decided to go for a walk in the woods. She came across two paths. One looked like a lot of people had traveled on it and the other went deeper into the woods." On the scenario card would be two buttons, one that goes to each path. The students worked in groups in this project, first outlining some story choices and events, and then dividing up to do the different scene pages.

Finally, students wrote their own interactive stories modeled after CD-ROM books like *Just Grandma and Me*. All of the students reading skills improved. In addition, the teacher discovered this was a wonderful way to get to know each child's interests and skills. Every story was so different and told her a lot about each child's development and learning preferences. For example, some stories had lots of text and few pictures, while others had elaborate pictures and little text. The teacher was able to appreciate each child's unique contribution.

Similar features are demonstrated in the multimedia science program, *Curious Creatures.* In this series, vocabulary hotlinks display and narrate a description of selected words related to creatures such as wolves, spiders, owls, and bats. Learners can view video clips of the creatures in their natural habitats and listen to a narration of the text as they read the story and develop vocabulary within a rich context. By clicking on underlined words, students are taken to hypertext explanations of the words (see Figure 5.6).

The latest electronic dictionaries designed specifically for English language learners have several built-in aids that their book counterparts cannot provide. The *Longman Interactive English Dictionary (LIED)*, for example, allows students to select from a wide assortment of component books, including various types of dictionaries and picture and video libraries. With these resources, students can compile and save pictures, audio, and video excerpts to contextualize the meanings of words and concepts. Icons for highlighted words indicate a wide range of help features, including access to the main dictionary entry, audio pronunciation, phonetic transcription, grammar guide, verb formation, typical errors, pictures, video, and grammatical and functional uses demonstrated via video. Navigation among the

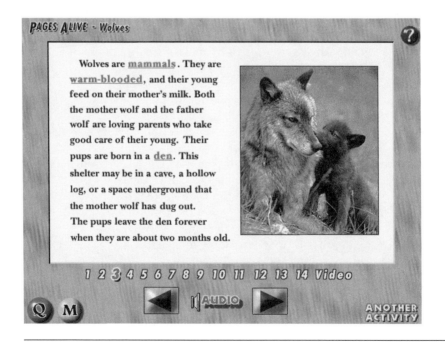

FIGURE 5.6   *Curious Creatures*

Source: Curriculum Associates. Reproduced by permission of the publisher.

different data is accomplished in a hypertext format that lets the reader click on words within the definition to get further clarification of the word's meaning.

Another effective type of dictionary for English language development is illustrated by the *Oxford Picture Dictionary Interactive,* a theme-based dictionary that groups vocabulary associated with particular situations or places, such as a shopping mall (see Figure 5.7). Students see and hear words related to a mall via pictures, graphics, and sound, thereby building multiple pathways to memory.

The theory that lexical information is stored in our memory system in clusters centered around a theme or situation and that key words in one cluster can activate others is the premise for a Web vocabulary activity called *lingonets* (http://www. linetti.com/nets.htm). This game presents situations like "At an Airport Check-In" and provides clusters of words and spaces for missing words in three categories: things to have, actions to take, and problems. As students play this game, they are grouping vocabulary into meaningful clusters that enhance memory (see Figure 5.8).

In his lexical approach, Michael Lewis (1997) suggests an alternative to Grabe's vocabulary and structural knowledge category, arguing that language has traditionally been erroneously divided into two distinct categories: (1) grammar

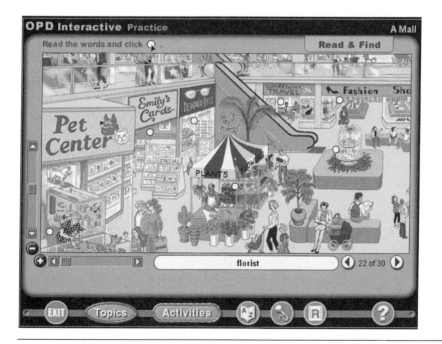

FIGURE 5.7   *Oxford Picture Dictionary Interactive*

Source: Reproduced by permission of Oxford University Press from the Oxford Picture Dictionary Interactive © 2000 Oxford University Press.

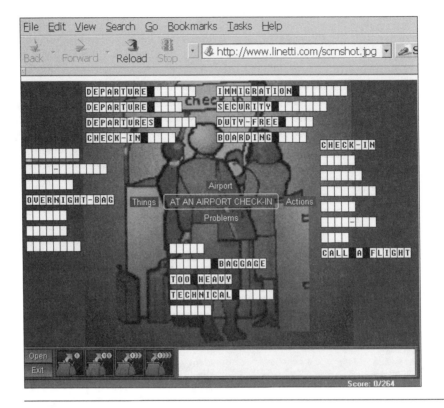

Figure 5.8   Lingonets

Source: The picture is a courtesy of Lingonet Ltd. Used with permission.

typically assigned generative powers and (2) vocabulary considered to be "fixed non-generative words" (p. 255). Based on his lexical approach, Lewis proposes, instead, the existence of different types of lexical items that he defines as "socially sanctioned independent units . . . [that] may be individual words or full sentences." These "institutional utterances" are positioned on a generative continuum ranging from fixed to free and "convey fixed social or pragmatic meaning within a given community" (p. 255).

Such lexical items include pairs or groups of words that occur together with a high frequency such as *to make a determined effort* or *to raise venture capital* (p. 256). Lewis asserts that these collocations, or "partnerships," should be presented and practiced as a whole rather than as individual words. Similarly, he maintains that institutionalized utterances that are typically remembered as one entity, such as *If I were you, I'd* . . . and text sequencing devices such as *in conclusion* (p. 257), can be successfully learned and used as wholes, rather than analyzed as separate words or grammatical parts. Lewis suggests teachers use instructional strategies that raise student awareness of these types of lexical items and provide nonthreatening classroom experiences in which students can practice them as a way of improving reading and vocabulary skills.

An effective strategy for this purpose is the use of a *concordancer,* a computer program that allows students to search large amounts of authentic text for multiple examples of selected words or phrases. Allen-Juarez demonstrated this practice in her eleventh-grade sheltered language arts class. She modeled for her students how to use a simple concordancer available at the *Virtual Language Centre* website of Hong Kong Polytechnic University http://www.edict.com.hk/concordance/default.htm) to search for collocations such as "on the other hand." The students were able to scan multiple pieces of text containing these items and then view the full sentences in which the collocations appeared. Dictionary entries and text-to-speech sound files were also available for further assistance with each lexical item (see Figure 5.9).

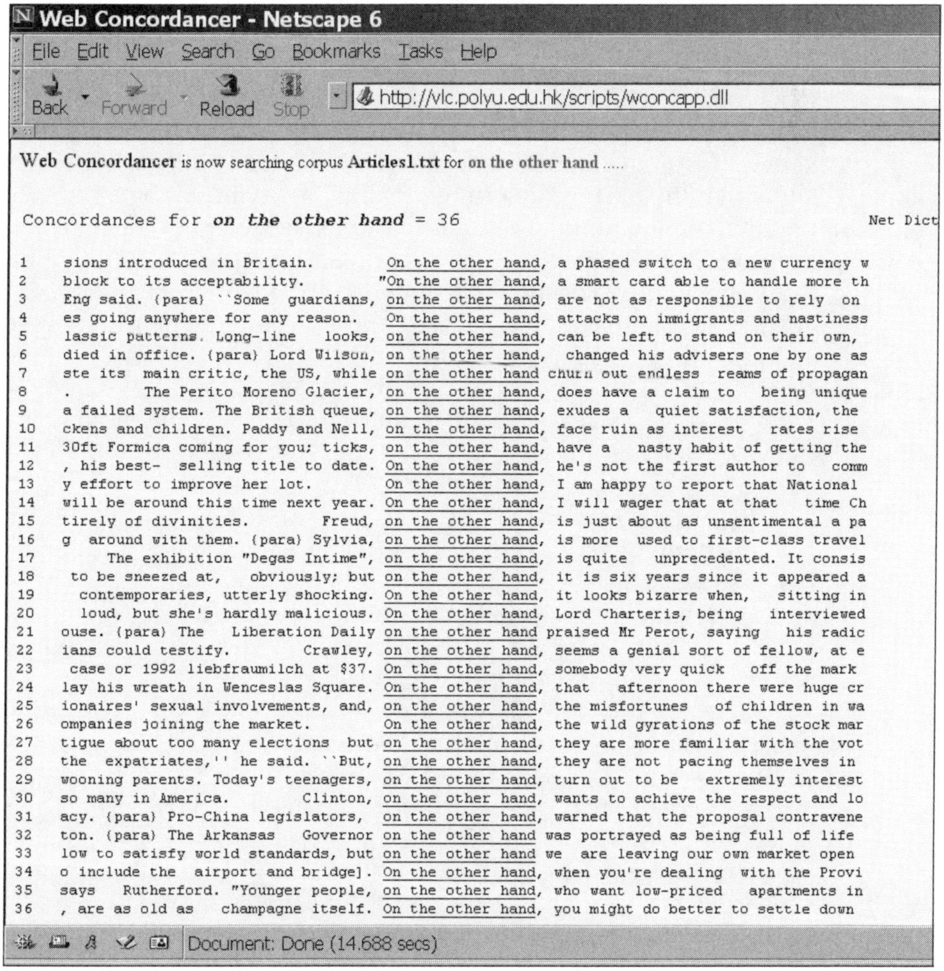

FIGURE 5.9 *Virtual Learning Centre* **of Hong Kong Polytechnic University**

Barlow (1997) described other techniques using a concordancer that went beyond observing lexical patterns in context. For example, using specified sort features of the *MonoConc Pro* software program, he produced a reconstruction exercise consisting of lines of text with gaps where either the word *for* or *since* was missing. Students had to analyze the context and determine the meaning of these phrases or sentences in order to fill in the correct missing word. Additional Web-based concordancing resources include *CobuildDirect's* corpus site http://titania.cobuild. collins.co.uk/form.html and *Conc,* a Macintosh program that can be accessed via the TESOL's Computer-Enhanced Language Instruction Archive (CELIA) maintained at Latrobe University http://www.latrobe.edu.au/gse/celia/celia.html.

Formal Discourse Structure Knowledge

Knowledge of the structure of formal discourse (formal schemata) assists the learner in understanding and remembering the text. Research (Carrell, 1984) suggests that texts utilizing certain types of expository organization, such as comparison, problem/solution, and causation, facilitate the recall of specific ideas from the text by second language learners to a greater extent than texts that are more loosely organized around a collection of facts or descriptions. Furthermore, Carrell found that the extent to which each particular type of discourse facilitated recall varied according to the particular native language group. In a later study on the explicit teaching of rhetorical organization of text (Carrell, 1985), results indicated that such training facilitated ESL students' reading comprehension as measured by quantity of information recalled and, specifically, recall of major topics, subtopics, and supporting detail.

What technology is available to assist English learners in developing knowledge of English rhetorical patterns?

Software programs that provide models and that practice rhetorical organizational patterns can assist ELLs in developing this type of background knowledge that is so crucial to their reading skill development. Teachers can assure that students unfamiliar with certain patterns in their native language receive sufficient practice with that type of English discourse to facilitate their encoding, retention, and retrieval of information from the reading text.

Software such as *Writing Process Workshop* (see Figure 5.10) and *Scholastic Process Writer* provide models of different forms of writing, ranging from types of poetry to persuasive essays.

Exercises that come with process-oriented programs guide the beginning reader and writer through the process of writing a letter or composing various types of writing genres. The use of devices such as topic sentence, transition words, supporting details, and examples are demonstrated for the student. For example, in the case of a comparison and contrast essay, students are guided in identifying differences and similarities associated with the subjects of their topic. With both of these programs, students can transfer their topic sentences, supporting details, and other computer-prompted notes into a built-in word processor to compose their

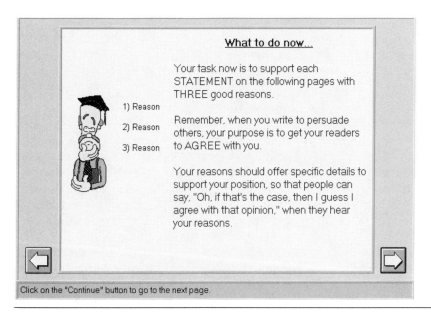

FIGURE 5.10 *Writing Process Workshop*

Source: Educational Activities Software, a division of the Siboney Learning Group, St. Louis, MO. Used by permission.

essays. Process writing and discourse structure are examined later in this chapter as we discuss teaching English language learners to write.

Using the software program *Postcards,* students write in different genres based on multimedia journeys they take to Mexico, Turkey, Ghana, and Japan. Students select the country they wish to visit and one of four companions who assign writing projects in the text structure that corresponds to their character. Students who select the *author* companion respond to prompts that require them to write in a narrative genre. The *filmmaker* uses persuasive language structures; the *investigator* compares and contrasts; and the *archeologist* writes descriptive prose. In this highly interactive program, students can simultaneously access multimedia presentations about their selected country and can take notes in their electronic travel log for later use in writing postcards to their classmates and teacher.

Content and World Background Knowledge

Researchers (Carrell, 1987; Floyd and Carrell, 1987) have presented compelling data that suggest that activating the readers' knowledge of the subject matter and cultural content of the text is a significant factor in both reading comprehension and recall. English language learners can better recall information from text on topics familiar to them than readings of equivalent difficulty level on subjects with which they are less familiar (Anderson and Pearson, 1984). Readers can comprehend and recall texts that presuppose cultural content of their own culture more easily than they can recall syntactically and rhetorically similar texts based on unfamiliar and more remote cultures (Pritchard, 1990; Steffensen and Joag-Dev, 1984). The implication for classroom instruction is that readers can benefit from learning about the culture-specific and subject matter content of a reading before attempting to read a particular text. Technology can be helpful in filling in these content and cultural gaps in the readers' background and content knowledge.

How can technology provide content and schema knowledge?

Computer-based reading programs allow second language learners the flexibility to interact with the text in ways not possible with books alone. Comprehensive interactive reading programs and multimedia reading software utilize CD-ROM video clips to provide readers the background knowledge needed to form mental models of the text before reading passages on subject matter topics. With programs such as *Scholastic's Read 180,* students access video clips prior to reading the text in order to establish background knowledge needed for comprehension. Though all the students view the same video clip on a particular subject, the reading passage that follows is adjusted to each student's individual reading level. In this way, even beginning-level readers can share in this schema-building activity.

Several websites supply readings, multimedia presentations, project ideas, and software that address specific content areas and themes. For young English language learners, the *Kids Domain* website supplies an extensive collection of shareware, freeware, and demos of content material that can be accessed by subject areas. The *Eduhound* website (www.Eduhound.com), sponsored by the *T.H.E. Journal,* offers an extensive free directory of theme-based and subject matter links to rich resources for K–12 classrooms.

Popular websites for study of science, the environment, and nature include *Discover Magazine* (http://www.discover.com), *Environmental News Network, NASA's Space Science News, National Geographic News,* and the *Scientific American* (http://www.sciam.com), which provides a list of science related articles with reference links, and an interactive service that lets students ask questions of the experts. Additionally, Web-based news services such as *USA Today* (http://www. usatoday.com/) and the *Global Newsstand* (http://www.mcs.net/~rchojnac/www/tgn.html), which links to newspapers around the world, are excellent sources for filling in missing social, political, and cultural schemata. (See Technology Resources at end of this chapter for website addresses.)

Synthesis and Evaluation Skills and Strategies

Fluent readers are able to synthesize and compare information from a text to other relevant sources of information on the same topic. Readers are called on not only to comprehend the text, but to make judgments about the information, the author's purpose, and the usefulness of the text. Fluent readers typically use strategies like predicting to assist them in anticipating text development and evaluating the author's perspective as they read (Grabe, 1991).

How can technology encourage students learning to synthesize and evaluate reading text and other data?

Several websites present graphs and other nontext information that gives students practice in interpreting various forms of data, including graphs, tables, and timelines. Engaging readers in a communicative, task-based activity supported by the Web is one way to help beginning English readers gain more cognitive strategies for reading. For instance, if students are invited to obtain information about the local weather, population, and geography of their area as required in a community-based project initiated on the *MathStar* site (http:// mathstar.nmsu.edu), they can learn to search associated links such as weather sites, demographic sites, and geographic sites to answer the questions provided with the task. Students will learn to read, for example, a weather information table and quickly find local weather information required by the task (see Figure 5.11).

With exposure to unlimited sources of information on the Internet, students need to develop skills in evaluating data and differentiating facts from opinions. Highly interactive software that require students to evaluate and synthesize information from multiple sources are good resources for teaching these skills. The problem-solving software, *Ace Detective*, requires the reader to compare and evaluate two or more sources of information about a crime to determine such things as

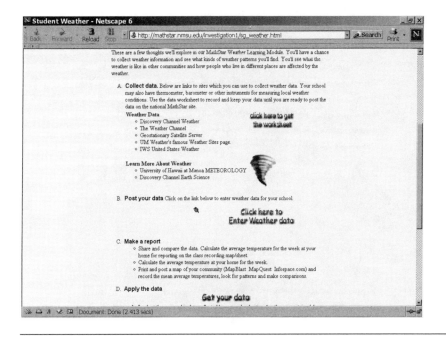

FIGURE 5.11 *MathStar*, **New Mexico State University**

Source: Used with permission.

which witnesses are telling the truth and which suspect had the motive, opportunity, and means to commit the crime (see Figure 5.12).

Similarly, the *Learning English: Neighborhood* program asks the readers to assume the role of news reporter and, based on their reading of an article, decide which headline and picture are most appropriate for the story. In order to make the best matches, students consider the main idea of the news article and the author's purpose for writing it.

For adults, software such as the *Reading for the Workplace* program use functional context passages to develop evaluative skills like recognizing the problem, determining the main idea, making inferences, determining cause and effect, and drawing conclusions. In this program students read materials relevant to job-related tasks and, through interactive computer instruction, experience and respond to real workplace situations.

Metacognitive Knowledge and Monitoring

Metacognitive knowledge is knowledge about how learners think and self-regulate their cognitive processes. The ability to effectively apply metacognitive strategies to the reading process is a key ingredient to skilled reading, especially for older readers. Metacognitive knowledge includes knowledge about language and encompasses recognizing structural and rhetorical features of the text using suitable strategies for accomplishing particular goals. In the reading process, this knowledge would include such skills as recognizing main ideas; adjusting reading rate as comprehension of text dictates—skimming, scanning, paraphrasing, and summarizing; guessing meaning from word formation rules, prefixes, and suffixes; and taking notes (Grabe, 1991). In a study of students in an undergraduate ESL reading

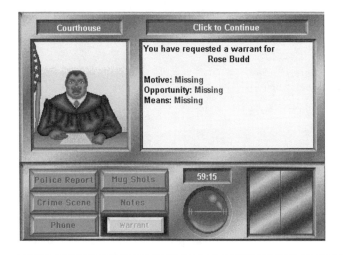

FIGURE 5.12 *Ace Detective*

Source: Mindplay. Used with permission.

course, Auerbach and Paxton (1997) found that when second language readers researched and reflected critically on their own reading strategies, they increased their metacognitive awareness and control of their reading, and also their enjoyment of reading in English.

How does technology assist in developing metacognitive skills?

Bickel and Truscello (1996) identified ways the computer is a valuable tool in assisting students in the development of metacognitive learning strategies. Applying these strategies to reading development, students can *self-monitor* and *self-evaluate* by checking their reading speed and comprehension evaluation records of the software and writing in their electronic learning logs about their progress. Readers utilize *directed attention* to follow a preplanned sequence of reading software lessons and plan activities on the Web, which would give them additional reading resources and practice.

In order to develop *selective attention* strategies, in which students decide in advance to focus on particular items, students can search for specific vocabulary in authentic writing on the Internet links, in listserv discussions, or with any text using a concordancer. With a concordancer, learners observe multiple uses of the same word in a wide variety of contexts and draw their own conclusions about the meaning and usage of the word. This approach is especially helpful with words such as prepositions, conjunctions, and lexical items that do not easily lend themselves to concise definitions, but are more readily understood by their usage. The search capability of the Internet can serve the same function of displaying lexical items in extended discourse.

Affective Factors in Reading

So far in this chapter, we have examined some of the cognitive processes involved in reading, as well as the knowledge and skills required of fluent readers and the multiple ways technology can be used to facilitate their acquisition. Of equal importance is the affective domain with factors of self-esteem, motivation, and anxiety having an important impact on the reader's ability to comprehend the text. Gee (1999) makes a strong case for the importance of the reader's perception of his or her reading ability to the development of reading competence. He notes that students who feel self-confident to read and expect to understand a story are intrinsically motivated to engage in reading (Spaulding, 1992). Motivated students read more with the result of improvement in their reading skills.

How does technology support a positive affective development in learning to read?

Technology offers English language learners several features that foster high self-esteem and increased motivation and that serve to diminish anxiety and inhibitions. By providing the reader a nonthreatening source of reading practice with feedback and help features, computer-based reading programs encourage student autonomy and motivation. Students feel free to guess answers to comprehension questions, seek vocabulary assistance, reread the text as frequently as needed for understanding without fear of embarrassment, and are empowered to monitor their own progress over extended periods of time. Since students are reading material based on their individual reading proficiency levels, they expect to be able to succeed and are motivated to progress to a higher level.

Motivation is also stimulated by interactive software games ranging from arcade-style vocabulary games that foster rapid letter and word recognition to computer-generated activities such as crossword puzzles. The game *That's a Fact Jack! Read* is a good illustration of how games can add interest and motivation to reading (see Figure 5.13). This program is done in a game show format and appropriate for upper elementary grades through high school. The game requires that students read specific books and then answer comprehension questions. This quiz-type game asks students to connect statements with supporting points. In this manner students are engaged in a highly motivating activity while developing skills in evaluation and rhetorical structures.

FIGURE 5.13   *That's a Fact Jack! Read*

Source: From That's A Fact, Jack!® Read, published by Tom Snyder Productions. © Copyright Tom Snyder Productions, Inc. Reprinted with permission.

Technology resources also motivate readers by fulfilling a variety of purposes for reading. For example, students working on collaborative Web-based projects must read and gather information on their topic in order to feed data into the larger group project and shared data bases. The World Wide Web gives the reader immediate access to extensive and up-to-the-minute information that meets all types of reading purposes, whether they be to gather data on subject-specific academic topics, read about a topic of personal interest, or read the day's international news stories.

Summary

As we conclude this section of the chapter on teaching English language learners to read, we find that technology is a tool that can assist in the development of reading skills and, as such, can be employed by TESOL teachers using a wide variety of approaches. Specific strategies, techniques, and approaches will depend on the principles and theories held by the teachers and the needs and goals of their students. For example, technology is well suited to support teachers who practice a balanced approach to early literacy, since it offers unique features for developing recognition, structure, and vocabulary skills and a wealth of resources for providing content and schema knowledge. With equal ease, technology could be integrated into instruction that features extensive reading (Krashen, 1989; Coady, 1997) as students access the rich network of extensive reading resources, including large online databases, magazine articles, and full-length books. The *Online Books Page* website, developed by John Mark Ockerbloom at the University of Pennsylvania, offers over 15,000 listings of books published on-line (see Figure 5.14).

In summary, technology can be a vehicle to practice specific skills and strategies such as timed reading, recognition exercises, cloze exercises, and other vocabulary development exercises. It can also serve as a major resource for reading materials of interest to the reader for silent, extensive reading over sustained periods of time. The computer can be a motivational tool for literacy development as students work on collaborative projects on the World Wide Web to do pre-reading and post-reading tasks in a content, cross-curriculum context.

Regardless of which approaches are used, research has repeatedly shown that a strong relationship exists between the processes involved in reading and writing (Reid, 1993). Simply put, those students who are good readers are most often also good writers; conversely, good writers make good readers. The next part of the chapter examines the other half of the reading-writing connection and the important ways in which technology can facilitate the development of writing skills of English language learners.

Developing Writing Skills

It has long been recognized that reading and writing are integrally linked and in fact share many of the same cognitive and social processes. Just as we saw that readers are active participants in the reading process bringing background knowl-

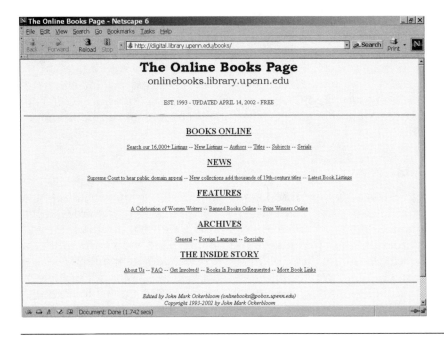

FIGURE 5.14   *Online Books Page*

Source: The Online Books Page. http://onlinebooks.library.upenn.edu/. © 1993–2002 by John Mark Ockerbloom. Used with permission.

edge to bear on interpreting and constructing meaning from text, the same is true with writers. Writers have schemata in mind about the content and form of their writing as they compose and revise their mental and written drafts of the text. Like reading, writing is a complicated, interactive, and recursive process in which the writer is engaged. We will look now at different approaches that have been used in teaching English language learners to write.

Raimes (1991) identified four approaches to teaching second language writing that emerged at different times over the last few decades and continue to have an impact on writing pedagogy today. Each of these approaches represents a particular focus in the teaching of writing to second language learners: form, the writer, the content, or the reader. We would argue that depending on the particular students and their purposes for writing, each of these focuses is important to developing writing skills. Good writing instruction draws on each approach in varying degrees and attends to the interaction among these different focuses. We will discuss these approaches and investigate ways technology enhances their effectiveness in developing second language writing skills.

Focus on Form

What is the role of form-focused instruction in teaching second language writing skills?

Dating back to the era of the audio-lingual method in the 1960s, when writing was predominantly viewed as a means of reinforcing speech patterns, writing instruction focused on sentence-level linguistics forms. Writing was largely limited to the teaching and testing of grammatical rules and the manipulation of transformation, substitution, and completion exercises. By the 1970s, instruction moved beyond the sentence level to controlled discourse in the form of sentence combining and controlled compositions that required learners to manipulate certain features of whole paragraphs, such as changing the text from active to passive voice or from present tense to future tense. This was also a time when attention was directed toward rhetorical forms and the impact of culture on the formation of the writer's dominant thought pattern and rhetorical organization. Native English writers, it was hypothesized (Kaplan, 1966), utilize a dominantly linear approach to writing as compared to other cultures that organize discourse in a variety of other manners. Based on this observation, form-focused instruction included practice in recognizing and using basic elements of well-written essays, such as introductory and concluding paragraphs, topic sentences, supporting details, and transitions (Raimes, 1991). Attention was given to the organizational patterns and forms of different types of written text, such as expository, descriptive, and narrative.

A focus on form continues to be a crucial aspect of second language writing instruction with researchers and practitioners probing the pivotal question of what role grammar instruction should have in the teaching of writing. Proponents of form-focused instruction point to studies that indicate that students who receive grammar instruction progress at a more accelerated pace than those following a natural acquisition path (Ellis, 1990; Long, 1988; Pienemann, 1984) and that form-focused instruction is instrumental in improving the learner's grammatical accuracy (Larsen-Freeman, 1995). The explicit study of form even within a communicative approach has found many supporters (Williams, 1995). Fotos (1994) argued for the use of grammar consciousness-raising tasks within communicative classrooms, and Spada and Lightbrown (1993) found that "form-focused instruction and corrective feedback provided within the context of communicative interaction can contribute positively to second language development in both the short and long term" (p. 205).

Celce-Murcia (1991) offered a practical guide for teaching grammar in a second language, suggesting that the teacher consider both *learner* variables of age, proficiency level, and educational background, and also *instructional* variables including skill areas, degree of formality, and purpose or need for using the language. She advocated, for example, less attention on form when teaching younger and beginning learners listening skills than when instructing adult learners who are literate in their native language and need advanced writing skills to meet academic or professional writing requirements.

How can technology be used to support form-focused instruction?

Grammar was one of the first areas of language development to be addressed by the computer-based instruction. Even the original drill and practice style programs offered some noticeable advantages over a book. Students could get immediate feedback, could be branched to the correct difficulty level, and could have information repeated without embarrassment. These programs also frequently included various types of games to add interest and motivation.

Technology today offers focused practice of grammar structure in interactive formats for all ages and proficiency levels. Research by Pellettieri (2000) strongly suggests that synchronous networked-based communication (NBC), in which students view their writing and that of their interlocutors simultaneously on a split screen, contributes to the development of grammatical competence. Pellettieri's study found that students who were engaged in NBC negotiated meaning and made necessary form-focused modifications in their writing.

Grammar practice is found in different types of programs ranging from simple games that feature a few points of grammar to comprehensive interactive software that cover all major grammatical structures from beginning to advanced levels. While comprehensive grammar programs teach explicit grammar rules, with the addition of multimedia and hypertext, they do so in an interactive format, usually integrated with other English skills. With the *Focus on Grammar Series,* for example, students engage in activities in which they discover the rule, practice the structure in several types of guided exercises, see the rule applied in a reading, listen to its use, and finally incorporate it into their writing using their word processors (see Figure 5.15). Students also have the option of seeing grammar notes that include usage rules and examples, grammar charts depicting the relevant rules, and appen-

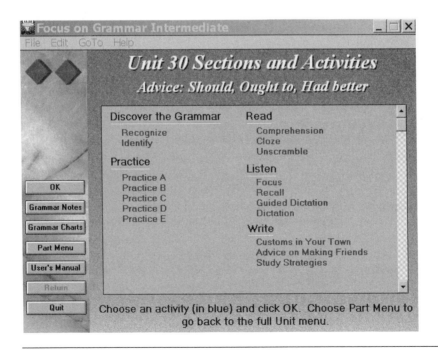

FIGURE 5.15   *Focus on Grammar*

Source: Reprinted by permission of Pearson Education, Inc., White Plains, New York.

dices that give further information on spelling and pronunciation rules. Students can also check their scores on each unit to monitor their progress.

Focused practice within an integrated approach attempts to address the long-standing concern that students learning grammar in isolation of other skills were unable to transfer that grammatical knowledge to their writing and speaking.

The comprehensive CD grammar program, *Azar Interactive,* is a companion program for the Azar series of grammar books (see Figure 5.16). For each structure, the program provides exercises and further exposure to the rule through some combination of a reading passage, video, or audio tape. The Azar grammar chart and other help menus are also available to them. Students may have the text read to them or view the correct answers at any time. This program has a very intuitive interface that students find easy to manipulate as they navigate through its various components.

Another CD program that supports a book series is *Grammar 3D,* a supplement to the *Grammar Dimensions* series based on the work of Diane Larson-Freeman's model of form, meaning, and use as critical components of English language learning. This program has a click-and-drag feature in some sections to correctly complete sentences. For usage practice, it presents a short, concise description of a situation and then requires students to determine the best choice of words. If a student gives an incorrect answer, grammar clues are given and grammar help rules are easily accessible.

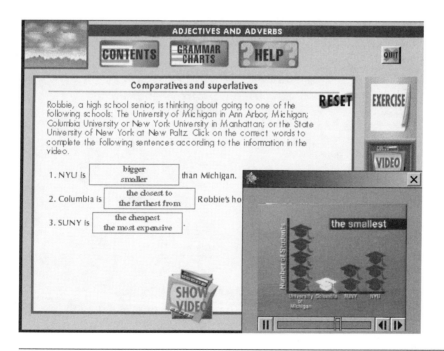

FIGURE 5.16   *Azar Interactive*

Source: Reprinted by permission of Pearson Education, Inc., White Plains, New York.

We offer one caveat about the use of intensive grammar programs; these programs need to be carefully incorporated into a broad language-development approach that gives students substantial practice using these grammatical forms in authentic language in real-life situations.

Grammar practice is frequently a component of programs based on a listening comprehension approach, as in the case of *English Your Way,* which offers practice with basic grammar rules and provides a grammar help menu to support the learner's listening and speaking skills. Other programs, including the *Grammar Mastery* series, embed grammar structures in narrations about everyday situations such as "Anna's First Day," in which an exchange student visits her host family's home for the first time. Students practice the situational narratives by recording and typing in the correct answer to the missing words of a dialog.

Some software are more specific in their focus offering one particular type of practice. For example, *Easy Writer: The Interactive Software for ESL Students,* authored by Jane Boris, utilizes a technique that has been a mainstay in ESL and EFL classes (see Figure 5.17). Students' essays containing various types of errors are displayed to the class accompanied by clues as to the number and nature of the errors. Students then try to locate and correct these errors. This can easily be a small group

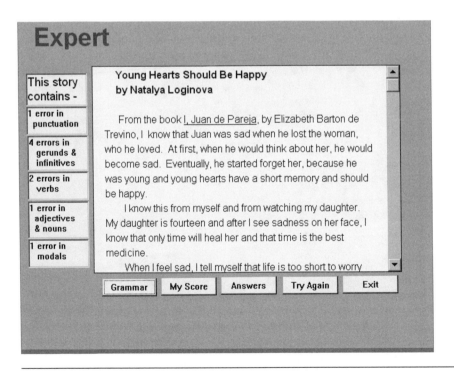

FIGURE 5.17   *Easy Writer: The Interactive Software for ESL Students*

Source: Published by Software for Students. Authored by Jane Boris. Distributed by Linguatronics. Used with permission.

activity where it becomes a game to see who can make all the needed corrections in the least amount of time.

In addition to commercial software that focus on grammatical form, freeware and shareware grammar programs can be downloaded from the World Wide Web from sites such as *Kids Domain* (http://www.kidsdomain.com/down/pc/) for children and the TESOL/CELIA collection, available from TESOL, Inc. (http://www.tesol.org) for adults and younger learners. Excellent grammar tutorials, extensive support materials, and on-line exercises for college-level ELLs can be obtained at Purdue University's *OWL,* on-line writing lab (http://owl.english.purdue.edu/), *Grammar Safari* (http://deil.lang.uiuc.edu/web.pages/grammarsafari.html), and *The Grammar Help Page* (http://www.hut.fi/~rvilmihelp/grammar_help). The University of Illinois at Urbana-Champaign sponsors the electronic *Writer's Workshop* (http://www.english.uiuc.edu/cws/wworkshop/grammar.me nu.htm), which provides an extensive grammar handbook on parts of speech, phrases, clauses, sentences, and common usage problems. It is also a source for tips on technical writing and writing websites.

Focus on the Writer and the Writing Process

How did a focus on the writer change teaching practices in second language writing classes?

The 1970s witnessed a shift in second language writing research and pedagogy from an emphasis on the final written product to interest in the cognitive activities and strategies students experience as they write. This new process approach, which was largely a reaction against form-dominated instruction that placed a premium on accuracy, had a profound impact on classroom practice (Zamel, 1987). The focus of instruction moved "from language focused activities to learner-centered tasks in which students assume greater control over what they write, how they write it, and the evaluation of their own writing" (Richards, 1990, p. 109). Teachers allowed time for pre-writing activities, including brainstorming and bridging to students' background knowledge, before students began to compose. Students were encouraged to write multiple drafts, communicate with authentic audiences, share feedback with peers, and publish their writing in one of numerous forms. Content and student expression were viewed as more important than linguistic correctness, though many practitioners of the process approach did not abandon attention to grammatical features and, in fact, included skill development as one of the final stages of the writing process.

How has technology supported the writing process approach?

One of the earliest uses of technology in the English as a second language curriculum was to support the process approach to teaching writing. Technology enhances this approach in terms of providing both collaborative writing opportunities and individualized skill development using computer-based programs. Each stage of the writing process is supported by technology use (see Table 5.1).

TABLE 5.1   *Technology-Enhanced Writing Class for English Language Learners*

The Writing Process Stages	Individual Skill Development	Collaborative Group Learning Activities
1. Prewriting activities	• Prompted writing • Brainstorming programs • Outlining programs • Research	• Accessing Web databases • Brainstorming • List making • Electronic bibliography writers
2. Writing the draft	• Composing with the word processor	• Collaborative Web-based writing projects
3. Responding	• Individual teacher-student conferencing	• Networked peer response groups • Electronic prompted peer review
4. Revising and editing	• Word processing • Thesaurus programs • Spelling and grammar checkers	• Incorporating peer suggestions
5. Evaluating	• Teacher-student interaction assessing skills and assigning software; self-correct	• Class critique of student writing using an LCD panel
6. Developing skills	• Use assigned grammar software • Web-based writing labs and grammar software	• Small group use of prompted writing and grammar software
7. Showcasing or publishing work	• Display final copy of student writing • Desktop publishing • Web publishing	• Desktop publishing group products such as school magazines, newspapers, brochures; web pages and publications

   In the pre-writing stage, students can use word processors and brainstorming software, such as *Inspiration,* to stimulate and organize their thoughts and make notes about what they want to write (see Figure 5.18). Using the graphical drawing tools of these programs, students are able to create mind maps of key vocabulary and concepts they wish to express.

   Students can also brainstorm as a whole class using an electronic whiteboard or "smart board." By connecting a computer with an electronic whiteboard, ideas generated by students and recorded on the board can be captured and saved as a text file for later use by students when writing their compositions. Notes written on a smart board can also be saved as html files that all students can readily view

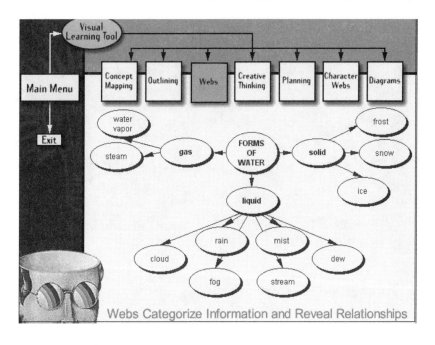

FIGURE 5.18 *Inspiration*

Source: Used with permission from Exploring Inspiration®, an interactive training CD-ROM, published by Inspiration Software, Inc.

using any Web browser. Special features of the smart board also assist students in grouping ideas into meaningful clusters.

Another popular and creative application of technology in the pre-writing stage is the use of prompts to assist students in getting past a blank page. Teachers can create their own prompts to guide students into a particular type of composition. For instance, when studying persuasion-style compositions in his high school writing class, Mr. Bargeron created an opening prompt that read, "There are many reasons why students should be allowed to leave campus at lunch time." Since this was a real issue being considered by their school board, students were very motivated to write.

There are also highly interactive software programs, such as *Rainbow, Storybook Weaver,* and *Imagination Express,* that have "story starters" to encourage students to author their own stories (see Figure 5.19). Typically, students are prompted with an opening phrase or sentence that relates to the picture on the screen.

These programs give students the power to illustrate their stories by choosing from a collection of backgrounds, objects, and people. *Storybook Weaver* and *Imagination Express* have special features such as sizing of the objects and people in the story to make them larger or smaller, flipping them to face to the left or right side, and adding appropriate music—all of which help to foster a sense of ownership in the story by the students engaged in writing (see Figure 5.20).

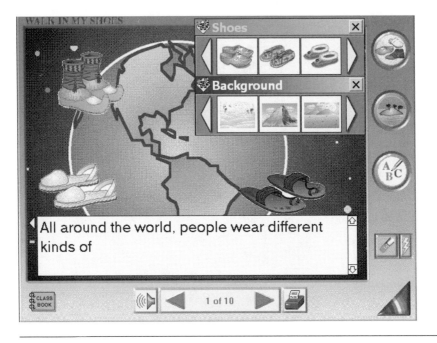

FIGURE 5.19   *Rainbow*

Source: Curriculum Associates. Reproduced by permission of the publisher.

FIGURE 5.20   *Imagination Express*

Source: © 1995 Riverdeep Interactive Learning Limited and Harcourt Brace & Company. Used with permission.

Word processors make composing much easier, since students find it less intimidating to write when they discover how easy it is to edit and revise their writing. Programs such as *Writing Process Workshop, Scholastic's Process Writer,* and the Daedalus Integrated Writing Environment (DIWE) have specific components to address each step of the writing process. The DIWE is a networked program that allows students to interact with each other electronically as they compose their compositions. They can easily read and critique their classmates' work and revise their own work to incorporate suggestions from peers. The *Daedalus Online* program presents a comprehensive writing process program that also features research sites via the World Wide Web (see Figure 5.21).

After students have composed the first draft of their writing on the word processor, they can edit and revise their work by utilizing the peer review capabilities of the software. Programs like *The Process Workshop* and *Scholastic Process Writer* have peer-editing components that give clear prompts to students as they respond to various types of essays. For example, one prompt that a student was using as he responded to his classmate's persuasive essay asked him to identify the writer's solutions to the problem and comment if he thought they were clearly stated. Similarly, a compare and contrast peer response prompt might ask the reviewer to find all the differences and similarities proposed by the writer. At this stage students should be encouraged to revise their writing to incorporate the suggestions of their peers and to utilize the spelling and grammar checkers and thesaurus features of their word processor to self-correct mechanical errors.

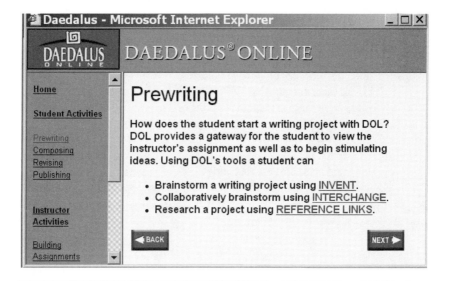

FIGURE 5.21 *Daedalus Online*

Source: Reprinted by permission of Longman Publishers.

In addition to peer feedback, teacher conferences are especially useful in assisting students to determine which areas of their writing need improvement. Several computer-based grammar programs described earlier in this chapter provide opportunities for further individualized practice in grammatical structures. At this stage of the process, computer use supports explicit teaching and conscious learning.

Technology can provide the three conditions proposed by Krashen (1981) as prerequisites for conscious learning to take place: sufficient time to consult and use rules, a focus on form, and knowledge of the applicable rule. Effective grammar software provide explanations of grammar points, allow students to study and manipulate these structures at their own speed, and provide feedback and correction of their answers. Teachers could utilize software that assists students with particular structural and discourse elements that emanate from the students' own writing in contrast to teaching "the rule of the day." In their role of facilitator, teachers need the skills to identify writing problems displayed in students' compositions and communicative activities and to be able to suggest appropriate software that provide relevant practice.

The focus on skill development in the second language classroom does not have to be boring and alienating for students. In one eighth-grade class, the students wrote their own grammar book to pass along to the entering sixth-grade class. Working in pairs, students helped each other select a grammar rule they had studied and then, using a word processor, wrote the rule and sentences to practice the grammar structure. After peer reviewing their work using electronic prompts created by their teacher for this purpose, each student submitted a disk with her or his grammar lesson. After final revisions, the teacher collected the students' disks and assisted student editors and artists in publishing the final book using the *Student Writing and Learning Center* desktop publishing program.

Other exciting ways are available to publish student work either by using multimedia with programs such as *Multimedia Workshop* or one of the numerous websites like *ExChange* at University of Illinois–Urbana–Champagne (http://www2.lei.uluc.edu/Echanges/, which specializes in providing a forum for publication of student writing by non-native English speakers from around the world (see Figure 5.22). Students engaged in communicative projects on the Web, like those described in Chapter 3, find their work published on the project's website, thereby providing a world audience for their writing. Students can also be encouraged to develop class and school websites where their writing can be displayed.

Several websites with on-line writing labs provide detailed information on every stage of the writing process. One of the most comprehensive sites for this purpose is the *Online Writing Lab* at Purdue University (see Figure 5.23).

What does research tell us about the effectiveness of using technology to support the writing process?

The writing process has proven to be an effective approach with second language learners (Kroll, 1990). Providing these types of writing activities not only

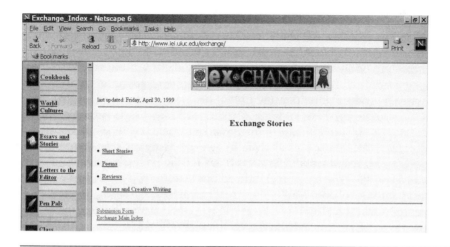

FIGURE 5.22   *ExChange* Website

Source: Copyright 1995–2001 by the Board of Trustees of the University of Illinois. All rights reserved. Reproduced with permission.

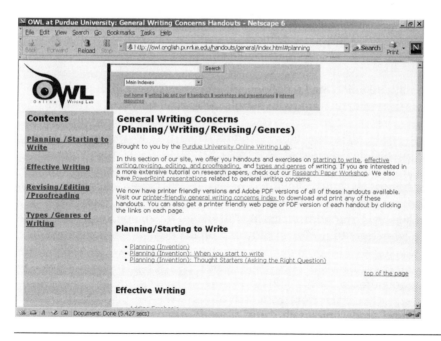

FIGURE 5.23   *Online Writing Lab,* Purdue University

Source: Purdue Research Foundation. Used with permission.

improves English learners' writing but also promotes other aspects of second language acquisition (Peregoy and Boyle, 2001). In a study of university-level ESL writing classes using the technology-enhanced model (Butler-Pascoe, 1994), findings showed significant improvement in student writing skills and control over targeted grammatical forms. Additionally, several advantages of a computer-based writing process were identified:

1. Students' estimate of their own writing ability improved significantly.
2. Word processors allowed students to easily revise and edit their compositions, thereby avoiding tedious recopying and increasing student enjoyment of writing.
3. Students demonstrated pride in producing a legible, professional looking paper and in developing word processing skills which they viewed as very valuable.
4. Student enthusiasm for writing with word processors resulted in their spending additional time on revisions outside of class hours.
5. Instructors could view students' writing on the computer monitors without interrupting them as they composed their compositions.
6. With computer-based skill development taking place in the lab, more class time and teacher attention could be devoted to writing tasks.
7. There was an increase in student interaction and oral communication as students collaborated on word processing and on-line database projects.
8. Writing pen pals via a telecommunication network provided students an authentic audience and acted as a motivating force for revising and editing. (p. 617)

Other research indicated similar findings. Cohen and Riel (1986) reported positive results from the use of computer networks to provide authentic audiences for student writing. Other studies indicated improvement in motivation and pride of authorship (Phinney, 1989; Engberg, 1986) and reduction in anxiety (Berens, 1986; Piper, 1987).

Focus on the Content

Largely as a reaction to what they considered the process approach's excessive attention to "the writer's making of personal meaning" (Raimes, 1991, p. 410), some teachers and theorists (Mohan, 1986; Horowitz, 1986) began to focus on the content of the writing and the academic expectations placed on their students. Research by Cummins (1984) and others demonstrated the need for students to develop cognitive academic language proficiency required for success in subject matter courses. Similarly, college-level ESL and EFL students benefit from a content approach for developing writing skills for academic purposes. In an adjunct model, ESL instructors team with subject-area instructors to provide advanced ESL students language instruction that reinforces the concepts and material presented in their degree courses.

Research has also shown that for English language learners of all ages, literature serves as rich content for language development (Reid, 1993). Literature serves as a model for good writing and reflects the culture of the target language (Ibson, 1990; Carter and Long, 1987).

How can technology facilitate writing in content areas?

Content-based instruction with ELLs can draw on subject matter software to enhance language skills and develop content knowledge. Programs that are ideally suited to the needs of English language learners are those that have the following characteristics:

1. Incorporate some combination of audio, video, and graphics to support comprehension.
2. Stimulate critical thinking through problem-solving tasks.
3. Use easily identifiable icons for easy navigation of the program.
4. Are not heavily dependent on text.

Examples of software meeting these criteria include simulation programs such as *Oregon Trail,* in which users take on the role of American pioneers who must make strategic decisions planning their trip to the West. Students are engaged in critical thinking while doing cross-curriculum tasks with math and social sciences.

An illustration of a task-driven multimedia program that can be effectively used for content writing across the curriculum is *USA Explorer.* This software presents the learner with a mystery that can only be solved by tracking down clues across the United States. In this highly engaging program, students learn geography and history, study weather patterns and, via a video, observe ocean life of the Pacific Ocean. In the process of learning content material, the students are practicing their language skills in context. For example, their search for the longest river or tallest building requires them to practice the superlative form of adjectives. The real benefit for language development is the language production required to talk to classmates about the task and clues as they work to solve the mystery and with the follow-up writing assignments. Students using *USA Explorer* could be asked to choose their own mystery location and write clues for a partner to follow. It would be important for students to write clearly in hopes that their partner will be the first to find the mystery location. For adult learners, there are software programs specializing in content areas such as business. For example, the *Dynamic Business English* series uses video and speech recognition to provide simulations of real-life business situations, such as a job interview or a business lunch meeting.

In addition to content-based software, the World Wide Web offers numerous resources for authentic content materials and lesson plans. Websites of world news agencies and magazines such as *CNN News, World News Headlines,* and *National Geographic News,* and on-line encyclopedias and libraries serve as rich resources for content-based instruction. The *CNN Newsroom* and the *Weekly Reader* are designed specifically for students. Several textbook publishers maintain websites that provide sample lesson plans and teaching activities in content areas.

Focus on the Reader

Paralleling and complimenting the attention to content that emerged in the 1980s was a movement toward greater consideration of the reader and reader expectations in the academic community. In this audience-dominated approach, the reader is not just an individual, but rather the larger academic discourse community into which the writer will become socialized (Raimes, 1991). In this approach, ESL teachers typically develop theme-based lessons that practice various rhetorical forms and assist students in the development of academic writing skills that are transferable across the curriculum (Johns, 1988). As was noted earlier, several software packages model and practice various essay genres such as compare and contrast, giving instructions, persuasion, and cause and effect. Websites like *Writing-DEN* serve a similar service (see Figure 5.24). Here students can get information about and see models of writing at the sentence, paragraph, and essay levels. In her advanced college ESL writing class, Ms. Santana-Williams has her students work in pairs or small groups to complete a task that requires them to research this website. In this way she feels they learn the rhetorical English patterns for academic writing, increase their technology and research skills, and develop their group dynamic and social skills as they strive to accomplish the assigned task.

Through technology students now have access to an academic audience that is worldwide. Electronic discussion groups make it possible for students to engage in the language of a common discipline as they discuss issues in their fields of interest. Latrobe University maintains the *SL-Lists: International EFL/ESL Email Student Discus-*

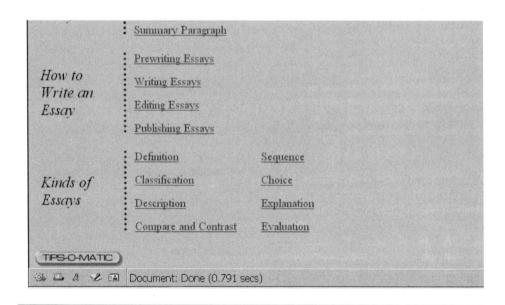

FIGURE 5.24   *WritingDEN*

Source: WritingDEN is copyright 2001 ACT360 Media Ltd. All rights reserved. Used with permission.

sion Lists (http://www.latrobe.edu.au/www/education/sl/sl.html) which include discussion groups in business and economics, science, technology, and computers.

Bringing It All Together: Reading, Writing, Listening, and Speaking

Whereas Chapters 4 and 5 examined each of the language skills individually, listening, speaking, reading, and writing are intertwined components of a student's language ability, and ample time should be devoted to the integrated use of these skills. Ideally, students will have the opportunity to advance at their own pace with tools that facilitate individual efforts and also engage in collaborative tasks and projects that require oral and written communication with real audiences. Figure 5.25 summarizes the features of these two elements of a computer-based functional learning environment.

This type of technology-enhanced learning environment offers students the support and learning experiences needed to develop their English skills. The following vignette of a fifth-grade sheltered ESL class illustrates how technology can be used to support a content-based, integrated skills approach to language development.

Classroom Vignette

As you enter Lara Baumgarten's fifth-grade sheltered ESL classroom in a culturally diverse sschool and community, you see students engaged

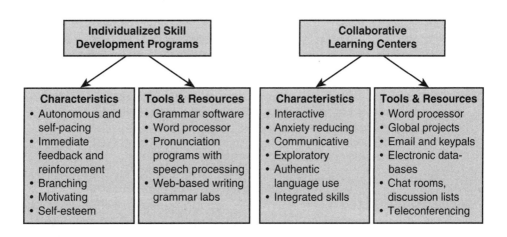

FIGURE 5.25   A Model of Computer-Based English Language Learning

in a task at their computers, taking notes on what they are investigating at a website and discussing their findings with each other. Another group of six students is gathered around a circular table in a discussion with their teacher and each other. This class is participating in the Monterey Bay Habitat WebQuest that Ms. Baumgarten created as part of a district-wide federally funded program.

Baumgarten explained the goals that she had in participating in the project and developing this unit for her students. It was important to create a cooperative and supportive learning environment that would encourage her English language learners to feel free to take risks in using their English. By carefully designing the project so that students could experience success, she hoped the unit would promote student self-confidence and encourage personal goal setting: two ingredients for further success. She selected a science-related project to draw on the intrinsic motivation and high interest students usually bring to this subject.

Baumgarten also wanted her students to develop higher order thinking skills. This she felt could best be accomplished through a content-based reading program that would provide sequential development of reading skills and the purposeful development of a desire to read. With these objectives in mind, she designed the unit on the Monterey Bay Habitat which had two key components: the webquest and literature circles that provided guided reading of text that students selected from the webquests.

The quest website explained every aspect of the project to the students. First an introduction described the environmental perils that the sea life of Monterey Bay was experiencing. This was followed by a clear definition of the task in which students were told that they had been selected to investigate the reasons for the destruction of the Monterey Bay habitat. To accomplish this, they would select one specific area to study and would serve as a member of a team that was responsible for writing a proposal on how to save the marine life in the habitat. It was up to their team to prove to the U.S. Congress that the Monterey Bay habitat must be protected by the National Marine Sanctuaries.

A key to the success of a project such as this is that students understand exactly what the process is and what is expected from them. The process section outlining the seven steps each student needed to take to complete the project was clearly explained on the website (Baumgarten, 2002) as it appears in Table 5.2.

In the previous vignette, the students had already selected their roles and were busily looking at the related websites. As they discovered information on the website, they made notes which they would later use to fill out their research report to present to their cyber team. Ultimately all six members of the team would work together to produce a report to present to the U.S. Congress that would argue

TABLE 5.2   *Direction for Monterey Bay Habitat Project*

Process

Step 1   **Choose One of the Following Roles**
- *Environmentalist:* In charge of threats to Monterey Bay
- *Oceanographer:* In charge of investigating needs of Monterey Bay Habitat
- *Marine Mammal Specialist:* In charge of identifying marine mammals that live in the Monterey Bay
- *Fish Specialist:* In charge of identifying the fish that live in the Monterey Bay
- *Kelp Specialist:* In charge of identifying kelp that is important to the Monterey Bay habitat
- *Educational Expert:* In charge of stating why the Monterey Bay habitat is important from an educational standpoint

Step 2   **Click on Evaluation**
There is a rubric to help you understand what you have to do during this unit. Be sure to discuss this page with your teacher. You want to know how you will be graded, right?

Step 3   **Research Page**
Click on the link that is connected with your role.
(Here the students could see a research sheet to take notes on the role they had selected in step 1. They were then provided a hard copy of this sheet by their teacher)

Step 4   **Get on the Internet**
Click on the following sites as they apply to your role. You may need to go back and reread certain parts, as some words may be difficult to understand. Go to the online dictionary if you want to look up the definition of a word. (Here students see the name and a picture representing each role.)

Step 5   **Putting It All Together**
Now you must write up your proposal to present to Congress. Work with the other members of your group to make sure that information is not repeated in the presentation and important facts are not left out. Your proposal must include the following:
- One paragraph per group member
- Correct grammar and punctuation
- Accurate information written in your words
- A visual aid either hand-drawn or printed from the Internet with credit given to illustrator/artist
- Evidence to explain why the Monterey Bay Habitat must be protected

(continued)

TABLE 5.2 *Continued*

Step 6 **Presenting to Congress**
Your last activity, as a group, is to present your proposal to "Congress." Unless you are really going to Washington, DC, this year, you will present to your peers. Check out the Presentation Rubric with your group members so that you know how you will be graded on this portion of the project.

Be sure to
- Take turns with other members when speaking.
- Speak in a clear loud voice.
- Speak slowly.
- Use "key vocabulary terms" found in your research.

Step 7 **Additional Resources**
Have a hard time finding information? Check out the additional resource page to help you. (Here students find links to additional resources for each of the roles.)

Source: Baumgarten (2002). Used with permission.

their case for actions required to protect the Monterey habitat from further destruction.

Other students seated at the table with their teacher were reading a section of text from the WebQuest website that they had selected as a group. These students were engaged in a literature circle in which students have roles with specific duties. The most challenging role, *Discussion Director*, has to develop a list of questions related to the predetermined portion of the website that will be read. The *Passage Picker* gets to select favorite sections of the text that were especially comical, interesting, or otherwise noteworthy to be shared aloud. The *Clever Connector* relates what the students have read to outside events. The *Super Summarizer* gives a short description of the main ideas of the text while the *Word Wonderer* watches out for words that are unfamiliar, significant, or perhaps confusing. This day the students were deciding who would have which role the following day when they would read and discuss the agreed on text. They were expected to come prepared with notes to help them fulfill their assigned duties. Their teacher had previously modeled exactly what was expected of each role. Baumgarden had found this approach to teaching reading successful because, as she explained, "Literature circles allow teachers to give students ownership of the task at hand. Students gain greater insight by sharing literature instead of reading in isolation."

It is easy to see what a powerful learning experience this webquest would be for these English language learners. Through cooperative learning and multiple sheltering techniques, students are able to do tasks at a higher level of development. Students are given autonomy to make selections based on their own interests and encouraged to use divergent thinking and problem-solving strategies to complete situated learning tasks.

Conclusion

Although this chapter looked separately at reading and writing, it is important to combine the reading, writing, listening, and speaking components into one holistic approach to the development of language. This chapter looked at issues involved in teaching reading and writing to English language learners and examined the ways in which technology can facilitate that goal. The uses of technology were organized around the different strategies that can be used to develop reading fluency and an understanding of English language structure. The second part of the chapter discussed four major focuses of second language writing instruction over the last few decades that impact writing instruction today and looked at the support technology offered in each of these areas. Next, as a way to combine all the skills discussed in Chapters 4 and 5, a classroom vignette of fifth-grade sheltered ESL classroom participating in a webquest was presented. The chapter concludes with a summary of the key ideas, suggested learning activities, references, and a list of technology resources.

Summary of Key Ideas

1. The reading process involves the reader, the text, and the interaction between the two. Within this interactive view theorists have proposed three basic models of how reading occurs: bottom-up, top-down, and interactive (Barnett, 1989; Aebersold and Field, 1997; Carrell, Devine, and Eskey, 1988).

2. Research on literacy development of second language learners, such as that by Elley and Mangughai (1983), supported the use of a holistic activities for ELLs that merged all four skill areas—listening, speaking, reading, and writing.

3. According to interactive theorists, reading is a process of constructing meaning from text through the use of both bottom-up and top-down processes, strategies, and skills. Current reading theory in TESOL combines an emphasis on all skill areas with both bottom-up and top-down approaches, known in the reading field as a *balanced literacy* approach.

4. Some theorists have argued that the psycholinguistic model of reading did not adequately emphasize the pivotal role that background knowledge plays in ESL/EFL reading (Carrell and Eisterhold, 1988). This led to schema theory, which pays particular attention to reader background knowledge and experience. According to schema theory, the reader brings previously acquired background knowledge organized into interrelated patterns, or schemata, to the reading process.

5. Grabe (1991) identified and described six key characteristics of fluent reading—rapid, interactive, flexible, purposeful, comprehending, and gradual—and proposed that this general perspective of the reading process was equally fitting for ESL students who had not attained fluency but aspired to do so for academic purposes. There are a variety of ways that technology can help build fluency.

6. Several software programs assist students in developing phonemic awareness and alphabet knowledge. Phonics programs like *Kid Phonics 2* and *Reader Rabbit's Learn-*

ing to Read can help students connect sounds and clusters of letters. Interactive stories are available via CD-ROM that help students build vocabulary and understanding of the structure of language.

7. There are a variety of software programs such as the *Rosetta Stone* and *English Your Way* that help adults learn the structure and vocabulary of English. The latest electronic dictionaries such as the *Oxford Picture Dictionary Interactive* provide additional support for reading that is not available in textbooks.

8. Software programs such as *Writing Process Workshop* (Educational Activities) and *Scholastic Process Writer* (Scholastic) provide models and practice of rhetorical organizational patterns that can assist ELLs in developing this type of background knowledge that is so crucial to their reading skill development.

9. Comprehensive interactive reading programs and multimedia reading software utilize CD-ROM video clips to provide readers the background knowledge needed to form mental models of the text prior to their reading passages on subject matter topics. With programs such as *Scholastic's Read 180,* students access video clips before reading the text in order to establish background knowledge needed for comprehension.

10. Several websites present graphs and other nontext information that gives students practice in interpreting various forms of data, including graphs, tables, and timelines. Engaging readers in a communicative task-based activity supported by the Web is one way to help beginning English readers gain more cognitive strategies for reading

11. Reading and writing are integrally linked and in fact share many of the same cognitive and social processes. Writers have schemata in mind about the content and form of their writing as they compose and revise their mental and written drafts of the text. Like reading, writing is a complicated, interactive, and recursive process in which the writer is engaged.

12. Raimes (1991) identified four approaches to teaching L2 writing that emerged at different times over the last few decades and continue to have an impact on writing pedagogy today. Each of these approaches represents a particular focus in the teaching of writing to second language learners—form, the writer, the content, or the reader.

13. Grammar was one of the first areas of language development to be addressed by the computer-based instruction. Technology today offers focused practice of grammar structure in interactive formats for all ages and proficiency levels. Grammar practice with programs such as *Azar Interactive* provides an integrated approach that helps to diminish concerns about isolated grammar practice. Practice of grammar points is most effective when derived from students' needs as indicated in their own writing.

14. The writing process approach to writing has gained popularity in recent years and allows time for students to brainstorm and bring their own ideas to the process, to write and respond to multiple drafts, and then to edit and publish their final work. Technology provides numerous tools for supporting each stage of the writing process as elaborated in the text of this chapter.

15. The Internet provides websites with on-line writing labs such as the lab at Purdue University that serve as resources for the writing process for writers throughout the world. There are also highly interactive software that have "story starters" to prompt students to author their own stories—for example, *Rainbow* (Curriculum Associates*)*, *Storybook Weaver* (The Learning Company), and *Imagination Express* (Edmark).

16. Content-based instruction with ELLs can draw upon subject matter software to enhance language skills and develop content knowledge. Programs that are ideally suited to the needs of English language learners are those that have the following characteristics: incorporates audio, video, and graphics; stimulates critical thinking; is easy to navigate; and is not dependent on text only.

Learning Activities _____

1. This chapter gives numerous examples of software and websites that can be used to assist in developing reading skills. Working in small groups, identify software or websites for a specific student population (K–3, secondary sheltered, college ESL, etc.) that would be beneficial to the students' development of a particular reading skill, such as vocabulary development or content or schema building. Explain how you would use this software or website in a lesson for this group and explain your rationale for its selection.

2. Discuss Internet sites and software that present a variety of different types of text formats, such as literature, news media, poetry, dialog, advertising, graphics, and so on. Then, select a text from one format and identify the types of formal, content, and linguistic schemata which a student would need in order to achieve (nearly) complete comprehension of a selected text. Finally, devise a series of activities which would maximize the student's level of comprehension of the selected text.

3. Design a writing unit using a technology-supported writing process approach for an ESL/ELL/EFL writing or language arts class. Describe how you would incorporate technology at each stage and explain your rationale for its use.

4. Design a task-based reading/writing project utilizing technology for a grade level or adult education program. Consider issues of importance to the students and ways in which students can use reading and writing to solve a problem or complete a task. In what ways does the technology support the effectiveness of the project?

Technology Resources _____

Software

Ace Detective. (1997). Mindplay/Methods & Solutions, Inc.
The Alphabet. (2000). Protea Textware Pty Ltd.
Arthur's Teacher Trouble. (1994). Marc Brown. Broderbund Software, Inc.
Azar Interactive. (1998). Prentice Hall, Inc.
Body Works. (1999). The Princeton Review.
Core Reading and Vocabulary Development. (1996). Priscilla Hamilton and Barbara Hombs. Educational Activities Co.
Curious Creatures. Curriculum Associates.

Daedalus Integrated Writing Environment (DIWE). (1997).
Discis Books. Harmony Interactive Inc.
Dynamic Business English. (2000). DynEd International.
Easy Writer. (1995–1999). Linguatronics. Jane Boris.
English Mastery. (1998). American Language Academy.
English Your Way Program. (1995–1997). Syracuse Language Systems.
Focus on Grammar Series. (1996–1998). Addison Wesley Longman.
Grammar Mastery. (1998). American Language Academy.
Grammar 3D. Newbury House/Heinle and Heinle.
Hyper Studio. (1993–1997). Roger Wagner Publishing, Inc.
Imagination Express. Riverdeep Interactive Learning Limited.
Inspiration. (1998). Oregon: Inspiration Software, Inc.
Issues in English. (2000). Protea Textware Pty Ltd.
Just Grandma and Me. (1998). Mercer Mayer. Riverdeep Interactive Learning Limited.
Kids Phonics II. (1996). Davidson & Associates, Inc.
Leap Into Phonics. (1999). Leap Into Learning, Inc.
Learning English: Neighborhood. Contér. (1994). Life Software.
The Longman Interactive English Dictionary (LIED). Longman Allyn-Bacon/Addison Wesley.
MonoConc Pro. (2000). Athetstan Publishers.
Multimedia Workshop. (1994). Davidson Co.
Oregon Trail Pioneer Adventures 3rd Edition. (1997). The Learning Co.
Oregon Trail Pioneer Adventures 4th Edition (1999). The Learning Co.
Oxford Picture Dictionary Interactive. (2000). Oxford Publisher.
Postcards. (2000). Canada: Curriculum Associates, Inc.
The Process Workshop. Educational Activities.
Rainbow. Curriculum Associates.
Read 180. (1999). Scholastic, Inc.
Reader Rabbit's Learn to Read. (1999). The Learning Co.
Reading for the Workplace. Educational Activities.
Rosetta Stone. (2000). Fairfield Language Technologies.
Scholastic Literacy Place. (1996). Scholastic, Inc.
Scholastic Process Writer. Scholastic, Inc.
Storybook Weaver. (1998). Riverdeep Interactive Learning Limited.
Student Writing and Learning Center. The Learning Co.
Student Writing and Research Center. (1997). The Learning Co.
That's a Fact Jack! Read. Tom Snyder Productions.
USA Explorer. (1999). New York: Dorling Kindersley Interactive Learning.
Wiggleworks. (1994). Scholastic Inc.
WorldWalker: Destination Australia. (1998). Soleil Software, Inc.
Writing Process Workshop. (1999). Educational Activities.

Websites

Book On-line website (http://digital.library.upenn.edu/books/)
Computer Enhanced Language Instruction Archive (CELIA) (http://www.latrobe.edu.au/gse/celia/celia.html) of TESOL at Latrobe University
Daedalus Online, The Daedalus Group, Inc.
Discover Magazine (http://www.discover.com)
Eduhound.com
ExChange (http://deil.lang.uiuc.edu/exchange/filler/html)
The Global Newsstand (http://www.mcs.net/~rchojnac/www/tgn.html)
The Grammar Help Page (http://www.hut.fi/~rvilmihelp/grammar_help)
Grammar Safari (http://deil.lang.uiuc.edu/web.pages/grammarsafari.html)

Hot Potatoes. University of Victoria Humanities Computing and Media Centre (http://web.uvic. ca/hrd/halfbaked/v5preview/jcloze.htm)
Kids Domain (http://www.kidsdomain.com/down/pc/)
Lightspan's Global Schoolhouse (http://www.lightspan.com)
Lingonet (http://www.linetti.com/nets.htm)
MathStar site (http:// mathstar.nmsu.edu)
Online Writing Lab (OWL), Purdue University (http://owl.english.purdue.edu/)
Scientific American (http://www.sciam.com)
SL-Lists: International EFL/ESL Email Student Discussion Lists, Latrobe University (http://www. latrobe.edu.au/www/education/sl/sl.html)
TESOL, Inc. (http://www.tesol.org)
USA Today (http://www.usatoday.com/)
Virtual Language Centre at *Cobuild* (http://titania.cobuild.collins.co.uk/form.html)
Virtual Language Centre of Hong Kong Polytechnic University (http://www.edit.com.hk/ concordance/default.htm).

References

Aebersold, J., and Field, M. (1997). *From Reader to Reading Teacher: Issues and Strategies for Second Language Classrooms.* Cambridge: Cambridge University Press.
Adams, M. J. (1990). *Beginning to Read: Thinking and Learning about Print.* Cambridge, MA: The MIT Press.
Anderson, R. C., and Pearson, P. D. (1984). A schema-theoretic view of basic processes in reading comprehension. In P. D. Pearson, R. Barr, M. L. Kamil, and P. Mosenthal (Eds.), *The Handbook of Reading Research* (pp. 255–292). New York: Longman.
Auerbach, E., and Paxton, D. (1997). "It's not the English thing": Bringing reading research into the ESL classroom. *TESOL Quarterly* 31 (2): 237–261.
Barnett, M. (1989). *More Than Meets the Eye: Foreign Language Reading Theory and Practice.* Englewood Cliffs, NJ: Prentice Hall.
Barlett, F. C. (1932). *Remembering: A Study in Experimental and Social Psychology.* Cambridge: Cambridge University Press.
Barlow, M. (1997). Language teaching with a concordancer. *Athelstan Newsletter,* 6 (3).
Baumgarten, L. (2002). *Exploring the Monterey Bay Habitat: The Process.* Retrieved from url http:// projects.edtech.sandi.net/encato/habitats/process.htm on January 2002.
Berens, G. L. (1986). Using word processors in the EFL composition class part II. *TESOL Newsletter* 20 (6): 13.
Bickel, B., and Truscello, D. (1996). New opportunities for learning: Styles and strategies for computers. *TESOL Journal* 6 (1): 20–24.
Birch, B. (1998, Winter). Nurturing bottom-up reading strategies, too. *TESOL Journal,* 18–23.
Butler-Pascoe, M. E. (1994). The effects of introducing computer technology into a university-level English as a second language writing course. *Technology and Teacher Education Annual 1994.* Proceedings of the Annual SITE Conference, AACE.
Cambourne B. (1979). How important is theory to the reading teacher? *Australian Journal of Reading* 2: 78–90.
Cambourne, B. (1988). *The Whole Story: Natural Learning and the Acquisition in the Classroom.* New York: Ashton-Scholastic.
Carr, T., and Levy, B. (Eds.). (1990). *Reading and Its Development: Component Skills Approaches.* San Diego: Academic Press.
Carrell, P. (1983a). Background knowledge in second language comprehension. *Language Learning and Communication* 2 (1): 25–34.
Carrell, P. (1983b). Some issues in studying the role of schemata, or background knowledge, in second language comprehension. *Reading in a Foreign Language* 1 (2): 81–92.

Carrell, P. (1984). The effects of rhetorical organization on ESL readers. *TESOL Quarterly* 18 (3): 441–469.

Carrell, P. L. (1985). Facilitating ESL reading by teaching text structure. *TESOL Quarterly* 19 (4): 727–752.

Carrel, P. L. (1987). Content and formal schemata in ESL reading. *TESOL Quarterly*, 21 (3): 461–481.

Carrell, P. L., Devine, D., and Eskey, D. (Eds.). (1988). *Interactive Approaches to Second Language Reading.* New York: Cambridge University Press.

Carrell, P., and Eisterhold, J. (1983). Schema theory and ESL reading pedagogy. *TESOL Quarterly* 17 (4): 553–573.

Carrell, P., and Eisterhold, J. (1988). Schema theory and ESL reading pedagogy. In P. Carrell, J. Devine, and D. Eskey (Eds.), *Interactive Approaches to Second Language Reading.* Cambridge: Cambridge Press.

Carter, R., and Long, M. N. (1987). *Literature in the Language Classroom.* Cambridge: Cambridge University Press.

Celce-Murcia, Marianne. (1991). Grammar pedagogy in second and foreign language teaching. *TESOL Quarterly* 25 (3).

Chall, J. (1987). Two vocabularies for reading: Recognition and meaning. In M. McKeown and M. Curtis (Eds.), *The Nature of Vocabulary Acquisition* (pp. 7–17). Hillsdale, NJ: Lawrence Erlbaum.

Coady, J. (1979). A psycholinguistic model of the ESL reader. In R. Mackay, B. Barkman, and R. R. Jordan (Eds.), *Reading in a Second Language* (pp. 5–12). Rowley, MA: Newbury House.

Coady, J. (1988, March). *Research on L2 Vocabulary Acquisition: Putting It in Context.* Paper presented at the 22nd Annual TESOL Convention, Chicago, IL.

Coady, J. (1997). L2 vocabulary acquisition through extensive reading. In James Coady and Thomas Huckin (Eds.), *Second Language Vocabulary Acquisition.* Cambridge: Cambridge University Press.

Cohen, M., and Riel, M. (1986, August). Computer networks: Creating real audiences for students' writing. La Jolla, CA: UCSD, *Interactive Technology Laboratory Report 15.*

Custodio, B., and Sutton, M. (1998). Literature-based ESL for secondary school students. *TESOL Journal* 7 (5): 19–23.

Cummins, J. (1984). *Bilingualism and Special Education: Issues in Assessment and Assessment and Pedagogy.* San Diego, CA: College-Hill Press.

Devine, J. (1988). The relationship between general language competence and second language reading proficiency: Implications for teaching. In P. Carreell, J. Devine, and D. Eskey (Eds.), *Interactive Approaches to Second Language Teaching.* Cambridge: Cambridge Press.

Elley, W., and Mangubhai, F. (1983). The impact of reading on second language learning. *Reading Research Quarterly* 19: 53–67.

Ellis, R. (1990). *Instructed Second Language Learning.* Oxford: Basil Blackwell.

Engberg, R. (1986). Word processors in the English classroom. In T. Cannings and S. Brown (Eds.), *The Information Age Classroom: Using the Computer as a Tool.* Irvine, CA: Franklin, Beedle, and Associates.

Eskey, D. (1973). A model program for teaching advanced reading to students of English as a foreign language. *Language Learning* 23: 169–184.

Eskey, D. (1986). Theoretical foundations. In F. Dubin, D. Eskey, and W. Grabe (Eds), *Teaching Second Language Reading for Academic Purposes* (pp. 3–23). Reading, MA: Addison-Wesley.

Eskey, D. (1988). Holding in the bottom: An interactive approach to the language problems of second language readers. In P. Carrell, J. Devine, and D. Eskey (Eds.), *Interactive Approaches to Second Language Reading.* Cambridge: Cambridge Press.

Floyd, P., and Carrell, P. (1987). Effects on ESL reading of teaching cultural content schemata. *Language Learning* 37, 89–108.

Fotos, S. (1994). Integrating grammar instruction and communicative language use through grammar consciousness-raising tasks. *TESOL Quarterly* 28: 323–351.

Gee, R. W. (1999, Spring). Encouraging ESL students to read. *TESOL Journal:* 3–7.

Goodman, K. (1967). Reading: A psycholinguistic guessing game. *Journal of the Reading Specialist* 6: 126–135.

Goodman, K. (1985). Unity in reading. In H. Singer and R. Ruddell (Eds.), *Theoretical Models and Processes of Reading* (3rd ed., pp. 813–840). Newark, DE: International Reading Association.

Goodman, K. (1988). *What's Whole in the Whole Language?* Richmond Hill, Ont.: Scholastic-TAB.

Goodman, Y. M., and Burke, C. L. (1972). *Reading Miscue Inventory Manual: Procedure for Diagnosis and Remediation.* New York: Macmillan.

Grabe, B. (1991). Current developments in second language reading research. *TESOL Quarterly* 25 (3): 375–407.

Haynes, M., and Carr, T. (1990). Writing system background and second language reading: A component skills analysis of English reading by native speaker-readers of Chinese. In T. Carr and B. Levy (Eds.), *Reading and Its Development: Component Skills Approaches* (pp. 375–421). San Diego: Academic Press.

Horowitz, D. M. (1986). What professors actually require: Academic tasks for the ESL classroom. *TESOL Quarterly* 20 (3): 445–462.

Iancu, M. (2000). Implementing Fluency First Activities in an intermediate-level EAP reading class. *TESOL Journal* 9 (2): 11–16.

Ibsen, E. (1990). The double role of fiction in foreign language learning: Towards a creative methodology. *English Teaching Forum* 28 (3): 2–9.

Johns, A. (1988). The discourse communities dilemma: Identifying transferable skills for the academic milieu. *English for Specific Purposes* 7: 55–60.

Kaplan, R. B. (1966). Cultural thought patterns in intercultural education. *Language Learning* 16 (1): 1–20.

Kolers, P., and Katzmann, M. (1966). Naming sequentially presented letters and words. *Language and Speech* 9: 54–95.

Krashen, S. (1981). The case for narrow reading. *TESOL Newsletter* 15 (6): 23.

Krashen, S. (1981). *Second Language Acquisition and Second Language Learning.* New York: Pergamon.

Krashen, S. (1989). We acquire vocabulary and spelling by reading: Additional evidence for the input hypothesis. *Modern Language Journal* 73 (4): 440–464.

Kroll, B. (Ed.). (1990). *Second Language Writing: Research Insights for the Classroom.* New York: Cambridge University Press.

Larsen-Freeman, D. (1995). On the teaching and learning of grammar: Challenging the myths. In F. Eckman et al. (Eds.), *Second Language Acquisition Theory and Pedagogy.* Mahwah, NJ: Lawrence Erlbaum.

Lewis, M. (1997). Pedagogical implications of the lexical approach. In J. Coady and T. Huckin (Eds.), *Second Language Vocabulary Acquisition.* Cambridge: Cambridge University Press.

Long, M. (1988). Instructed interlanguage development. In L. Beebe (Ed.), *Issues in Second Lanuage Acquisition: Multiple Perspectives* (pp. 115–141). Rowley, MA: Newbury House.

MacGowan-Gilhooly. (1996). *Achieving Fluency in English: A Whole Language Book* (3rd ed.). Dubuque, IA: Kendall/Hunt.

MacGowan-Gilhooly. (1996, February 27). *Fluency Fist Reading Activities.* TESLFF-L [Discussion list]. Retrieved February 27, 1996, listserv@cunyvm.cuny.edu.

McQuillan, J., and Lucy, T. (1998, Summer) What's the story? Using the narrative approach in beginning language classrooms. *TESOL Journal*: 18–23.

Mohan, B. A. (1986). *Language and Content.* Reading, MA: Addison-Wesley.

Nagy, W., and Herman, P. (1987). Breadth and depth of vocabulary knowledge: Implications for acquisition and instruction. In M. McKeown and M. Curtis (Eds.), *The Nature of Vocabulary Acquisition* (pp. 19–35). Hillsdale, NJ: Lawrence Erlbaum.

Nation, P. (1990). *Teaching and Learning Vocabulary.* New York. Newbury House.

Nunan, D. (1991). *Language Teaching Methodology.* New York: Prentice Hall.

Pellettieri, J. (2000). Negotiation in cyberspace: The role of chatting in the development of grammatical competence. In M. Warschauer and R. Kern (Eds.), *Networked-Based Language Teaching: Concepts and Practice.* Cambridge: Cambridge University Press.

Peregoy, S., and Boyle, O. (2001). *Reading, Writing, and Learning in ESL: A Resource Book for K-12 Teachers.* New York: Addison Wesley Longman, Inc.

Phinney, M. (1989). Computers, composition, and second language teaching. In M. Pennington (Ed.), *Teaching Languages with Computers: The State of the Art.* La Jolla, CA: Athelstan Publishers.

Pienemann, M. (1984). Psychological constraints on the teachability of languages. *Studies in Second Langauge Acquisition* 6: 186–214.

Piper, A. (1987). Helping learners to write: A role for the word processor. *ELT Journal* 41: 119–125.

Pritchard, R. (1990). The effects of cultural schemata on reading processing strategies. *Reading Research Quarterly* 25: 273–295.

Raimes, A. (1991). Out of the woods: Emerging traditions in the teaching of writing. *TESOL Quarterly* 25 (3): 407–430.

Reid, J. (1993). *Teaching ESL writing.* Englewood Cliffs, NJ: Prentice Hall Regents.

Richards, J. (1990). *The Language Teaching Matrix.* Cambridge: Cambridge University Press.

Savage, J. F. (2001). *Sound it Out: Phonics in a Balanced Reading Program.* Boston: McGraw Hill.

Saville-Troike, M. (1973). Reading and the audiolingual method. *TESOL Quarterly* 7(2): 395–405.

Schmitt, N., and Carter, R. (2000, Spring). The lexical advantages of narrow reading for second language learners. *TESOL Journal*: 4–9.

Swaffar, J., Arens, K., and Byrnes, H. (1991). *Reading for Meaning: An Integrated Approach to Language Learning.* Englewood Cliffs, NJ: Prentice Hall.

Silberstein, S. (1987). Let's take another look at reading: Twenty-five years of reading instruction. *English Teaching Forum* 25: 28–35.

Silberstein, S. (1994). *Techniques and Resources in Teaching Reading.* New York: Oxford University Press.

Smith, F. (1971). *Understanding Reading.* New York: Holt, Rinehart & Winston.

Spada, N., and Lightbrown, P. M. (1993). Instruction and the development of questions in the L-2 classroom. *Studies in Second Language Acquisition* 15: 205–224.

Spaulding, C. L. (1992). The motivation to read and write. In J. W. Irwin and M. A. Doyle (Eds.), *Reading/Writing Connections* (pp. 177–201). Newark, DE: International Reading Association.

Stanovich, K. (1990). Concepts of developmental theories of reading skill: Cognitive resources, automaticity, and modularity. *Developmental Review* 10: 72–100.

Steffensen, M., and Joag-Dev, C. (1984). Cultural knowledge and reading. In C. Alserson and A. Urquhart (Eds.), *Reading in a Foreign Language* (pp. 48–61). New York: Longman.

Widdowson, H. (1979). The process and purpose of reading. In H. Widdowson (Ed.), *Explorations in Applied Linguistics* (pp. 171–183). New York: Cambridge University Press.

Williams, J. (1995). Focus on form in communicative language teaching. Research findings and the classroom teacher. *TESOL Quarterly* 4: 12–16.

Yorkey, R. (1970). *Study Skills for Students of English as a Second Language.* New York: McGraw-Hill.

Zamel, V. (1987). Recent research on writing pedagogy. *TESOL Quarterly* 21 (4): 697–716.

Zimmerman, (1997). Do reading and interactive vocabulary instruction make a difference? An empirical study. *TESOL Quarterly* 31 (1): 125.

Teaching Thinking and Inquiry-Based Learning with English Language Learners

Chapter Overview

In this chapter we argue that students who are learning English must be provided with opportunities to engage in high-level thinking and problem solving. We discuss the use of inquiry and problem-based learning as appropriate strategies for ELL students to use when learning content and we provide examples of these instructional strategies in different classroom contexts. An extensive discussion of information processing theory as well as CALLA (Cognitive Academic Language Learning Approach) provides the foundation for teaching thinking in the ELL classroom.

The use of technology is tied to strategies for teaching thinking and shown in terms of practical examples of teacher work in TESOL or bilingual classrooms. The use of problem-based learning is discussed, and a classroom vignette involving teaching science to English language learners is presented. Guiding questions are used throughout the chapter in relation to teaching thinking in the linguistically diverse classroom.

Introduction

Sometimes people unfamiliar with the dynamics of learning a second language assume that if students have a low level of English skills then their thinking may also be low level. In another publication, Wiburg (1998) told the story of Victor, a Mexican American high school student who talked excitedly about the upcoming Mexican election with his uncle and then went off to his school social studies class where all of his understanding of political systems was lost behind a wall of silence. There is a danger when working with English language learners (ELLs) of confusing a student's ability to use English with his or her thinking abilities.

We believe that students who are learning English must be provided with opportunities to engage in high-level thinking and inquiry learning. In terms of language learning, the use of inquiry is tied closely to the cognitive academic language learning approach (CALLA) for supporting language and content learning (Chomot and O'Malley, 1994). These researchers described, analyzed, and classified strategies and combinations of strategies used by students who had success in learning language, then set out to teach these strategies to other students. Both inquiry learning and CALLA envision the student as a co-constructor of deepened content learning aided by the development of cognitive strategies.

Technology and Thinking in the ELL Classroom

How can the use of technology support thinking?

The world today is a fundamentally different place from the world in which many teachers grew up. Technology has changed human activity while greatly increasing the demand for humans to manage and evaluate large amounts of information. English language learners (ELLs) will need to be able to function, and hopefully thrive, in a world in which computer-based technologies are used routinely at home and work. It is important to teach cognitive strategies for using and managing these technologies. Technology itself can help because it provides tools and programs that scaffold thinking and support collaborative problem solving. Technology environments like the Web provide visual and auditory cues that make it easier to understand English text. The students' lack of English language ability should not keep a teacher from designing an inquiry-based learning environment that supports student thinking using multiple forms of information and computer-based cognitive tools. In fact, in areas such as science and math, there are times when words can even get in the way. Kanim (2000) shows one example of this— experimentation with correctly hooking up batteries and bulbs. Students without English just kept experimenting until they hooked up the bulbs correctly, while students who could read English spent too much time trying to figure out the meaning of the technical instructions without spending enough time experimenting with the connections.

Technology can be used to support thinking if teachers design classrooms in which (1) learning activities are informed by an understanding of the cognitive processes involved in language learning and thinking; (2) technology tools are carefully selected to support a wide range of thinking and problem-solving opportunities; and (3) these tools are used within an approach to learning based on an understanding of inquiry, problem-based learning, and language learning. Our coverage of these strategies begins with a review of human information processing.

Theories of Information Processing

Why does perception matter?

As a cognitive scientist, Norman (1982, 1993) has written extensively about learning and memory. He suggests that learning requires managing three things successfully: the acquisition, retention, and retrieval of information. An understanding of how information is initially acquired is necessary, as well as how it can be encoded and later retrieved from memory.

Everything students learn must first come through the senses. The initial stage of cognitive processing requires perception. Teachers might remember the notion of *anticipatory set* as part of a five- or six-step lesson plan developed by Hunter (1971). Hunter, whose theory into practice (TIP) was based on Gagne's theory of learning (1965), taught that in order for students to learn, the teacher must first get their attention.

How can learning to use technology improve perceptual skills?

Learning to pay attention to the essential features of an environment is an essential step in learning and one that may be easily taught to ELL students by teaching the use of software. When teaching students to use a technology program, it is important to help them pay attention to the meaning of computer icons and menus and how each menu contains related functions. For example, the teacher can direct students' attention to the File menu and guide learners to discover what the items on that menu have in common. For example, explain that the File menu includes opening, closing, or printing documents. Or ask students to focus on the Edit menu and notice that it includes options for moving text, changing fonts, and inserting pictures (editing things).

Sometimes teachers give students a set of written directions to follow exactly when learning software. However, students taught this way may later be lost without the exact directions and might not be able to create a different application of the same program. In order for students to become self-directed learners, they need to understand the program and how it works. They need to understand the generic features of menus and icons used in computer applications. Fortunately, computer manufacturers have learned to provide similar interfaces across integrated software packages. For example, if a teacher uses an applications package like Microsoft Office, students will soon notice that the menus on all the applications have very similar functions. Edit means the same whether the student is using a spreadsheet, a word processor, or a publishing program. Teachers can provide QuickStarts that orient the student to the software without giving exact directions. (See the QuickStart example in Learning Activities at the end of this chapter.)

Students may also find learning computer applications an easy way to learn some powerful and practical English. One of the authors recently improved her Spanish vocabulary by teaching the Spanish version of *PowerPoint* in Mexico. In summary, computer programs require attention to the *display* of information and its relevance to the processing of information. Improving students' perceptions of important words and functions in a computer-based learning environment can assist thinking and language learning.

How can visual perception help content learning?

Visual perception is important not only in learning technology tools but also in learning content, especially in fields like mathematics and science in which problem-solving processes are important and much important work occurs that is not based solely on verbal information. Researchers (Linn, 1985) have found that for many students, especially girls, skills in visual perception may relate to mathematics ability. Providing ELL students the opportunity to use a variety of visually oriented, technology-based, problem-solving environments in mathematics, such as *The Factory* or *KaleidoMania* (Sandpiper Software) can result in improved mathematics performance (see Figure 6.1).

Visually oriented programs such as these help students build a visual and intuitive understanding of objects in relationship to each other, an important idea in mathematics. In addition to helping students think about mathematics, visual problem-solving environments can provide a nonverbal way to think about any concept.

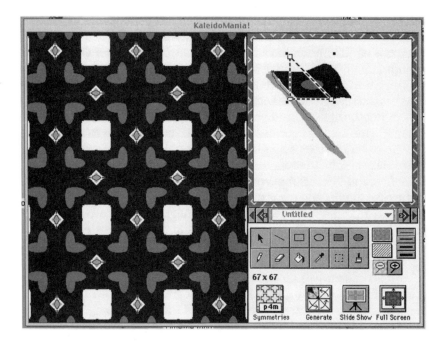

FIGURE 6.1 *KaliedoMania*

Source: KaliedoMania! Interactive. Used with permission.

Declarative and Procedural Knowledge

How does the brain process and retain information?

Beyond perception is the development of conception, the mental manipulation of ideas and concepts. Chamot and O'Malley (1994) emphasize the importance of understanding how the brain processes information in order to provide effective language and content learning environments. For example, they describe how two different types of knowledge are used in language learning and how each of these types of knowledge is processed differently in the brain. One type, *declarative knowledge* involves the mental manipulation of concepts, principles, and vocabulary. The second kind of knowledge, *procedural knowledge*, involves the processes of learning. In order for the brain to be able to remember and later recall declarative knowledge such as conceptual ideas, these ideas and accompanying vocabulary must pass through short-term memory and stay there long enough to be encoded in long-term memory.

The nature of short-term memory is visual and auditory (Norman, 1982). Think about the last time you wanted to remember a phone number. You probably repeated it to yourself until you could get some place and write it down. Or you wanted to remember how to get to a certain location in the city, so you paid attention to the visual cues in the environment. Presenting information using different modalities can help students remember information as they interact with it in short-term memory. As students draw pictures, sing songs such as *Grammar Rock* or *Multiplication Rock,* or find images to connect to vocabulary words, information it is more likely to be remembered.

How is long-term memory different from short-term memory?

Long-term memory is semantic in nature and organized in terms of meaningfulness to the learner. Things are most easily stored and retrieved if they are connected to already existing mental schema. Piaget pointed out how students make meaning of their experiences by adapting and adopting them to existing ideas and relationships. His ideas, as well as the ideas of Dewey, Bruner, Piaget, and Vygotsky, lead to modern day constructivist learning theory.

How can understanding in a first language help students think in a second language?

Theories of language learning recognize that concepts and learning strategies the ELL student uses in his or her native language can be helpful in assisting students to connect the concepts in the new language (Cummins, 1980, 1996; Ovando and Collier, 1985). For example, if the student has a well-developed schema of what a classroom or a garden looks like, adding names to the pictured objects using both the old and the new language can help him or her develop vocabulary. Using a multimedia program that contains many pictures of objects and backgrounds such as *StoryBook Weaver* or *Imagination Express* can help students gain vocabulary within a comprehensible context. The reason the teacher using *PowerPoint* in Spanish found it easy to function in a new language is that she knew the program so well in the first language.

How can technology help ELL students gain declarative knowledge?

Cissy Barrara is teaching her bilingual students about ecology and wants them to create a scene that shows interactions between animals and their environment by using a visual storytelling program—in this case, *Storybook Weaver*. She will be using the many pictures that accompany words to help students understand in a new language, and understand a science concept in a different language. The students will click on the picture objects to create a background scene and then add animals and vegetation. Through visual images they will show interactions between animals or plants and their environment.

Across the hall, Scott Miller is using the visual program *Imagination Express* to help his beginning-level ELL students construct pictures related to families and neighborhoods. This group of students is using a multimedia environment to express ideas about interactions. They place a mother and daughter in a bedroom, arguing about the appropriate clothes to wear to high school.

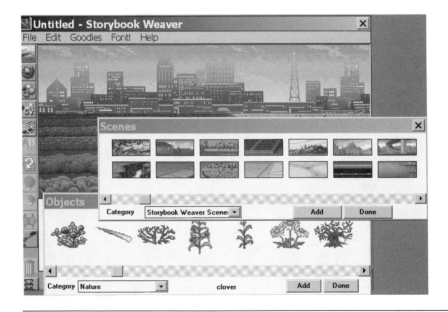

FIGURE 6.2 *Storybook Weaver*

Source: © 1994 Riverdeep Interactive Learning Limited. Used with permission.

How do students learn procedural knowledge?

In the last section we discussed ways in which technology can help students think about and learn vocabulary and concepts—types of declarative knowledge. *Procedural knowledge* is also important for language and content learning. Learning strategies involve the processes of managing and obtaining knowledge, the how and when of learning. Procedural knowledge ranges from cognitive strategies for solving types of problems to metacognition, or the ability to think about one's own thinking. Procedural knowledge is best learned by "practicing a complex procedure that has meaning and achieves an important goal" (Chamot and O'Malley, 1994, p. 17). Procedural knowledge is supported by problem-based learning and inquiry.

Using different types of instructional strategies for different types of learning was first developed into a theory of instruction by Robert Gagne (1965, 1985). He calls procedural knowledge *problem solving* and describes how students must be actively involved in solving problems in order to gain these cognitive strategies. Problem solving and/or procedural knowledge cannot be taught by asking students to read, memorize, and report back information. Students must struggle with puzzling problems and construct satisfying solutions for themselves in order to gain procedural knowledge.

Multimedia and Thinking

How can multimedia environments be used to help students think about content?

Blanca Aranjo, a bilingual social studies teacher, decided to use a multimedia encyclopedia and the Web to help her ELL students think about weather. She wanted them to think about how weather affects human lives. She had already selected and book-marked on an Internet browser (Explorer, Netscape) several weather sites such as *Weather.com* for her students and had helped them find weather on the class multimedia encyclopedia (see Figure 6.3). Prior to letting the students work in small groups, she modeled for the class how to copy images and save them to their own disks and then how to insert images into the word processing program they were using.

She asked the students to include information on different types of weather and to try to find some that were very different. They should look for extreme differences such as floods, earthquakes, droughts, and hurricanes. She asked them to prepare a one- or two-page report with pictures of the weather and questions for other students. Later they will work in small groups and do a multimedia presentation for the class and school about weather.

There are many sites on the Web that offer information about weather. In addition to the *Weather.com* site, it is useful to use search engines to find weather pictures. We recommend *Yahooligans* for educational information and pictures (www.yahooligans.com).

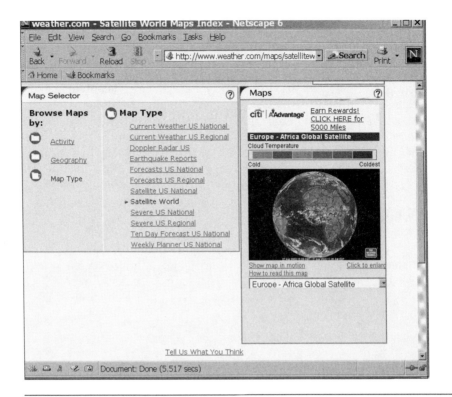

FIGURE 6.3   The Weather Channel

Source: Copyright © The Weather Channel Enterprises, Inc. Used with permission.

The Web and Thinking

In addition to the uses of the Web for thinking already discussed, there is a type of Web page specifically designed to support thinking and problem solving on the Web known as a WebQuest. WebQuests are Web-based environments organized to support inquiry learning in authentic contexts. First developed by Bernie Dodge at San Diego State University, they are now being developed at many universities and in teacher professional development projects. You can visit Dr. Dodge's site at http://edweb.sdsu.edu/webquest/webquest.html (see Figure 6.4). WebQuests include the following elements:

- An introduction or scenario
- A task that is meaningful and doable
- A process for completing the task, often in groups

- Information resources to support the task
- Guidance on how to organize the information acquired
- A conclusion that brings closure and reflection

WebQuests can be short, taking only a few class periods and focusing on knowledge acquisition and integration or they can take from a week to a month or more and require refining knowledge. WebQuests provide teachers with an already developed problem-based learning environment on the Web. They are useful for linguistically diverse learning environments because they facilitate cooperative learning, are rich in different kinds of resources including pictures and sound, and provide a variety of ways to access and demonstrate knowledge. The *MathStar* website at New Mexico State University (NMSU) (http://mathstar. nmsu.edu/teacher/webquests.html) has an excellent WebQuest page that provides additional examples and sources of information about WebQuests. WebQuests are also available on this site in Spanish and English such as *Yerbos y Remedios* in which students are asked to become ethno-botanists, museum curators, and biologists in their quest for natural remedies for human sickness (see Figure 6.5).

Technology tools such as multimedia authoring programs and WebQuests are known as *cognitive enhancers* (Jonassen, 1998). Such technology tools can assist all students with the problem-solving process. The characteristics of cognitive

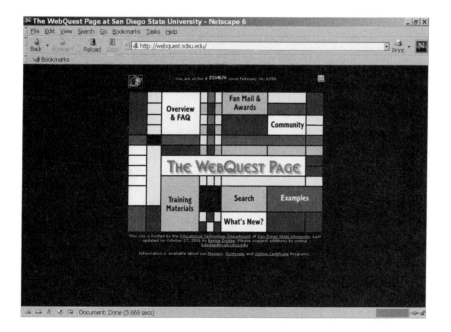

FIGURE 6.4   The WebQuest Page

Source: Bernard J. Dodge, Ph.D., San Diego State University. Used with permission.

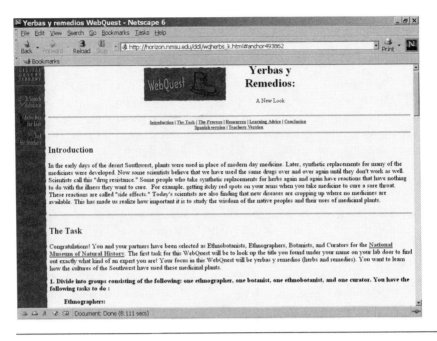

FIGURE 6.5   *MathStar* **WebQuest**

Source: Used with permission.

enhancing tools are described below. By utilizing these tools and recognizing the dual roles of declarative and procedural cognitive strategies, teachers can help English language learners think about and manage learning.

Computers as Cognitive Enhancers

Computer environments that provide students with continuous access to tools such as notebooks, drawing programs, calculators, and microphones facilitate remembering through writing, sketching, or recording information. Using visual environments to teach vocabulary and concepts was discussed previously, as was the use of multimedia authoring and WebQuests. These computer-mediated environments assist with problem solving, because they provide a source of *scaffolded* information. For example, as the students thought about the causes and impact of weather on human life, a visual database of weather events was available via the Web. This provided students access to multiple images for thinking about weather. After finding what they wanted, computer applications helped English language learners to store and reorganize their saved images. Such technology-rich environments provide a way to share the cognitive load of a task, especially when students are struggling with new language. All of the computer applications, such as spreadsheets, databases, and presentation tools, can be great cognitive enhancers. Visual and auditory tools, such as the multimedia and hypermedia environments available via the Web or on CD-ROM or DVD, may also be especially helpful in the ELL classroom.

How can a teacher decide which technology tools can support increased thinking in the ELL classroom?

Research and our common experience suggest that after the home and parents, the teacher is the most important factor in creating a good learning environment for kids. However, the kinds of tools chosen by the teacher matter. Not all computer software supports thinking. In order to understand how technology tools support thinking we'd like to introduce the term *affordance*. Norman (1993) used this term to describe what a tool or an environment enables the user to do. This concept of affordance was first introduced into social psychology by Eleanor Gibson (1991), who describes affordance as a property of the environment with consequences for the perceiver or actor. A chair, for example, affords support. A toothbrush affords brushing between the teeth. A classroom environment may afford competition or cooperation, thinking or mimicking. A computer program may afford the use of graphics or sound to help students communicate ideas or only afford the typing of words. It may afford student-directed learning or the passive answering of yes or no questions.

Norman provides an interesting illustration of the different affordances provided by television as compared to reading. Even though television and reading are kinds of displays, they are quite different. Television requires the user to be passive and to simply watch. It is fairly easy to use, but provides no user control. Reading is harder; it requires effort by the reader but also provides user control. Reading allows us to randomly access information, stop and reflect, and construct understanding as we interact with words. Television affords experience; reading affords reflection. Yet neither are interactive in the sense that a conversation or a problem-solving environment on the computer can be interactive. Multimedia and hypermedia environments can also be interactive and afford a person control over visual images, animation, sound, and text. The capability of the computer to provide this interactivity and user-control is one of the reasons computers and the networks to which they are connected are likely to have a longer instructional shelf life than traditional media, such as language labs or instructional television.

How can the teacher select software that affords thinking?

If we want students to learn generatively, to analyze, synthesize, and apply information, to reflect on information, and to create new knowledge by combining diverse ideas in a variety of forms, the computer tool must be examined in terms of how it supports a thinking-oriented environment. Such environments are an important part of a constructivist view of learning that suggests students learn more deeply when they are allowed to construct meaning for themselves (Fosnot, 1996).

In discussing the need for computer tools that support a constructivist view of learning, Linda Polin (1992) suggests the following characteristics of tools to be important:

1. The learner performs a whole, meaningful task, not a subskill.
2. The tool carries some of the burden of the task. It "scaffolds" the elements of the task the learner cannot accomplish alone.
3. The tool allows increasingly complex versions of the task to be carried out by turning back some of the task burden to the learner. (pp. 6–7)

Wiburg (1995) and Norton and Wiburg (1998) discuss criteria that can be used by teachers to select tools that support thinking environments. In this book we have expanded these criteria in light of choosing thinking tools for the English language classroom:

Proposed Criteria for Selecting Software
1. What is the theoretical approach to learning used in the design of the tool? Does the software provide opportunities for students to interact with complex problems in a variety of different ways and at different levels? Or does the approach to learning suggest students learn best when presented with information and asked questions?
2. Are there opportunities to process information using all modalities—print, graphics, sound, video, and/or animation?
3. Are there opportunities for students to work together in groups as they interact with the computer-based material or does the software afford only individual use?
4. Is the computer-learning environment well organized? Is it easy to navigate? Are visual cues as well as text provided to guide navigation?
5. Can students use the software to generate a variety of different types of answers or products?
6. Can the teacher modify the program to meet the needs of students learning English, and is clear documentation provided on how to do this?

All of the tools we have mentioned in this chapter, from multimedia environments to the use of computer applications, can meet these criteria. They afford student-directed generative learning. However, just selecting good tools is not enough. Teachers need models that can help them use software as part of an instructional approach that supports inquiry and problem solving.

Designing Learning Environments That Require Thinking

The tools and the memory enhancing strategies mentioned earlier are not enough. The selected tools must be integrated into what has been called problem-centered (Norton and Wiburg, 1998), problem-based, project-based, or inquiry-based learning. While each of these approaches is slightly different, they have in common roots within a social constructivist view of learning.

What is social constructivism?

As mentioned earlier, constructivism is drawn from the work of Dewey (1938, 1966), Piaget (1929, 1970, 1973), Vygotsky (1978), and Brunner (1990). Although each of these theorists contribute different aspects to this theory of learning and knowledge construction, their collective work points to the need to design a curriculum in which students are afforded opportunities to construct their own meaning through student-directed interaction with rich resources and problems.

Bruner developed a cognitive theory of instruction based on the individual's construction of knowledge as a result of active engagement with his or her environment and guided discovery. Vygotsky added the crucial role a social group plays in helping students to construct knowledge, arguing that students first learn ideas in social context and then later integrate these words and thoughts into their own developing cognitive structures. More recently, theorists (Brown, Collins, and Duguid, 1988) have argued for the importance in learning of what has become known as *situated cognition*. The idea is that how something is learned may be as important as what is learned and that learning is more meaningful when it relates to authentic experiences that are similar to what might be encountered in the real world.

There are a variety of ways in which technology, tied to teaching methods, can situate learning. First of all, students can learn content like mathematics or reading in the context of solving real problems related to the world in which students live. Students can redesign their classrooms or playgrounds, and teachers can replace some of their textbooks with interactive computer-based learning tools that support students in doing their own research. They can design better lunches or lunch times, better desks, more exciting learning activities, school gardens, greenhouses, publication or counseling centers, or review educational software for the school community. For these kinds of tasks, technology can be a valuable tool. To design a better lunch program, for example, it may be useful to create a survey, using a desktop publishing program, gather data and then compile it, and display the results in graphical form using spreadsheets. Computer-assisted drafting software can assist teams of students in designing gardens or parks.

Designing Problem-Based Learning

Teachers can help students think by providing problem-based learning opportunities. In order to do this, teachers must design rich, problem-centered learning situations. One model for designing problem-centered learning suggests following four stages of design (Norton and Wiburg, 1998).

The first step is to introduce and then help students to further define the problem. This often involves developing questions that are essential to answer as part of solving the problem. The second stage is to help students build a knowledge base related to the problem through print and electronic resources, simulations, presentations, and discussions. The third step involves acting as a facilitator to provide the students with the additional time, resources, and necessary scaffolding to answer their essential questions. Finally, the teacher needs to help the students to evaluate and possibly modify their alternative solutions to problems and to reflect on and evaluate their own learning.

If educators want students to improve their thinking abilities, it is necessary to provide a problem-centered curriculum in which there may be more questions than answers. Students will need practice in coming up with alternative solutions and then evaluating their ideas. Teachers may find it uncomfortable to introduce problems that have no clear and simple solutions. However, doing so is really the best way to stimulate student cognitive abilities. It also makes teaching and learning more exciting.

In addition to introducing problems it is also necessary to structure the classroom so that students are encouraged and assessed positively for working together to solve problems. Educators need to change their current assessment practices to value higher-level thinking and group collaboration, and provide rich tools and resources for students, in order to make progress in developing thinking classrooms.

Teaching Thinking to ELL Students in the Science Classroom

Science is such a rich field for encouraging both language and content learning. Everyone can do experiments, trying different variables and looking for effects. All students can learn to use scientific processes, generating questions about the natural world, sharing guesses about what might happen, analyzing what happened and why, and suggesting other ways to answer the questions posed. While such activities require thinking and promote language learning, they aren't necessarily dependent on high-level English language skills. The same is true in mathematics, where universal symbol systems supported by technology-based communication tools make students less dependent on the English language

> **Susan Brown's Middle School Science Classroom: A Classroom Vignette**
> Sierra Middle School is located in a low-to-middle-income city near the border between New Mexico, Texas, and Mexico. The school district in which it is located is about 60 percent Hispanic, and for around 40 percent of the district's students, English is not their home language. Sierra is located in an especially poor area of the border city, but has been successful over the last five years in turning what had once been a gang and problem school into a school that exemplifies the best of middle school teaching. All of the teachers work in teams and the school day has been restructured so that the teacher teams can meet for planning during each regular school day. The curriculum emphasizes

thematic teaching and close coordination between each student's regular and resource teachers and parents, with a focus on meeting each student's individual needs.

Susan Brown has taught school for over 17 years and welcomes the opportunity to teach English language learners in her science classroom. She has a well-developed instructional approach for teaching science that is successful even with the students from her middle school's Newcomer Center for monolingual Spanish speakers. She uses a project-based approach to science teaching and insists that all students engage in inquiry as they learn science.

Early in the fall, when students first enter her room, they notice a sign that indicates that they are entering the Sierra Sands Scientific Company. Below the sign is an employee manual for each student that states:

> We are proud to welcome you as a new employee to our company. The Sierra Sands Scientific Company is committed to excellence in science education. As a new employee you must complete each of the center activities to ensure that you are familiar with all the scientific equipment we sell to the schools. Again, welcome! We are so excited to have you as a member of our team!" (Brown, 1999, Student manual, Sierra Middle School)

Ms. Brown had carefully constructed centers in which the students will become familiar with the pieces of equipment used in science, including tools for experimentation, computer software, and calculators. In this first project-based activity, she asks students to work in pairs and provides enough centers that there is always one available for a pair to work in. She also pulls half the class at a time into an orientation and discussion group with her during each period. She knows that for many students, especially her monolingual Spanish speakers from nearby Mexico, a special orientation to the way in which she teaches science is necessary. In fact, as an experienced teacher, she follows the principle that one should never assume students know something.

Recently Ms. Brown shared with us how a group of newcomer students entered her room last fall, wide-eyed and afraid to touch things, and yet how quickly these same students became excited and motivated learners once they had experienced success at a center or two. She also talked about how her students from Mexico were often better at estimating than her other students and definitely better at using metric measures, which were standard in their country.

There are 16 different centers in this introductory science session in Ms. Brown's classroom. Some involve simple tasks that teach basic science experiment tools. Students are asked to measure colored water in a beaker; to look at slides under a microscope and a magnifying lens and sketch what they see; to filter tea leaves from a cup of tea and to weigh them; to measure the temperature of different colored boxes; and to simply measure and weigh objects using the metric system. Students are also invited to do a variety of different simple experiments such as float a boat, discover mystery powders, or investigate the properties of mystery liquids using petri dishes and test tubes. Some of the centers include using computers for graphing and accessing resources on the Web and using calculators for computation and graphing. Many of the key scientific words and procedures are provided in Spanish in this classroom, but more importantly the manual contains multiple pictures and diagrams that help all students be successful in the centers.

Ms. Brown tells the story of one Spanish-speaking student from Mexico who figured out a better way to measure the room than using a meter stick along the sides. She had figured out that because the room had tiles, all she had to do was measure one tile and then multiply this measurement by the number of tiles along the wall. The student was using body language and kept saying *uno, dos, tres* as she pointed at the tiles. Finally the students in the room got it! It was an incredible learning moment as other groups measuring the room quickly adopted the girl's suggestion.

How did this teacher design successful problem-based learning?

After these successful student orientation activities, Ms. Brown moved students into complete problem-based units that followed the basic design for problem-based learning suggested in this chapter. At the beginning of each unit she introduced the problem, provided questions and facilitated student formulation of questions and hypotheses. Next, she provided resources, mini-lectures, and demonstrations to ensure that students had an adequate knowledge base for solving the problem. Then she provided time for students to move through the centers, reflect on their work, and meet with her for additional questions and discussion. One of the centers was a teacher conferencing space. This is where she made sure the students were understanding the science content. She asked them to explain to her what they observed and what they did. Finally, students were asked to present their findings and helped to evaluate their solutions.

Introducing the Problem

The Sierra Sub Sandwich is an example of one of the many project and problem-based units developed in Susan Brown's middle school science classroom. Each of the projects has an opening scenario designed to engage students in the topic to be studied, which in this case is the human body digestive system. However, before looking at the opening scenario for the sandwich unit, Ms. Brown asked that we remind teachers of the importance of extensive advanced planning when designing a problem-based unit. Each of the centers must be developed in order to meet student needs and interests and to ensure that all content and process science standards are included. The centers must have everything students need to complete the tasks or management becomes a nightmare. And before doing a unit like the sandwich, the students should have completed introductory work like that described in the science company simulation.

This is the opening scenario for students to read, and have read to them for this unit. In this classroom, the scenario is also read in Spanish.

Sierra Sub Sandwich

Let me introduce myself. I am the sierra sub sandwich. Most people have thoroughly enjoyed my brothers and sisters. To let you know me better, I guess I should describe myself. I am a foot-long white bun with ham, salami, lettuce, onions, olives, mayonnaise, a touch of mustard, pickles, and tomatoes. I always go out with a 9 oz. package of potato chips and a 16 oz. Pepsi. Now, here is what I would like from you! I would like to know beforehand what is going to happen to me when I am eaten. To save me a lot of worry, please write a story about what will happen to me when you order and begin to eat. Your story should include an on-the-spot report of what happens at each part of the alimentary canal that I will be traveling. I realize that I will not all be digested at the same time. I know that different parts of the digestive system will take care of different parts of me. Please let me know what part of me I will lose first. Just tell me! Also make the report long and thorough. Please take the time to look up the alimentary canal and describe the parts of what enzymes will be attacking me at what time. Time . . . time . . . how long will I have in your digestive tract before I am completely gone?

I would also like to know the good that I am doing for your body. Please make a chart listing the calories, vitamins, and minerals that I am contributing to your body.

A picture of my trip would be nice. If it is possible, please draw a picture, with labels, of course, of your alimentary canal. I do not want to make any wrong turns.

Finally, how many calories are you allowed for your age and height and frame? What percent is this meal of your total calories for the day?

Thank you for taking the time to tell me the truth. I will feel better knowing that I am contributing to your healthy, growing body!

Clarifying the Questions and Developing a Knowledge Base

After presenting this scenario, there is much discussion about how to meet the sandwich's request. Lists are made of what students know and want to know. Questions are asked and clarified. Videos and websites related to the study of the human body are introduced along with all the center activities. Students work in peer reading groups with relevant sections of the text, begin to write about their ideas and predictions, and draw pictures and tables in their science notebooks about the project. The centers are all introduced to the whole class before Ms. Brown divides the students into heterogeneous work groups of four. She is careful to ensure that students who are new to English have a partner who is also a second language learner, and then two partners fluent in English, but maybe not as skilled in math or computer operation or some other skill as the non-English speakers. This describes the second stage of problem-based learning in which the teacher is ensuring that students construct an adequate knowledge base to work on the problem in their small groups.

Providing Students Time to Work on Carefully Structured Tasks Related to the Problem

During the third stage of problem-based learning, students are provided with time and resources to further understand the digestive system and the properties of different kinds of foods. In this example, tasks include the following:

- Using iodine to test for the foods that contain vitamin C
- Testing for fats using foods and a brown paper bag
- Reading cereal nutrition labels to compare nutrients in different cereals
- Drawing and/or building the digestive system
- Comparing the digestive systems of different animals
- Estimating and creating graphs of calories contained in different foods

During this center time the teacher pulls out small groups of students to meet with her and asks questions about their work. Sometimes they ask questions and want a quick teacher answer, but this teacher is careful to ask them how they might find out and to guide them to answering the questions themselves. She also checks to make sure they are writing in their science journals about what they have learned and want to learn.

The teacher has given them an activity to do at home as well. The activity involves reading the labels of the foods they like with their families and answering questions such as, *Which foods contain minerals such as calcium, potassium, or iron, or vitamins including A, B, C, D, and K?* During the first week of the project she holds an all-class meeting to discuss what the middle school children found out about food nutrients from their homework.

Helping Students Design their Presentations and Evaluate Their Answers

After the students finish their center activities they return with their group to a large table workspace to design their report/presentation for the Sierra Sub Sandwich. Each group answers the teacher's questions (see following list) as well as questions they generated. The students may use word processing as well as the *PowerPoint* program for their presentation. They may also generate graphs and charts with the *Excel Spreadsheet* program. If students have the skills, they can also design their own Web page or WebQuest. Students are reminded that the report must include the following:

1. A story that will describe what happens to the sandwich. Where does each part of the sandwich get digested?
2. An estimation, supported by charts and drawings, of how long the sandwich's parts will be in each part of the digestive system.
3. A chart that shows what nutrients (vitamins, minerals, protein, fats, water, and carbohydrates) are in each of the items that makes up the sandwich.
4. A picture or three-dimensional representation of the alimentary canal with all parts labeled correctly.
5. An estimation of the number of calories contained in the sandwich and what percentage of calories are provided by the sandwich in terms of the daily requirements of calories needed by each member of the group.

As students assemble their presentation, Ms. Brown meets with them to evaluate their solutions and their group problem-solving processes. She helps them reflect back on their process of learning, helping them to develop metacognitive skills and self-directed learning skills. The students have kept individual science journals throughout the class and she also goes over the journals and asks additional questions, extending students' thinking whenever possible.

Conclusion

This chapter focused on the idea that all students learn best when provided with opportunities to investigate problems and construct their own solutions. It examined what we know about information processing and strategies for helping students to gain both declarative and procedural knowledge. Examples of classroom applications in which technology was used were offered as well as suggestions for how to select software that supports thinking. A classroom vignette involving teaching science to beginning English speakers was described fully.

Summary of Key Ideas

1. In this chapter we argue that students who are learning English must be provided with opportunities to engage in high-level thinking and problem solving. The world today requires technology, and English language learners (ELLs) will need to learn to use technology tools and manage information to be able to function well in society.

2. Technology itself can help because it provides tools and programs that scaffold thinking and support collaborative problem solving. Technology environments like the Web provide visual and auditory cues that make it easier to understand English text and content presentations. The students' lack of English language ability should not keep a teacher from designing an inquiry-based learning environment, which

supports student thinking using multiple forms of information and computer-based cognitive tools.

3. In terms of language learning, the use of inquiry is tied closely to the CALLA (cognitive academic language learning approach) approach for supporting language and content learning (Chomot and O'Malley, 1994). Both inquiry learning and CALLA envision the student as a coconstructor of deepened content learning aided by the development of cognitive strategies.

4. Technology can be used to support thinking if teachers design classrooms in which (a) learning activities are informed by an understanding of the cognitive processes involved in language learning and thinking; (b) technology tools are carefully selected to support a wide range of thinking and problem-solving opportunities; and (c) these tools are used within an approach to learning, based on an understanding of inquiry and problem-based learning.

5. Both declarative and procedural knowledge are important and technology use supports these in different ways. For students who need to learn content, they can benefit from learning in multimedia and Web-based environments. To gain process skills, they are invited to participate in problem-based learning ranging from WebQuests to scientific experiments.

6. Technology tools can be considered in terms of the affordances for thinking that they provide. Criteria are offered for teachers to help them select software that support thinking.

Learning Activities _____

1. Think about a piece of software you plan to use with your English language learners. Use the software yourself to determine what crucial features you want to point out to the students and then prepare a QuickStart sheet for them to help them learn the essential functions of the software. Here is a QuickStart of an environmental science program.

QuickStart
A Field Trip to the Rain Forest
Sunburst

Science/Social Studies 3rd–Adult

Overview: In this program you can explore 34 detailed pictures of the rain forest. There are 70 different plant and animal species depicted in their habitats. You will learn about their interactions, habits, and life cycles.

To start: Open the Field Trip Folder on your hard drive. Your first view will be of the entire forest in the daytime.

Exploring software: Explore by clicking with the mouse on any part of this view. The place you select will be marked with a Selection Marker and information about it will appear in the Text Box. The Location Marker under the picture tells you where you are. The Action Buttons in the lower right enable you to explore further: zoom in, change to night, click to see a plant or animal in another place, or see the field guide. Try each of these. The Rainforest Day Button on the lower left returns you to the opening view.

Data: Use View on the Menu Bar to get to the Data Tables at any time. When selected it lists animals sorted by name. Use the Sort function (the key on the bottom) to sort animals by weight or length.

Question: Is there any relationship between weight of animals and their being active at night ?

Food chain: Explore the food chain of different animals by selecting the animal from the Food Chain menu. In the view that appears try to find something this animal eats. When you guess correctly the ? is replaced by the icon of the animal chosen.

Field guide: The field guide provides detailed information on each of the species selected, its food, enemies, and friends. Find takes you to a different entry.

2. Software evaluation and selection is an important skill for teachers to have. Students can use the criteria for selecting software for thinking presented in this chapter and evaluate a wide variety of software as well as websites, CD-ROMS, and other technologies including laserdiscs.

3. Remember the Web search and report prepared by students about the weather. Think of another topic that can be explored using visual information and design an activity for students using the Web and a computer application.

4. Think about a topic you introduce in your ELL class. Consider how to transform this topic into a problem-based learning activity. Begin by brainstorming what instructional strategies you will use.

   a. First, how will the problem be introduced in a way that motivates and interests the students? What questions will you ask and how will you encourage the students to generate their own questions and procedures they might use to answer the questions?

   b. Looking at the content material for the topic and the science process and content standards, list the key concepts and skills students will need to develop an adequate knowledge base about the topic. Then decide how you will introduce these concepts. What materials and technology tools will you use? Will you do some task-based centers or whole class activities? What kinds of groupings will you use? Begin to think about how you will assess student learning of the content and problem-solving skills. Develop a rubric, if appropriate, to share with students.

   c. Design a task-based structure for students to use in practicing and extending their understanding of the content. You might want to use project-based centers as described in this chapter. Consider additional alternative designs for encouraging student thinking, such as asking them to teach each other, having a classroom debate on a scientific or social question, doing surveys and gathering data, or doing a WebQuest activity.

   d. Students should be able to present their learning to at least the classroom community and, when possible, to larger groups. You may want to help them create a newspaper or a Web page that presents their findings. While students are creating their presentations and projects is an excellent time to ask them questions that help them evaluate their work.

Technology Resources _____

Software

Destination: *Rain Forest (Imagination Express)*. (1995). Riverdeep Interactive Learning Limited.
The Factory. (1995). Pleasantville, NY: Sunburst Communications, Wings for Learning.
HyperStudio (Version 3.1). (1997). San Diego, CA: Roger Wagner.
Inspiration. (1998). Lake Oswego, OR: Ceres Software.
Microsoft Publisher 97. (1997). Redmond, WA: Microsoft.
Microsoft Office (2000) [Word, Excel, Access, PowerPoint]. Redmond, WA: Microsoft.
Storybook Weaver Deluxe (Version 2). (1998). Riverdeep Interactive Learning Limited.

Websites

Problem-based learning (http://www.mcli.dist.maricopa.edu/pbl/)
Problem-based learning at San Diego State (http://edweb.sdsu.edu/clrit/learningtree/PBL/
    WhatisPBL.html)
Problem-based learning in math/science (http://www.imsa.edu/team/cpbl/problem.html)
A tutorial on problem-based learning and how to do it (http://www.imsa.edu/team/cpbl/whatis/
    whatis/slide1.html)
Weather Channel (www.weatrher.com)
Constructivism (http://www.sedl.org/scimath/compass/v01n03/)
A nice website of constructivist theories with their pictures (http://curriculum.calstatela.edu/
    faculty/psparks/theorists/501const.htm)
MathStar New Mexico (http://mathstar.nmsu.edu) has a unit-planning tool for teachers sup-
    ported with a collection of websites related to learning theories including problem-based
    learning; Go to Unit Planning Tool
A great search engine for educational resources is Yahooligans (http://www.Yahooligans.com)

Other Technology

Brooks, Jacqueline Grennon, and Brooks, Martin G. *In Search of Understanding: The Case for Con-
    structivist Classrooms*. Alexandria, VA: Association for Supervision and Curriculum Develop-
    ment, 1993.
Rader, J., & Wiburg, K. (1999) *Excel for Terrified Teachers*. Teacher-created materials. Lots of sample
    spreadsheet lessons for K–12 students across all areas of the curriculum.

References _____

Brown, A. (1995). The advancement of learning. *Educational Researcher* 23 (8): 4–12.
Brown, J., Collins, A., and Duguid, P. (1988). *Situated Cognition and the Culture of Learning*. Report
    No. 6886, BBN Systems and Technologies Corporation, p. 3.
Brown, S. (1999, Spring). Personal conversation/observation and unpublished student manuals
    and materials. Sierra Middle School, Las Cruces Public Schools.
Bruner, J. (1960). *The Process of Education*. Cambridge, MA: Harvard University Press.
Bruner, J. (1966). *Toward a Theory of Instruction*. Cambridge, MA: Harvard University Press.
Bruner, J. (1990). *Acts of Meaning*. Cambridge, MA: Harvard University Press.
Collins, A., Brown, J., and Newman. (1989). Cognitive apprenticeship: Teaching the craft of read-
    ing, writing and mathematics. In L. B. Resnick (Ed.), *Knowing, Learning, and Instruction: Essays
    in Honor of Robert Glaser*. Hillsdale, NJ: Earlbaum.
Chamot, A. U., and O'Malley, J. M. (1994). *The CALLA Handbook: Implementing Cognitive Academic
    Language Learning Approach*. Reading, MA: Addison-Wesley.

Clements, D. H., and Bastasi, M. T. (1992). Geometry and spatial reasoning. In D. A. Grouws (Ed.), *Handbook on Research on Mathematics Teaching and Learning* (pp. 420–464). New York: Macmillan.

Collier, V. (1995, Fall). Acquiring a second language for school. *Directions in Language and Education* (4). Washington, DC: National Clearinghouse for Bilingual Education.

Cummins, J. (1980). The cross-lingual dimensions of language proficiency: Implications for bilingual education and the optimal age issue. *TESOL Quarterly* 14: 175–187.

Cummins, J. (1996). Language proficiency, bilingualism and academic achievement. In Patricia A. Richard-Amato (Ed.), *Making It Happen*. New York: Longman.

Dewey, J. (1966). *Democracy and Education*. New York: Free Press.

Fosnot, C. (1996). *Constructivism: Theory, Perspectives, and Practice*. New York: Teacher's College Press.

Gagne, R. (1965). *The Conditions of Learning*. New York: Rinehart and Winston.

Gagne, R. (1985). *The Conditions of Learning and Theory of Instruction* (4th ed.). New York: Holt, Rinehart and Winston.

Gardner, H. (1983). *Frames of Mind*. New York: Basic Books.

Gibson, E. (1991). *An Odyssey in Learning and Perception*. Cambridge, MA: MIT Press.

Hunter, M. (1971). *Teach for Transfer: A Programmed Book*. El Segundo, CA: TIP Publications.

Jonassen, D. (1998). *Computers as Mind Tools for Schools: Engaging Critical Thinking*. Englewood Cliffs, NJ: Prentice Hall.

Kanim, S. (2000). Personal conversation with Science Education professor. New Mexico State University, August 15, 2000.

Linn, M. (1985) The cognitive consequences of programming instruction in classrooms. *Educational Researcher* 14 (5): 14–16, 25–29.

Norman, D. (1982) *Learning and Memory*. San Francisco: W. H. Freeman.

Norman, D. (1993). *Things That Make Us Smart: Defending Human Attributes in the Age of the Machine*. Reading, MA: Addison-Wesley.

Ovando, C., and Collier, V. (1985). *Bilingual and ESL Classrooms*. New York: McGraw-Hill.

Norton, P., and Wiburg, K. (1998). *Teaching with Technology*. Fort Worth, TX: Harcourt Brace.

Palinscar, A., and Brown, A. (1984) Reciprocal teaching of comprehension fostering and monitoring activities. *Cognition and Instruction* 1: 117–175.

Piaget, J. (1929). *The Child's Conception of the World*. New York: Harcourt, Brace Jovanovich.

Piaget, J. (1970). *The Science of Education and the Psychology of the Child*. New York: Grossman.

Piaget, J. (1973). *To Understand Is to Invent*. New York: Grossman.

Polin, L. (1992, May). Subvert the Dominant Paradigm. *Research Windows, The Computing Teacher, Journal of the International Society for Technology in Education* 19 (8): 6–7.

Richard-Amato, P. (1996). *Making It Happen*. White Plains, NY: Longman.

Snow, M. A., and Brinton, D. (1997). *The Content-Based Classroom: Perspectives on Integrating Language and Content*. White Plains, NY: Longman.

Sternberg, R. (1985). *Beyond IQ: A Triarchic Theory of Human Intelligence*. New York: Cambridge University Press.

Vygotsky, L. S. (1978). *Mind in Society: The Development of Higher Psychological Processes*. Cambridge, MA: Harvard University Press.

Vygotsky, L. S. (1984). *Thought and Language*. Cambridge, MA: MIT Press.

Wiburg, K. M. (1995). Becoming critical users of multimedia. *The Computing Teacher* 21 (5): 59–61.

Wiburg, K.M. (1998). Literacy instruction for middle school Latinos. In M. Gonzalez, A. Huerta-Macias, and J. Tinajero, (Eds.), *Educating Latino Students: A Guide to Successful Practice*. Lancaster, CA: Technomics.

Wiburg, K. M. (1987). *The impact of different types of computer-based learning environments on fourth grade students' cognitive abilities*. Unpublished doctoral dissertation, United States International University, San Diego, CA.

7

Culture, Community, and Diverse Learners

Chapter Overview

This chapter explores the importance of culture and community for second language learning. Current theories of learning, such as social constructivism, recognize that learning is influenced by the social and cultural context in which it occurs. The communities in which students live and have lived play a critical role in how these students make meaning out of the world around them. In addition, understanding language in terms of its cultural context is essential. Through the use of technology, students in diverse classrooms can come to know each other's culture while also practicing the target language.

The chapter continues by focusing on the need to serve diverse students through technology-integrated multicultural education. A vignette describes how technology was used to restructure a high school English class in a border community. This is followed by an in-depth discussion of learning styles and uses of technology to support multiple ways of learning. The chapter concludes with suggestions for creating classroom communities supported by appropriate uses of cooperative learning.

Culture and Language Learning

Students' experiences in learning language are deeply intertwined with the culture in which the language is being learned. It is not enough for the teacher of English language learners to teach in ways that he or she is used to. Teaching strategies in the mainstream culture may not be a good match for students coming from different cultures. Nelson (1995), after studying culture and learning in Hawaii, Oregon, China, and Japan, describes how children begin to acquire cultural styles of learning even before entering formal schooling.

An example of how ways of acting and thinking are culturally based was told to me by a friend who taught overseas. She had the interesting challenge of teaching several competitive American games to a group of students. The students were asked to run relays with two teams competing against each other. Yet whenever a student team got ahead, the students in the group invariably slowed down so that the other team could cross the finish line at the same time.

There are many differences between cultures that can be seen in day-to-day activities as well as classroom interactions. Among these differences are how time is viewed, how students believe they should act with people of status, how people greet each other, even how they walk and the amount of space that they feel is appropriate to place between themselves and others. In order to raise awareness of these differences, the teacher of linguistically and culturally diverse students might want to show videos, pictures, or slides of everyday interactions in different cultures and talk with the students about these differences. Once students have explored these cultural behaviors through media, they often become more comfortable with sharing some of their own anxieties about living and studying in a new culture.

Gebhard (1996) suggests that many minority language learners may have an especially hard time learning English, not because they are offered limited instruction in skills, but because these students may exist in a painful sort of cultural limbo. They have moved away from their traditional cultures and are faced with a rapidly moving American culture that may be difficult for them to understand.

Drawing from Damen's (1988) work, Scarcella (1990) addresses how middle-American cultural values in the United States might appear in contrast to students' home cultures. The idea of contrasting values is not meant to be related to any specific culture but reflects the kinds of perceptions of U.S. culture that students from places such as Mexico, China, Korea, the Middle East, Southeast Asia, and the Philippines might be experiencing. For example, Americans typically value individualism and personal control of their environment, whereas other cultures see nature as the controlling force and value their interdependency with others.

Americans also assume change is inevitable and so look to the future; other cultures value tradition and are more oriented toward the past. The middle-American culture is viewed as action and problem-solving oriented, as compared to cultures that stress a state of being and are more accepting of current situations.

Cultural Studies through Telecommunications

There is no question that global telecommunications has changed our perceptions of the world around us. We are now as familiar with the West Bank, Ethnic Albanians, South African apartheid, Indonesian independence movements, and revolution in the Philippines as we are with our own cities and states. Media has influenced commerce and politics and inevitably it will influence education. While the content we receive is mediated somewhat by the powerful networks and corporations that influence its interpretation, we are still in contact on a daily basis with diverse cultures and parts of the world that were certainly unfamiliar in the United States of the past.

Through the use of digital media, today's students have the opportunity to experience and communicate with people in cultures that are quite different from the ones in which they live. Tiene and Ingram (2001), in a chapter entitled "It Takes a Global Village," discuss the potential of multicultural studies through telecommunications. Cummins and Sayers (1995), in their book *Brave New Schools* introduced the notion of cultural literacy through the use of Web-based communication. These authors provide multiple examples of schools that are using technology to expand their students' understanding of diverse cultures.

Such multicultural understanding is essential in today's society for several reasons. The United States has always been a nation of many cultures and its diversity is growing. In the year 2010, one-third of the children in the United States will live in just four states—California, Texas, New York, and Florida—with "minority" children becoming the majority in these school populations (Hodgkinson, 1992). The recent 2000 census indicated a 46.7% increase in Hispanics from the 1990 census and it is projected that this cultural group will soon reach 34.7 million people in the United States, becoming the largest minority population in the country (African Americans are around 34.3 million) (Armas, 2001). By the year 2020, one-half of the nation's school children will be non-European American (Darder, Ingle, and Cox, 1993). Yet the curriculum used in many schools still reflects an older European American culture. An appreciation of the reality of diversity is essential for building a stable and strong political and social structure as the United States becomes increasingly diverse. Businesses recognized several decades ago that the ability to work within different cultural settings is important for economic well-being and that fluency in a second language is a valuable asset.

One of the ironies related to the value of languages in education in the United States is the "English-only" movement, which has grown in recent years, especially in California. Students fluent in a second language when they start school are asked to use *English only* in their classrooms. Then, when these same students graduate into a multilingual or bilingual community they are told they will be more likely to get a job if they speak a second language. Bilingualism seems to be valued in the global economy while being devalued in American education.

How can telecommunications build cultural literacy?

Warshauer (1996) suggests that "computer-mediated communication (CMC) —is probably the single computer application to date with the greatest impact on language teaching." He continues by describing how "for the first time, language learners can communicate directly with other learners or speakers of the target language twenty-four hours a day, from school, work, or home" (p. 9).

The World Wide Web is certainly appropriately named. It provides opportunities to connect students and classrooms with the rest of the world. The net provides opportunities for virtual travel, bringing scenes, artifacts, and information about other cultures into the classroom. Governments, tourist bureaus, and museums provide excellent websites for visitations to other countries. One site, *Teaching with the Web* (http://polyglot.lss.wisc.edu/lss/lang/teach.html), developed by Lauren Rosen (1995) at the University of Wisconsin, suggests activities that are linked to other sites and provides teachers with pedagogical information on how these links support language learning (see Figure 7.1). For example, one activity links teachers to the *City Net* website, where they can arrange virtual travel for their students to anywhere in the world. *City Net* is actually part of a commercial program that is helpful for planning trips but would work well in the classroom as a resource for learning about other places in detail.

Students can move beyond virtual travel to participate via the Web in real adventures going on around the world. Several sites offer choices of adventures and options for involvement. Some require a school or classroom fee, whereas others invite all to participate for free. An excellent free site is the *Global School Net* site (www.gsn.org), which provides opportunities to participate in expeditions as well as opportunities to participate in international projects (see Figure 7.2). The projects often involve studying global issues such as food distribution or environmental issues. Another popular site is *Adventure Online* (adventureonline.com). A complete curriculum is provided around the on-line adventures in which students can participate.

What is the Cultura Project?

Still being developed is a project between the Massachusetts Institute of Technology and the University of Paris (Furstenberg and Levet, 2001) that is structured

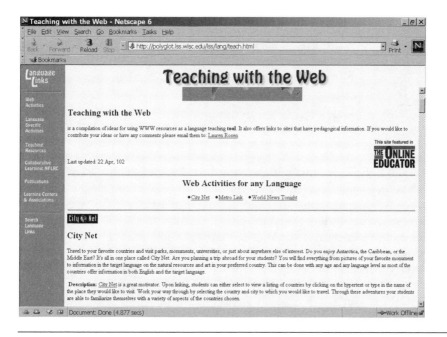

FIGURE 7.1   *Teaching with the Web*

Source: Teaching with the Web (Rosen, L., 1995). Used with permission.

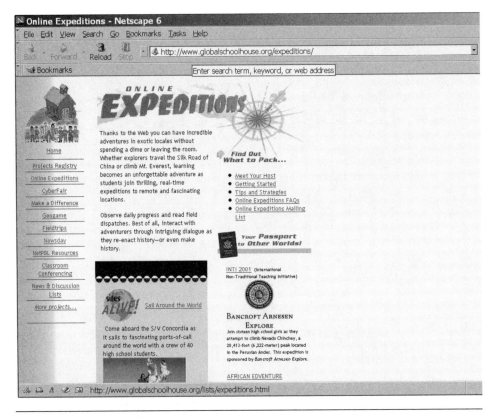

FIGURE 7.2   *Global SchoolNet*

Source: Copyright © Global SchoolNet Foundation. Used with permission.

around the meanings of words in the French versus the American culture. Students in a French class at MIT are communicating with students learning English in Paris. The project calls for the two groups to observe and compare similar materials from their cultures, such as news and magazine articles, which have been placed on the website. The students then exchange viewpoints about these materials. A discussion of the different meanings of words in their cultures is an important aspect of this project. For example, the meaning of individualism in English is quite different from the meaning of the same word in French because of the differences in cultural values connected to these words. Students are asked to build semantic nets of words by listing words they associate with a word such as *individualism*. These networks of meaning that the students in the two cultures bring to the words are quite different and serve to illuminate how culture influences language. The project promises to provide deeper insight into cultural connections to language.

Cultural Differences within Classrooms

How can technology be used to facilitate respect for cultural differences within an ELL class?

Not only are there important cultural differences between language groups, but in increasingly diverse ELL classrooms there are also cultural differences between students within the class. Ortmeier (2000) was surprised to find many prejudices within her classroom of diverse English language learners. She first discovered this when she was walking to her classroom with two of her advanced ESL students, one from Thailand and one from Mexico. The Thai boy was afraid that his father, who was there to pick him up, would see him with his Mexican friend. He told Ortmeier he had been told at home not to socialize with Mexicans. As a result of this interaction and her increased awareness that students were not only uncomfortable with their new American culture but also with their classmates from other cultures, she created the Homeland project. Ortmeier decided to do a Web-based project that involved students in finding and combining resources about their homelands into a multimedia presentation for the class. They were also required to use the new library electronic database to find books about their countries. As students shared interesting information about their homelands, there was increased respect within the class for each other and a sense of community began to emerge. We advise you to read the entire article on this unit, since the author did an excellent job of combining language skills, technology skills, and cultural literacy.

How can oral histories be used to build cultural understanding in the classroom?

Oral histories are another way for students to bring their own experiences and background into the classroom while studying history. Olmedo (1993) describes how she helps her students to see history from different points of view by asking her ESL and bilingual students to become junior historians. Many of these students live with or near grandparents and other relatives. They may not realize before doing this kind of project the rich cultural resources their own relatives can be. For example, if the class is studying the Vietnam War or the conflicts in the Russian and Eastern European countries, students whose families have experiences in these countries become valuable resources for the classroom curriculum. These older relatives are probably also important conservers of the students' families' language, stories, songs, and customs, and these oral interviews help students to realize the rich backgrounds they come from.

Another kind of oral history can be done by having the students work in small groups to research the history of their town, their school, or an important event in the community. For example, students at New Mexico State University researched the annual pilgrimage of the Tortuga Indians, who climb the mountain near the university every year as part of the festival of Guadalupe. A professor and several students climbed along on the pilgrimage and, with the tribe's permission, took pictures and interviewed members of the tribe in order to share their story.

Culturally Responsive Teaching with Technology

As can be seen from the preceding text, technology can be used to support a variety of strategies for addressing cultural differences in the classroom. In the rest of this chapter, we will focus on three general strategies for developing culturally responsive technology integrated learning environments. The first approach, bringing culturally relevant material into the students' studies, echoes the two examples described in the last section, which allowed students to be historians and cultural anthropologists. It is important that students see their own experiences and backgrounds included in the materials used in the classroom. In the communities and cultures from which diverse students come, there are valuable "funds of knowledge" (Moll and Greenberg, 1992; Goldenberg and Gallimore, 1991) that can be integrated into the content learning which is part of the goals of schooling.

Second, it is important to provide opportunities for students to construct their own knowledge by providing a variety of ways for students to learn and manage the material themselves. Technology can provide important tools and strategies for supporting student-centered constructivist learning. Third, in addition to providing culturally responsive learning opportunities and tools for student-controlled learning, technology supports the development of diverse ways for learning and demonstrating learning that meet the needs of students' different learning styles. Each of these strategies is discussed more fully in the sections that follow. Following this is a model for technology integration and a vignette that shows how one teacher integrated this model and the three strategies discussed into her border high school English class.

How can technology support these culturally responsive learning strategies?

Technology can be connected to the strategies mentioned. First of all, it can be used to literally bring each student's world into the classroom. Wiburg remembers bringing the interactive CD-ROM, *Just Grandma and Me* to one of her master's courses in technology and literacy. She demonstrated the program and how it could be played in Japanese, Spanish, or English, and noted how the face of a quiet Japanese student suddenly lit up upon hearing her home language. During the evening this student spent a lot of time with others playing this CD and sharing additional Japanese words with the other students. Another time, a beginning technology class went to the lab to learn about Web pages, and a student from Yemen connected to a site written in Arabic. It was a memorable class for this student and others who wanted to see and explore the Arabic language.

Constructivist Teaching with Technology

What role does constructivism play in engaging diverse students in learning?

Many students suffer from an instructional strategy that is all too common in classrooms and limiting to all students, not just second language learners. Tharp and Gallimore (1988) have named this type of instruction *recitation*, since students are continually asked to answer questions to which the teacher already has the answer. In this traditional form of instruction, students have not been provided with opportunities to construct meaning from comprehensible input.

Tharp and Gallimore (1988) describe the recitation they believe is very common in American Schools:

> What is this ubiquitous recitation? It consists of a series of unrelated questions that require convergent factual answers and student display of (presumably) known information. Recitation questioning seeks predictable, correct answers. It includes up to 20 percent yes/no questions. Only rarely in recitation are teacher questions responsible to student production. Only rarely are they used to assist students to develop more complete ideas. (p. 14)

Nunan (1996) echoes these concerns about the extensive use of recitation in K–12 schooling and begins his writing with a quote from a first-year student of his at the University of Hong Kong:

> When I was in secondary school, I seldom asked questions. The reason was that the teacher always tried to explain the stuff as detailed as possible, leaving no queries among students. This method is well-known as the spoon-feeding education system in which we are fed with piles of notes and text books. But in the universities, things are different. Lecturers only give a brief talk on the topics, leave a huge area for students to explore by themselves. (p. 35)

This recitation model is easily contrasted with the constructivist learning models that have been suggested throughout this book, based on the work of Piaget, Vygotsky, Brunner, and others (see Chapter 6 for more on constructivism and language learning). Constructivists believe that learning is based not on the individual, but on the child's developing mind as a result of social interaction. Followers of Vygotskian theory suggest that learning is not based on memorizing the information coming from the teacher and the textbook, but on participating in a social structure that supports the student in constructing information (Wertsch, 1979; Fosnot, 1989). Teaching becomes a process of assisting performance, rather than controlling and testing. Learning occurs as a result of specific types of social interactions—interactions that must be designed by the teacher to assist students in creating meaning.

The process of helping students to learn within a constructivist approach is tricky. Another Vygotskian concept, the zone of proximal development (ZPD), is helpful. What the ZPD suggests is that all students have a zone of development, which ranges, at the bottom, from being able to do something only with assistance to, at the top, being able to do something alone. The teacher cannot expect students to learn outside of their level of development; for example, a student who knows no English cannot suddenly converse in English. At the same time, a student who already knows much of the common vocabulary in English, and can often comprehend at a much higher level than he or she is speaking, should not spend days filling out worksheets with common words. It makes no sense to teach students what they already know or to teach them what they are not yet ready to learn. It is necessary to provide assistance at the right level in order to assist learners to move through this zone of proximal development.

How can ELL teachers help students to manage their own learning?

In addition to providing instruction at the appropriate level, it is important to assist students in gaining skills for managing their own learning. Nunan (1996) reported on an action research project designed to encourage students to become more active participants in their language learning. Students were given a strategy training that included helping them become aware of the processes for learning that they were using; focusing on the context and environment in which they learned and practiced English; and writing down the different strategies they were using for pronunciation, vocabulary, grammar, and discourse. Students kept detailed learning journals. These journals changed over time as learners become aware of their language learning strategies. Their entries indicated that the combination of strategy training and regular opportunities for reflection on the learning processes resulted in greater awareness of their learning process and increased ability to make connections between English and content courses. The students also appeared better able to decide what they wanted to learn and how best to do it.

Another successful strategy for sharing responsibility for learning in the classroom is the use of reciprocal teaching (Palinscar and Brown, 1984). Reciprocal teaching is a strategy for sharing the responsibility of bringing meaning to text with students. It involves four specific strategies:

1. *Summarizing* is a process in which students begin to summarize small amounts of text in their own words, eventually being able to summarize longer passages.
2. *Question generating* supports the students in developing their own questions about the text and asking them to refine and improve their questions. Teachers will need to model questioning first in most ELL classrooms.
3. *Clarifying* is an activity that helps students who have comprehension difficulty. Students are taught to be aware of barriers to comprehension such as word meanings or word structures that are difficult for them.
4. *Predicting* involves students hypothesizing about what might happen next in the text. It helps link the new knowledge gained from reading with previous background knowledge that can be used to make predictions.

These four strategies have been used successfully in many reading programs, but are also very useful for reading in any content area and may have great potential for helping English language learners to increase their comprehension abilities in English.

Technology and Diverse Learning Styles

What are some of the different kinds of learning styles?

Soo (1999) describes several different kinds of learning styles relevant to working with English language learners. First, there is the issue of cultural differences in what types of learning are valued. For example, in some societies students are encouraged to help each other to learn things, while in an individualistic culture such helping might be considered "cheating." Howard Gardner (1983) has developed a greatly expanded definition of intelligence grounded in cultural differences. He defines *intelligence* as "the ability to solve problems, or to create products, that are valued within one or more cultural settings" (p. x). His definition of multiple intelligence is built on biological and anthropological evidence, which reflects the differential values placed on diverse human abilities in different cultures. We live in a culture that places high value on only some of these intelligences, specifically linguistic and logical/mathematical skills. Yet, in other cultures, other types of intelligence are often of more value. Gardner gives the example of the Puluwat sailor who is considered intelligent only if he can sail by the stars. Whether or not he can read is not relevant to being considered intelligent in his culture.

What learning styles have traditionally been valued in schools?

Intelligence, like literacy, is related to the values held by a specific society. Eliot Eisner (1994) suggests that one of the major aims of education should be the development of multiple forms of literacy. By literacy he, and the authors, do not mean just print, but rather the ability to communicate and comprehend meaning in any of the forms of representation used in the culture. Schools to a large extent have focused primarily on the transmission of knowledge via print. Our minds are capable of comprehending and expressing ideas using a variety of forms of representation including visual, musical, and spatial. Limiting communication primarily to print and words has literally limited the development of students' minds to a single dimension.

What do we know about cognitive processing styles?

Many learning style differences have to do with differences in cognitive processing. In the study of cultural differences in learning, these processes were first conceptualized as *field dependent* or *field independent*. The field dependent person learned more easily if concepts were introduced as part of a larger context, while the field independent person could work from small pieces of information to construct a larger picture. The field dependent approach has now been reconceptualized in a broader way as a *global* learning style. Students who are global often like to learn in groups and like to have ideas introduced from the general to the more specific. The field independent approach is now called *analytical* and it is suggested that this type of learner enjoys going from the specific to the general and often prefers to work individually by putting ideas together in logical fashion (Soo, 1999).

A related type of learning difference has to do with the way in which the learner perceives information. There is a growing recognition among educators based on an explosion of research in the last ten years (Herrold, 1989) that there are distinct differences in the ways in which humans process information and in which modality (auditory, kinesthetic, visual, or kinesthetic) students prefer to learn. Rather than trying to teach to each favored modality, most teachers try to present information using all modalities and then provide opportunities for students to process content using a variety of different modalities and intelligences.

How does multimedia support multiple ways of learning?

Computers are natural multiple-modality learning tools. Students can type in information, read and write print, use a microphone to record sound, and draw pictures to illustrate concepts. Willetts (1992), in a review of technology and second language learning, noted that while the computer has many advantages for enhancing language learning, connecting it to other technologies such as videodisc players and CD-ROMS multiplies its benefits. Different types of technology support different aspects of language learning, for example, audio cassettes for listening skills. Interactive video-based systems provide the best environment for practicing all language skills including speaking, listening, writing, and reading.

How can students use multimedia to learn language?

It is much easier to learn a language in a rich context. Multimedia can provide the learner at any level with a visual kindergarten of words and pictures, which illustrate and illuminate words in context. Whole language approaches to language arts education stress the need to integrate speaking, listening, reading and writing. Using all of these processes within cooperative learning technology projects is a natural. Cooperative learning groups using the computer engage naturally in all four of these processes. Researchers have known for sometime that there is more communication in computer-based learning environments than in traditional classrooms (White, 1986).

The design of learning activities that support diversity requires the use of a variety of media as channels for students to both receive information and be able to show what they know and think. Students can demonstrate their understanding of a certain historical period by creating a play, drawing pictures, putting together a series of video images, making a radio show from the period, or creating a simulated newspaper from the day. Assignments should reflect new understandings of multiple intelligences by providing a variety of ways to demonstrate knowledge. For example, if students are studying the civil war, they should have a choice of a variety of assignments. Some examples might include the following:

Write a play (linguistic intelligence)

Create a pantomime or dance to demonstrate conflict (kinesthetic intelligence)

Draw a map to show where certain battles took place (spatial intelligence)

Write a song about the conflicting needs of the North and South (musical intelligence)

Engage other students in a discussion of the causes of the Civil War (interpersonal intelligence)

Use spreadsheets to demonstrate the economics that caused the defeat of the South (mathematical intelligence)

Write or tell an original story about what might have happened if the South had won the war (intrapersonal intelligence)

All of these would provide a variety of ways for students to demonstrate their learning.

All of the suggested strategies (the use of culturally relevant material and culturally responsive teaching strategies; the importance of providing constructivist learning opportunities; and the meeting of different learning styles) are integrated in a model for technology integration in the multicultural classroom, developed by Ines Chisholm (1998). This model is presented in the following text, followed by a vignette on the implementation of this technology-rich model in a border high school in southern New Mexico.

What does a multicultural technology integration model look like?

Chisholm (1998) advocates the inclusion of six elements when integrating technology in multicultural classrooms: *cultural awareness, cultural relevance, a culturally supportive environment, equitable access, instructional flexibility,* and *instructional integration.* In her article, Chisholm asked educators to try her model in their real-world classrooms. Michele Stafford-Levy used the model in her high school English classroom, which is the basis of the vignette on page 200.

A culturally supportive environment requires providing students with full exposure to technology so that technology can be used to bring culturally relevant materials into the curriculum and increase cultural awareness for all students. Historically, language minority students have used technology in limited ways (Wetzel and Chisholm, 1998), such as for drill and practice, rather than for student-directed productive activity. In the following vignette, a project-based approach utilizing technology was used in a high school English class in order to make the state-mandated literature curriculum more culturally relevant for bilingual/bicultural high school students in a southwest border community. Stafford-Levy used her language arts classroom as the venue for change in the face of adversity, poverty, and minimal technology infrastructure. She created a culturally supportive environment by encouraging her students to use technology to bring their life experiences into her English classroom. The students used computers to write their own poems and materials and bring in pictures and images that were meaningful for them.

Technology use in any classroom is most powerful if tied to constructivist learning using the content being studied. In order for this to be achieved, it is incumbent on educators to integrate constructivist designs that allow students to explore, question, and discover. Norton and Wiburg (1998) state, "Constructivist notions of learning start with a simple proposition: Individuals construct their own understanding of the world in which they live" (p. 29). Stafford-Levy (2001) integrated a constructivist philosophy in order for her Chicano high school students to bridge their rich local experience with an increased awareness of the world through English literature. For example, Shakespeare's *Romeo and Juliet* was recast and rewritten by the students in the context of a Latino barrio and then videotaped and shared in the school. Constructivist teaching relates to what Chisholm calls the *instructional integration* element, which she defines as the "degree to which technology becomes an integral part of classroom learning, student productivity, and information gathering for all learners across a variety of academic disciplines" (p. 261). This constructivist approach framed within the context of the multicultural classroom can create meaningful experiences for all learners, especially for minorities and second language learners.

A project-center approach that had been developed earlier through work in another university project also supported the element of *instructional flexibility* in our example classroom. This project-based approach asks students to complete a variety of tasks including ones that require computer access and tools. Yet, students have choices about the order in which the tasks are done and have long periods of time in which to work on their tasks. The approach contrasts with typical activity structures in which students must rotate between different activities within a limited and artificial time period. In the project approach, the students have a list of tasks to complete and complete these at their own pace, stopping now and then to reflect with themselves and their teachers on their progress. This approach is closer to work in the real world than to the traditional information dissemination classroom.

This project-based classroom strategy also facilitates a new approach to assessment for diverse students. Students are aware of the tasks they need to complete and are given time to do them. They also all have opportunities to use the classroom computers to complete their work, even if there are only a few computers. These practices support Chisholm's element of *equity*. The use of the computer by all students is in direct contrast to the still present practice of telling faster students they can use the computer as a reward when they have finished their work.

A Project-Based English Literature Class: A Vignette

The high school class in this case study is located in a poor, desert community in southern New Mexico. For the most part, the students here are the children of recent immigrants and are bilingual/bicultural. An enormous duality exists for them in that they speak Spanish at home and English at school. Wong-Filmore (1991) warns educators that this dichotomy can create an enormous gulf between parents and children, and grandparents and grandchildren—even alienation from the family.

As a language arts teacher in this border community, Stafford-Levy tries to inspire her students to become empowered by modeling new teaching practices. In her high school class, her teaching style is radically different from most of what her students have experienced in their previous education. Of all the in-service workshops Stafford-Levy had attended in the district, she found the information on how to juggle thirty kids and one computer most enlightening and she immediately implemented the project-center approach that she had learned. There were no computers available for English classes in her high school at the time she decided to begin this approach, but she was able to receive two new computers from the district as part of an ongoing staff development project. While she was determined to integrate the project approach with technology in her classroom, she admits that it was very frightening to try out new ideas at first—especially when "I was schooled one way and yet practicing another." Stafford-Levy also worried that it might be hard to utilize technology and a project approach in her field of language arts. "Prior to my training, I simply believed that projects were relegated to the Science classes and I thought that English Literature didn't lend itself to such a concept."

At the start of a new project/unit, the students are introduced to the tasks displayed on a large teacher-made board. Students are each given a folder that includes a checklist of tasks to help them manage their work. The checklist reads something like, "At Center One you will. . . . At Center Two there are. . . ."One of the centers is a meeting with the teacher, who is now the acting supervisor. (The teacher suggests that the tasks are much like ones that would occur in the workplace. Students begin to feel more like workers within this approach.) After visiting each center, students check off the completed task and then they move on to the next center. All tasks are completed at each student's own pace, contributing to a lower affective filter (Krashen, 1982) and increased learning opportunities.

There are several things Stafford-Levy recommends that should be included in the centers in order to support instructional flexibility and the meeting of diverse learning styles. She uses a project-center approach, combined with the use of different modalities and intelligences for learning (Gardner, 1985). When planning the centers, she includes a writing component where students can word process and publish their work. She makes sure that there is some sort of art project to supplement the lesson: chalk drawings, painting, cutting and pasting, or creating a collage from magazines. Stafford-Levy maintains that all learners enjoy relief from the linear work of reading and writing, and so she incorporates an art center in her English class. Stafford-Levy also makes sure that there is some sort of communication component integrated into the lesson: giving a speech or presentation, discussing an article, recording a radio show on cassette, or presenting a dramatic interpretation by filming it on video. Performance is an important component of her redesigned classroom lessons. Incorporating all the different discourse forms that support the various learning styles is at the very heart of multicultural education.

The project supervisor/teacher holds a conference with each student halfway through the centers and at the end of the project for a final check off and evaluation. The students in this high school English classroom sit in regular student desks and face each other in clusters of about six chairs that serve as centers. In the middle of each cluster is a folder labeled with the center number. The computer center, with its two new computers and Internet access, has a host of possible activities: from Web searches to authoring multimedia presentations.

In one class, for example, the students interact with The Edgar Allan Poe Project Center developed by Stafford-Levy. It is an example of the variety of activities one can craft with this approach to learning with technology in the multicultural classroom.

She teaches how Poe mastered the mystery and how we still use his formula to this day. Students travel from center to center, reading his various works: *The Raven, Annabelle Lee, The Fall of the House of Usher, The Masque of the Red Death*. Each work center has an activity to supplement the learning. For example, there is a listening center for *The Fall of the House of Usher* where students can listen to a dramatic interpretation on cassette of this great work. Another center involves students designing T-shirts for *The Masque of the Red Death* after they've read this story. At *The Raven* center, they can join the Raven Society by logging on to the website. This Internet center allows students to fill our certificates of membership after they have read this piece by Poe. Students go on to write their own Poe-like stories and poems using a second writing center computer.

Stafford-Levy asserts that technology and the project-based model have helped her address the problem of her previously unmotivated students. For almost all the students in her class, English is not their first language and reading classic English literature had not been attractive to them. Prior to placing the computers in Stafford-Levy's classroom, she admits that the kids sat in rows reading out of thick literature books, filling out handouts ("dittos"), and writing (by hand) responses to the traditional great works they read. This traditional classroom was not much fun for the students or the teacher.

The attitude of her high school students changed for the better after the project-center approach with its multicultural orientation to the use of technology was introduced into her classroom. The only problem was that some of her students started bugging the other English teachers to teach like Stafford-Levy, and this made staff meetings a little uncomfortable. Eventually, several other teachers also began creating centers, expanding learning opportunities further in this high school.

In the vignette above the high school students were provided with a learning environment that followed the three general strategies that should be kept in mind for building culturally responsive learning environments. Students were encouraged to bring their knowledge and experiences into the class; they were given opportunities to construct their knowledge; and they were able to do so by using their own learning strengths and preferred learning modalities.

Building Community

It has been suggested that there are three sorts of goal structures in classrooms: competitive, individualistic, and collaborative (Joyce and Weil, 1996). Many traditional classrooms are based on a competition goal structure in which there are limited rewards/grades available, and students need to compete for those rewards as well as for the teacher's attention and time. The relationship in these classrooms is between the teacher and each individual student. Most students see themselves in competition for the teacher's attention and reinforcement. In some situations an effort is made to provide a more individualistic goal structure, such as that advocated as part of mastery learning. Students are provided with individual learning packets and given the opportunity to complete learning tasks in their own time, giving them repeated opportunities to succeed. This is a model frequently seen in special education classrooms as part of an individualized educational plan (IEP). Again, however, the teacher is interacting primarily with each individual student, and many teachers find it difficult to provide individualized learning for their many students. A third type of classroom focuses on collaborative learning and shared power between the teachers and the students, with the teacher being in charge of the process but not necessarily the originator of all knowledge and assessment. This model relies on well-developed strategies for using cooperative learning.

What is cooperative learning? How can it be used with ELL students?

In the last ten years, there has been a significant growth in the use of a cooperative learning model for classroom learning. Cooperative learning, when designed so that students have interdependent tasks (Cohen, 1994), has been shown to be of benefit to diverse students and lower-achieving students (Johnson and Johnson, 1990, 1994). Cooperative learning is also an important practice for language learning (Willis, Stephens, and Matthew, 1996) and has been growing in importance as technology has provided increased opportunities for computer-mediated communications (CMC). However, its successful use is dependent on understanding appropriate uses of cooperative learning with students learning English.

Not all English language learners—and especially learners in college ESL classrooms who come from individualistic cultures based on memorization and success at testing—are comfortable with learning in this way. Kate Kinsella (1996), while describing the potential benefits of ESL classroom collaboration, notes that not all ESL students embrace cooperative learning and many feel uncomfortable when required to work in groups. In some cases the students might not feel like they have enough linguistic skill to participate in the generative-type language required as groups negotiate, agree, disagree, and work together.

What strategies can be used to implement cooperative learning in the ELL classroom?

Putney and Wink (1997) adapt the work of Faltis (1997) in order to implement a kind of cooperative learning they have found effective with ELL students. They suggest the importance of allowing students to use their native language when working in groups to construct meaningful options. They support students in constructing meaning by speaking to each other in their native language. In their experience, if this does not happen, there may be no conversation at all. For example, if a teacher insists on English, she or he may have only silence, since many ELLs are not yet ready to negotiate complex ideas in English. Putney and Wick believe "it is the teacher's responsibility to establish interactive exchanges for all students regardless of their level of English proficiency" (p. 31). It doesn't matter if the teacher speaks only English, as long as each student has at least one peer who speaks his or her native language. Putney and Wink are adamant that "to learn from interaction, language is still the key" (p. 31) and that students need to be able to use their native language to tap into their experiences and conceptual understanding and to formulate questions. When this is not possible, and no student can speak the students' native language, other kinds of scaffolding and support will need to be used, including charts, pictures, and supportive coaching that allow students lacking in English to begin to contribute to group work.

We encourage students to discuss, organize thoughts, summarize, and generate ideas through social interaction. We often ask groups to write a contract about how they will work together to meet a given assignment. This often involves allowing groups to modify research projects. We provide general topics within the content learning required in the class and ask students what they would like to research; we then group the class based on research topics. The group creates a contract on how they will complete their research.

We also suggest that teachers recognize that language proficiency exists in various levels. A student may have conversational but not academic proficiency in English. The vocabulary of different content areas may have to be explicitly taught to the students. Finally, we recognize the importance of involving the students' parents in their new classroom experiences and try to contact all the parents and explain how we are working to build a classroom community.

How did a teacher use cooperative learning and technology to build community with monolingual Spanish high school students?

John Sandin was a bilingual history teacher charged with helping high school–age monolingual Spanish speakers learn high school content while also developing their English proficiency. Because Sandin was bilingual, he could help the students in their native language while also teaching English language skills. He also had about 15 computers that he could use with the program. While the computers came loaded with several English tutorial programs, he found the use of computers as constructivist tools for the students to be far more powerful. He also used cooperative learning, often pairing the stronger English language speaker with a student weaker in English but strong in terms of using the technology. Each pair or triad of students were responsible for gathering information from the Web about topics such as the weather, news, and/or movies, and then translating this information to weekly newsletters for the class created on the computers.

Sandin decided also to use a project-based learning approach to organize as much of the content as possible around Nuestra Tierra (our land). The students worked in groups to research the people, history, plants, animals, geography, and weather of the area. They were able to go on field trips and take digital pictures. They were taught how to use a multimedia authoring tool to put together their findings about New Mexico, and in the spring of their first year in an American high school, they presented their findings to the community as part of a district presentation in the local downtown mall. The program developed by Sandin, which combined culturally responsive teaching strategies and cooperative learning, resulted in far more students than usual transitioning into the regular high school the next fall.

Building a Professional Community and Technology

How can technology be used to build communities among language teachers?

It seems fitting to end this chapter on culture and community with the suggestion that teachers of English language learners also use technology to build their own community of learning. One important place to start is to use the *TESOL Inc.* website (http://www.tesol.org/index.html) not only to share information about teaching strategies but also to find new job opportunities, opportunities to publish, and resources and ideas for the classroom (see Figure 7.3).

Another popular website for teachers is *Teachnet* (http://www.teachnet. com). On this site, teachers can find information ranging from already developed lesson plans to commentaries from teachers around the world.

Conclusion

This chapter considered the impact of culture on language learning. The use of technology to build cultural literacy was considered as well as the use of technology to build learning environments appropriate to diverse students. Three types of strategies were highlighted: the use of culturally relevant materials; the construc-

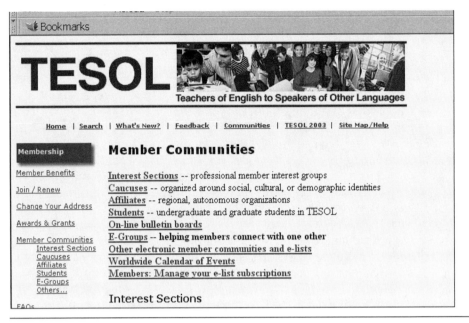

FIGURE 7.3   *Teachnet—Lesson Plans*

Source: Copyright © 2002 by Teachers of English to Speakers of Other Languages. All rights reserved. Reprinted with permission.

tivist uses of technology to support learning; and the use of technology to meet the diverse learning styles of students.

Summary of Key Ideas

1. Current theories of learning such as social constructivism recognize that learning is influenced by the social and cultural context in which it occurs. Language and culture are closely connected. Through the use of technology, students in diverse classrooms can come to know each other's culture while also practicing the target language.

2. Teaching strategies in the mainstream culture may not be a good match for students coming from different cultures. Teachers need to understand the culturally based behavior of their students.

3. There are many differences between cultures that can be seen in day-to-day activities as well as classroom interactions. Using videos, television, and the Web, students can observe and discuss these differences and often talk more comfortably about their own differences.

4. Through the use of digital media, today's students have the opportunity to experience and communicate with people in cultures that are quite different from the ones in which they live.

5. Such multicultural understanding is essential in the United States as the diversity of its classrooms continues to grow. The recent census showed increases in diverse students, especially Hispanic students.

6. Warshauer (1996) suggests that "computer-mediated communication (CMC)—is probably the single computer application to date with the greatest impact on language teaching." He continues by describing how "for the first time, language learners can communicate directly with other learners or speakers of the target language twenty-four hours a day, from school, work, or home" (p. 9)

7. Not only are there important cultural differences between language groups, but in increasingly diverse ELLs classrooms, there are also cultural differences between students within the class. Teachers need to learn how to apply multicultural strategies supported by technology in their classrooms.

8. Three strategies are emphasized for meeting the needs of diverse ELL students: the use of culturally relevant material and culturally esponsive teaching strategies; the importance of providing constructivist learning opportunities; and the meeting of different learning styles. These three are all integrated in a model for technology integration in the multicultural classroom, developed by Ines Chisholm (1998).

9. There are several different kinds of learning styles relevant to working with English language learners. First, there is the issue of cultural differences in what types of learning are valued. Second, learning styles may differ in terms of cognitive processing, specifically whether the students are more global or analytical in their thinking. Third, students may prefer different learning modalities such as auditory, kinesthetic, or visual. Technology provides a natural multiple learning styles environment in which students have choices about how to learn and how to demonstrate their learning.

10. Cooperative learning can be a powerful strategy for ELL students to learn, but it must be carefully designed to require both individual and cooperative tasks and to provide adequate support for language use in a high-demand language situation. One solution is to support students in speaking their home language in order to conceptualize their ideas and problem-solve. If there are no students who speak the same home language, the teacher will have to use sheltering strategies.

Learning Activities

1. A current educational issue is the existence of a digital divide between rich and poor students and schools. The issue involves more than access to technology but suggests that how technology is used is as important as whether it is used. The digital divide applies to family use of technology as well as use in school. The end of this chapter contains on-line resources for studying the digital divide. Students should explore this topic and suggest possible solutions to this problem.

2. There are several examples in this chapter of students using technology to study their homelands and/or other cultures. These range from the use of the Internet to developing multimedia presentations. Ask students in the class to design a project using technology to literally bring different cultures into the classroom.

3. Chisholm offers a model for multicultural technology integration. Discuss this model and what aspects the students in the class might be able to apply in their own classrooms.

4. Consider developing a project-based unit like the one developed by Michele Stafford-Levy for her border high school English class. Be sure to include learning activities that reflect different learning styles and cultural preferences.

Technology Resources

On-line Resources

These on-line resources will be helpful to teachers who want to learn more about using technology to meet the needs of culturally diverse students in the United States:

Becker, H. J. (1992). Equity and the "big picture."' *Technos Quarterly for Education and Technology,* 1 (1). [On-line]. Available: http://www.technos.net/journal/volume1/1becker.htm

Benton Foundation. (1997, July). *An education technology agenda.* [On-line]. Available: http:// www.benton.org/Library/Schools/two.html

Digital Equity Database. http://www.digital_equity.org

Edry, S. L. (1999, February). Bridging the digital divide. Newsweek.com [On-line]. Available: http://www.tbwt.net/misc/bridging_the_digital_divide.htm

Hoffman, D. L,. and Novak, T. P. (1998). Bridging the digital divide: The impact of race on computer access and Internet use. [On-line]. Available: http://www2000.ogsm.vanderbilt.edu/papers/race/science.html

NTIA. (1995). Falling through the net: A survey of the "have-nots" in rural and urban America. *NTIA Publication.* [On-line]. Available: http://www.ntia.doc.gov/ntiahome/net.html

NTIA. (1997). Falling through the net II: New data on the digital divide. *NTIA Publication.* [On-line]. Available: http://www.ntia.doc.gov/ntiahome/net2/falling.html

Tapscott, D. (1998). Closing the digital divide. NewsScan Exec. [On-line]. Available: http:// www.newsscan.com/exec/summer1998/divide.html

References

Armas, G. (2001, February 11). Schools look for help to teach Hispanic population. Associated Press. *Sun-News.*

Becker, H. J. (2000, Fall/Winter). Who's wired and who's not: Children's access to and use of computer technology. *The Future of Children: Children and Computer Technology* 10 (2) [On-line]. Available: www.futureofchildren.org

Bridis, T. (1998, July). "Digital divide" widens between whites and minorities. *Associated Press* [On-line]. Available: http://students.uww.edu/stdorgs/bsu/digital.htm

Chisholm, I. M. (1998). Six elements for technology integration in multicultural classrooms. *Journal of Information Technology Education* 7: 247–268.

Cohen, E. G. (1994) *Designing Groupwork: Strategies for the Heterogeneous Classroom* (2nd ed.). New York: Teachers College Press.

Cummins, J., and Sayers, D. (1995). *Brave New Schools: Challenging Cultural Illiteracy Through Global Learning Networks.* New York: St. Martin's Press.

Damen, L. (1988). *Culture Learning: The Fifth Dimension in the Language Classroom.* Reading, MA: Addison-Wesley.

Darder, A., Ingle, Y. R., and Cox, B. G. (1993). *The Policies and the Promise: The Public Schooling of Latino Children.* Claremont, CA: Thomas Rivera Center.

Eisner, E. W. (1994). *Cognition and Curriculum Reconsidered.* New York: Teachers College Press.

Faltis, C. (1997). *Joinfostering: Adapting Teaching for the Multilingual Classroom* (2nd ed.). New York: Merrill.

Fosnot, C. (1989). *Enquiring Teachers Enquiring Learners: A Constructivist Approach to Teaching Teachers.* New York: Teachers College Press.

Furstenberg, G., Levet, S., English, K., and Maillet, K. (2001). Giving a virtual voice to the silent language of culture: The Cultura Project. *Language Learning and Technology* 5 (1): 55–102.

Gardner, H. (1985). *Frames of Mind.* New York: Basic Books.

Gray, R., and Stockwell, G. (1998). Using computer mediated communication for language and culture acquisition. In On-Call (vol. 12 CALL-EJ online). http://www.cltr.uq.edu.au/oncall/gray123.html. Retrieved April 23, 2002.

Gebhard, J. (1996). *Teaching English as a Foreign or Second Language.* Ann Arbor, MI: University of Michigan Press.

Goldenberg, C., and Gallimore, R. (1991). Local knowledge, research knowledge, and educational change: A case study of early Spanish reading improvement. *Educational Researcher* 20 (8): 2–14.

Herrold, W. (1989, Fall). Brain research: Brain-compatible learning. *Educational Horizons.*

Hodgkinson, H. L. (1992) *A Demographic Look at Tomorrow.* Washington, DC: The Institute for Educational Leadership. (Information Analyses No. ERIC ED 359 087).

Johnson, D. W., and Johnson, R. T. (1990). *Cooperation and Competition: Theory and Research.* Edina, MN: Interaction Book Company.

Johnson, D. W., and Johnson, R. T. (1994). *Learning Together and Alone* (4th ed.). Boston: Allyn and Bacon.

Joyce, B., and Weil, M. (1996). *Models of Teaching* (5th ed.). Boston: Allyn and Bacon.

Joyce, B., Weil, M., and Showers, B. (1992). *Models of Teaching* (4th ed.). Boston: Allyn and Bacon.

Kinsella, K. (1996, Autumn). Designing group work that supports and enhances diverse classroom work styles. *TESOL Journal* 6 (1): 24–31.

Krachen, S. (1982). *Principles and Practice in Second Language Acquisition.* Oxford: Pergamon Press.

Moll, L., and Greenberg, J. B. (1992). Creating zones possibilities: Combining social contexts for instruction. In L. Moll (Ed.), *Vygotsky and Education: Instructional Implications and Applications of Socio-Historical Psychology* (pp. 319–348). New York: Cambridge University Press.

Moll, L., Arlmanti, C., Neff, D., and Gonzales, N. (1992). Funds of knowledge for teaching: Using a qualitative approach to connect homes and classrooms. *Theory into Practice* 31 (2): 132–141.

Nelson, R. G. (1995). Cultural differences in learning styles. In I. M. Reid (Ed.), *Learning Styles in the ESL/EFL Classroom* (pp. 3–18). Boston: Heinle & Heinle.

Norton, P., and Wiburg, K. (1998). *Teaching with Technology.* Fort Worth, TX: Harcourt Brace.

Nunan, D. (1996, Autumn). Learner strategy: Training in the classroom: An action research study. *TESOL Journal,* pp. 35–41.

Olmedo, I. (1993, Summer). Junior historians: Doing oral history with ESL and bilingual students. *TESOL Journal,* pp. 7–10.

Ortmeir, C. (2000, Spring). Project Homeland: Crossing cultural boundaries in the ESL classroom. *TESOL Journal,* pp. 10–17.

Palinscar, A. S., and Brown, A. L. (1984). Reciprocal teaching of comprehension-fostering and comprehension-monitoring activities. *Cognition and Instruction* 1 (2): 117–175.

Putney, L., and Wink, J. (1997.) Breaking rules: Constructing avenues of access in multilingual classrooms. *TESOL Journal* 7 (3): 29–34.

Rosen, L. (1995). City Net: Travel the world from your desktop. In M. Warschauer (Ed.), *Virtual Connections: Online Activities and Projects for Networking Language Learners* (p. 308). Honolulu: University of Hawaii Press.

Rosen, L. (1995). Metro your way around. In M. Warschauer (Ed.), *Virtual Connections: Online Activities and Projects for Networking Language Learners* (p. 310). Honolulu: University of Hawaii Press.

Rosen, L. (1995). World news abroad. In M. Warschauer (Ed.), *Virtual Connections: Online Activities and Projects for Networking Language Learners* (p. 268). Honolulu: University of Hawaii Press.

Scarcella, R. (1990). *Teaching Language Minority Students in the Multicultural Classroom* (p. 183). Upper Saddle River, NJ: Prentice Hall Regents.

Slavin, R. E. (1991). Are cooperative learning and "untracking" harmful to the gifted? *Educational Leadership* 48 (6): 68–70.

Soo, K. S. (1999). Theory and research: Learning styles, motivation, and the ESL classroom. In J. Egbert, and E. Hanson-Smith (Eds.), *CALL Environments: Research, Practice, and Critical Issues.* Alexandria, VA: TESOL, Inc.

Stafford-Levy, M., and Wiburg, K. (2001, January) Multicultural technology integration: The winds of change amid the sands of time. *Computers in Schools.*

Tharp, R. (1989, February). Psychocultural variables and constants: Effects on teaching and learning in schools. *American Psychologist* 4 (2): 349–359.

Tharp, R. G., and Gallimore, R. (1990). *Rousing Minds to Life: Teaching, Learning, and Schooling in Social Context.* New York: Cambridge University Press. (Original work published in 1988).

Tiene, D., and Ingram, A. (2001). *Exploring Current Issues in Educational Technology.* Boston: McGraw-Hill.

Vygotsky, L. S. (1962). *Thought and Language.* Cambridge, MA: MIT Press.

Warshauer, M. (1996). An Introduction. In S. Fotos (Ed.), *Multimedia Language Teaching* (pp. 3–20). Tokyo: Logos International.

Wertsch, J. V. (1979). From social interaction to higher psychological process: A clarification and application of Vygotsky's theory. *Human Development* 22: 1–22.

Wetzel, K., and Chisholm, I. (1998). An evaluation of technology integration in teacher education for bilingual and English as a second language education majors. *Journal of Research on Computing in Education* 30 (4): 379–397.

White, M. (1986). Synthesis of research on electronic learning. *The Information Age Classroom,* pp. 17–25.

Willetts, K. (1992). *Technology and Second Language Learning.* ERIC Digest. ERIC Document Reproduction Service ED 350883.

Willis, J., Stephens, E., & Matthew, K. (1996). *Technology, Reading and Language Arts.* Boston: Allyn and Bacon.

8

Assessment and Second Language Teaching

Chapter Overview

The purpose of this chapter is to suggest ways to assess student learning in alignment with the teaching methodologies described in this book. The different strategies for teaching English language learners (ELLs) are reviewed and tied to appropriate assessment strategies. It should be noted that our philosophy of teaching assumes that classroom assessment is most appropriate when it is embedded in instruction, and therefore references to evaluating learning are also found within other chapters. However, this chapter summarizes our approach to the assessment of English language learners and provides additional background on assessment. It is grounded in a short discussion of the changing nature of assessment and the influence of technology on the teaching, learning, and assessment process. Assessment is then reviewed in relationship to the attributes for successful technology-enhanced language learning environments that were introduced in the first chapter.

Reflections on the Nintendo Principle

I'm sorry I can't remember the name of the speaker I heard at a 1980s conference on restructuring education who first suggested what became a guiding principle for my work in connecting teaching and assessment. She suggested that teachers and curriculum designers should follow *The Nintendo Principle*. This principle states that every instructional activity should have embedded within it enough feedback so that students always know how they are doing. The idea, of course, comes from watching kids engaged in learning as they manipulate computer game environments to meet the goals of the game. At the heart of the engagement is the continuous feedback that occurs as students are allowed to rapidly try out different actions. The more engaging games come with complex problems that can be solved by the player in a variety of different ways and provide higher levels of challenge as the learner gains new skills.

This principle reflects a growing movement over the last 10 years toward instructional assessment. Yet, the metaphor, borrowed from interactive technology, is particularly powerful. The Nintendo Principle seems especially appropriate in language learning environments because learning a language requires opportunities for continuous practice, user control, and friendly feedback. Technology applications whether they are games, simulations, or productivity tools provide rich learning and assessment opportunities. The key for the second language teacher is to design the use of technology so that students gain control over their learning and opportunities for feedback on how they are doing.

Throughout this book we have suggested a variety of strategies for designing powerful language learning environments for the K–12 and college classroom. However, these environments will only succeed in improving learning if they are connected to assessment strategies that support them. As understandings about how people learn have expanded and as new technologies have made complex learning more accessible, new kinds of assessment are both possible and necessary. In this chapter we will look at these new forms of assessment as they apply to second language learning.

From Traditional Testing to Alternative Assessment

What are some of the problems with traditional testing?

Eisner (1994, 1999) suggests the serious limitations of a curriculum built only around behavioral objectives. When students and their teachers are evaluated on the basis of prespecified behavioral objectives, the performances that can be expected are limited to small units of behavior. Herman, Aschbacher, and Winters (1992) share Eisner's concerns and wonder if the standardized tests so often used in districts today are measuring the kinds of significant learning outcomes we want for our students. Wilson and Davis (1994) suggest that "standardized exams measure the kinds of knowledge that are becoming steadily less relevant to our definition of education" (p. 140). Darling-Hammond (1997), in a book on creating schools that work, suggests, "Focusing on testing without investing in organizational learning is rather like taking a patient's temperature over and over again without taking the necessary steps to promote greater health" (p. 241).

Chao (1999) talks about her experiences as a girl with traditional assessment in the English language learning classroom. Such assessment consisted primarily of vocabulary tests out of context and discrete multiple-choice options:

> Every week I took at least one vocabulary test, which normally included a long list of lexical items. The teacher would stand in the front of the classroom, carefully and slowly uttering the foreign words one by one. The girl sitting next to me would write furiously on her paper, but, unable to think of anything to write, I could only stare at the white piece of paper. (p. 243)

Functioning well in a second language requires much more than understanding isolated grammar and vocabulary. To be proficient in a language, it is also necessary to understand how language functions and to be able to use the language communicatively in different settings and for a variety of purposes (Brown, 1994). This reconceptualization of language learning implies a quite different approach to assessment than that experienced by Chao.

Fortunately, there is a growing and dynamic movement to provide expanded forms of authentic assessment. This movement speaks to the limitations of traditional testing, especially for English language learners, while advocating alternative assessment grounded in new theories of learning and assisted by technology. As Cummins mentions in the foreword to a book by O'Malley and Pierce (1996) on assessment for English language learners, testing and issues of diversity have a long and painful history ranging from the use of IQ tests to weed out "feeble-minded aliens" to the disproportionately large number of ELL students who have been placed in special education classes.

Why do some people consider standardized tests unfair?

The use of standardized tests is increasing. According to the U.S. Congress, Office of Technology and Assessment [OTA] (1992), revenues from standardized tests doubled between 1960 and 1989, while enrollment in schools only increased by 15 percent. The Educational Testing Service itself claims that there is *Too Much Testing of the Wrong Kind; Too Little of the Right Kind in K–12 Education* (ETS, 2000). The ETS article suggests that in the 1980s and 1990s it was elected officials—governors and state legislators—not educators, who have continued to press for more testing and that the original purpose in using standardized tests (i.e., evaluating programs and sampling student learning) is lost in a political bandwagon. Many voices in the evaluation field are now questioning the increased use of standardized, norm-referenced testing as the primary source for making decisions about student placement, grading, and achievement or the effectiveness of educational programs.

One concern raised by educators is that national standardized tests are often misaligned with the curriculum, affecting the students' opportunities to learn the material on which they will be tested (Madaus, 1991). For a test to be fair, it must match the curriculum and instruction that the tested students actually received. The Mathematical Sciences Education Board (1993) calls for the testing community to conscientiously rethink what is tested, how testing is done, and the effects caused by this testing. The board defines this concept as the *equity principle*. Every student must have the opportunity to learn the important concepts that are being tested in order for testing to be equitable. This is especially true when high-stakes decisions are made on the results of tests, such as graduation, promotion, or admission to restricted programs. In addition, students whose test scores are low are tracked into classes that emphasize drill on isolated facts and instruction, focusing on a narrow range of learning and lower-order cognitive skills (Darling-Hammond, 1994).

The problem of standardized testing is compounded for students from low socioeconomic and minority cultural groups who are more negatively affected by these tests than students from the dominant culture (Lacelle-Peterson and Rivera, 1994; Lam and Gordan, 1992; Cummins, 1996). A variety of factors influence lower test scores for students who are not proficient in English, including stylistic and interpretive language differences, time pressure, and cultural differences (Garcia and Pearson, 1993; Geisinger and Carlson, 1992; Harmon, 1995). Since our classrooms are becoming increasingly diverse (Lam and Gordan, 1992; *Newsweek,* 2000), it is important that the assessments used are supportive of education for all students.

How do theories of learning and technology use relate to assessment?

Traditional learning theories were grounded in behavioral theory, which was based on how well the student could master small units of information and provide evidence of this learning on objective and decontextualized tests. This orientation reflects Chao's early experiences with language testing. The newer social and cognitive constructivist views of learning emphasizes not just the product of learning, but the importance of cognitive processing by the learner and the influence of affective, social, and cultural factors on learning. The roots of modern learning theory can be found in the work of Piaget (1972) and Vygotsky (1962, 1978). Piaget, as a result of his work with assessment, became interested in how children learn developmentally and socially. Vygotsky suggested that learning occurs as a result of meaningful, social interaction. He questioned traditional testing, wondering about the educational usefulness of evaluating a student on the basis of what he already knows. Instead, Vygotsky claimed that all learners move through a zone of proximal development and can demonstrate a range of abilities, depending on the social and cultural context in which the learner is working. Vygotsky was interested in what a student could do in an intellectually supportive environment, not what the student might score on a test taken after the solution to a problem had been memorized.

It was also Vygotsky, over 50 years ago, who introduced the notion of mediation in learning. This mediation involves the social context in which learning is occurring, but it also includes a less mentioned aspect of Vygotskian theory—the use of tools as mediating factors (Rosa and Montero, 1990). As the student in a situational context begins to solve problems, various tools, including technology, can play an important role in the learning process. Technology can be used not only to assist in finding and evaluating information, allowing the manipulation of variables in simulations, but also as a media for storing evaluative information about the student. Newer networked environments store learners' interactions as they work together on-line or in shared writing spaces in the classroom.

What makes a student smart?

Work in intelligence theory has also influenced the development of a new pedagogy with its attendant requirement for new assessment (Gardner, 1985; Sternberg, 1994). Gardner suggests that there are at least seven different types of intelligence, only two of which (logical/analytical and verbal) have traditionally been taught or tested in schools. Sternberg describes the complex interplay of the different mental components that influence thinking and learning. *Metacognition,* for example, or the ability of a person to manage and think about his or her learning, is now recognized as an essential component of powerful learning yet is rarely measured on tests. Sternberg's notion of practical intelligence is also considered an important aspect of learning, especially as applied to real-world problems.

It is now generally recognized that each learner learns differently, organizing and synthesizing information into his or her own unique knowledge structures and schemas. To assess this more complex type of learning, evaluation must include an assessment of the learning *process* as well as product. The context for learning must also be considered, since we now know that learning is situational and cultural (Brown, Collins, and Duguid, 1988). Students learn best when instruction and assessment are related to what is meaningful to them and operate in a context with which they are familiar (Brown, 1995; Darling-Hammond, 1994). Finally, students are given the best chance to demonstrate what they know when they are provided with choices of how they want to represent and communicate their ideas. In addition, in language learning environments students benefit from opportunities to work collaboratively to solve problems and present information. Assessment of group work is a growing area of interest in the evaluation community.

Technology tools such as multimedia and telecommunications provide access to multiple resources and audiences and are just two examples of the many ways technology can support assessment within a constructivist, computer-rich learning environment. While technology has been useful in the past in making traditional assessment and evaluation more efficient, the stronger potential of technology is to support the new forms of alternative assessment, such as electronic portfolios, and performance. Newer alternative forms of assessment are discussed later in this chapter.

What is the alternative assessment movement?

Current movements in assessment reverse the emphasis on testing over learning. Educational researchers and writers have responded to what is perceived as a national need for new standards and alternative forms of assessment by becoming part of a growing movement for alternative assessment (Berklak et al.,

1992; Kulm and Malcom, 1991; Eisner, 1999). These educators are likely to begin with what is most worth learning and then move to assessment rather than have testing drive what students should be learning. Wiggins, a well-known leader in evaluation, suggests, "It's a common-sense case that says if we value it, we should assess it; if we don't assess it, we won't get it" (Hart, 1994, p. 11).

There is no single agreed upon definition of *alternative assessment*. It has been described as an alternative to standardized testing and all of the problems found with standardized, multiple-choice testing, such as not testing what students are learning, or testing in a biased fashion (Huerta-Macias, 1995). Knapp and Glenn (1996) suggest that "assessment is alternative when the tasks used in testing are equal or similar to the best tasks found in instruction" and when students are engaged in "using the knowledge and skills to solve the kinds of problems and do the kinds of things students will face in the world outside school" (p. 64). Hart (1994) prefers the term *authentic assessment*, which she defines as "assessment that both mirrors and measures students' performance in 'real life' tasks and situations" (p. 105). For example, if we want students to communicate effectively in writing, the authentic way to assess them is to evaluate actual samples of their writing.

Herman, Ausbacher, and Winters (1992) suggest that terms like *alternative assessment, authentic assessment,* and *performance-based assessment* are used synony-mously to mean variants of performance assessments that require students to *generate* rather than choose a response. The ability to generate communication in the target language is an important theoretical construct in communicative language teaching. As this goal has become more important, a different kind of assessment has emerged. Brown and Hudson (1998) describe how *alternatives in assessment* (their term) have developed in the language testing field.

> From discrete-point tests like the multiple-choice and true-false tests used predom-inantly in the 1950s and 1960s, to the integrative tests like cloze and dictation used in the 1970s and early 1980s, to the more communicative tests like task-based and other new assessments used in the 1980s and 1990s, language testers have tried out, researched, and argued about a wide variety of different types of tests. A variety of forms are available, including performance assessment, portfolio assessment, infor-mal assessment, situated, or conceptualized assessment, and assessment by exhibi-tion. (p. 657)

The authors then summarize some of the questions that have been asked about the purpose and reliability of tests and conclude "but the one idea that seems to get lost in the shuffle is that virtually all of the various test types are successful for some purpose, somewhere, sometime" (p. 657).

In summary, several common themes run through all alternative assessment efforts. First, process is as important as product and the students' explanations of how they developed, changed, or created a product as important as the product itself. Second, alternative assessment is instructionally based and relatively nonin-trusive. Assessment is built into the instructional tasks students are performing and used as criteria for continuously improving that performance. Third, alternative assessment seeks to provide students with expanded opportunities to demonstrate what they know. Students are evaluated on what they can produce, explain, or show, rather than on what they can recall or reproduce. Technology-mediated learning environments provide powerful ways to support new types of alternative assessment. Multimedia tools are useful for providing students with multiple ways to demonstrate and communicate their knowledge. Electronic writing spaces and portfolios can be used to save student work. Electronically stored work supports students in later revisiting and revising the work and assists the teacher, students, administrators, and parents in reviewing progress in learning over time.

How can technology support alternative assessment?

Wiburg (Norton and Wiburg, 1998) describes how she first discovered the importance of technology for providing time to assess student thinking when she was in the familiar role of the education professor supervising a student teacher.

> One day while visiting a student teacher, I found the pre-service teacher with a group of fourth-grade students in the computer lab using Sunburst's The Factory, a problem-solving program. In The Factory, students arrange a series of machines in such a way that running a blank square through the machines results in a design that matches a given model. To accomplish this, the students were arranging representational machines which could turn, strip, or punch the raw material in what they thought would be the correct sequence. As I entered the classroom, I noticed that the students were working in pairs at the computers and were quite engrossed in the task. A low buzz of self-talk, typical of children engaged in problem solving, was heard (Vygotsky, 1978).
>
> Observing the children, it occurred to me that assessing a teacher candidate in a situation that involved students using technology for problem solving would be quite different from evaluating a student teacher lecturing from the front of a classroom. In this new situation, while students were problem solving, there was actually time for the student teacher and myself to walk around and listen to the students talk as they manipulated a problem solving software program. Afterward we could talk not only about the teacher's presentation but also how she had designed the learning environment and how different students were interacting with that environment. (pp. 232–233)

More recently we observed a bilingual classroom using the program *Inspiration* as a support for thinking about a short book the students had read. *Inspiration* is a graphical organizer program that provides constructivist thinking tools for students, without requiring extensive English language skills. Pictures are abundant and can help students explain their ideas about the main character, the plot, and the setting of the story, which was about a young Spanish-speaking girl growing up in a United States/Mexico border city.

> Maria Lopez, the teacher, was skilled as managing her technology-enriched elementary classroom so that students worked in small groups on different projects and rotated easily through carefully designed centers. At the beginning of the day, she introduced the learning tasks by

using a graphical organizer that she projected from the teacher computer onto a large screen. The tasks were illustrated in four boxes with pictures and labeled with Tasks 1, 2, 3, and 4. They included meeting at the center table to do a drawing of Gloria, the main character in the story. On one side of a piece of paper students would draw a picture of her face and on the other the inside of her mind. The students were to draw pictures representing what the character might have been thinking about. Another group was working in *Inspiration* using an already developed template (see Figure 8.1) for describing a character in the story. A third group met with Ms. Lopez and discussed and drew attributes of one of the story's characters, while the fourth group learned more about the advanced functions of *Inspiration* from a classroom volunteer.

Because technology as well as other hands-on task-based activities supported the students in their work, the teacher and ourselves as observers were able to move around and interact with the students. The *Inspiration* program itself, because of an abundance of pictures and graphical tools, made it easy for all students to begin to express ideas about the story they were hearing and reading. The work they were doing was easily saved as part of an electronic portfolio and could be compared with more complex work on story analysis later in the year.

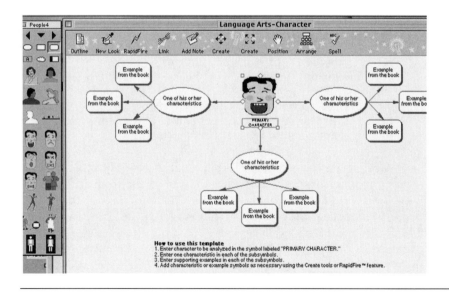

FIGURE 8.1   Character Template

Source: Used with permission from Exploring Inspiration®, an interactive training CD-ROM, published by Inspiration Software, Inc.

Standards-Based Instruction and Assessment

As part of a national educational reform effort to improve student learning, many national organizations (NCTM, 1993; NRC, 1996; TESOL, 1997) as well as states have developed content-based standards (see http://mathstar.nmsu.edu/standards for additional standards information). The purpose behind the standards-based movement is to provide students with a high-level curriculum focused on important ideas in each of the academic disciplines. The intention of standards-based instruction is to help all students to gain a deeper understanding of content and demonstrate high achievement.

Teachers of English language learners in the content classroom can benefit from learning to teach and assess using the standards. Teacher professional development in the area of standards-based instruction is aimed at moving teachers from dependence on textbooks and isolated activities to a focus on the big ideas in a discipline, moving away from a textbook and activity-based curriculum to one that is content driven. Since standards focus on what students need to know and be able to do, a strong emphasis on instructional assessment is also required. When working with teachers to develop standards-based instruction, we encourage them to start with unifying ideas and concepts, then to attach relevant national and/or state standards, and next to move directly to performance assessment. Specific activities are developed only after the standards and performance assessment is clear. An example of this approach to unit planning can be found in the interactive website shown in Figure 8.2, developed as part of a professional development project for implementing standards-based mathematics instruction.

Assessing the Attributes of Successful Language Learning Environments

What are the attributes of successful language learning environments and how can they be assessed? How can technology help in implementing these assessments? How can new interactive technologies assist in evaluating student learning?

The rest of this chapter is organized around the design of assessment strategies supported by technology for each of the attributes of successful language learning environments that were introduced in Chapter 1. Each attribute is introduced briefly and uses examples from the text. Questions about assessment related to the attribute are suggested followed by specific examples of assessment strategies.

It is important to point out technology's dual role in assessment. The existence of computer-based learning environments helps support alternative approaches to assessment simply because these types of environments support project-based and product-based learning. It is easier, with the use of technology, to develop products that demonstrate what students have learned and then to develop related rubrics,

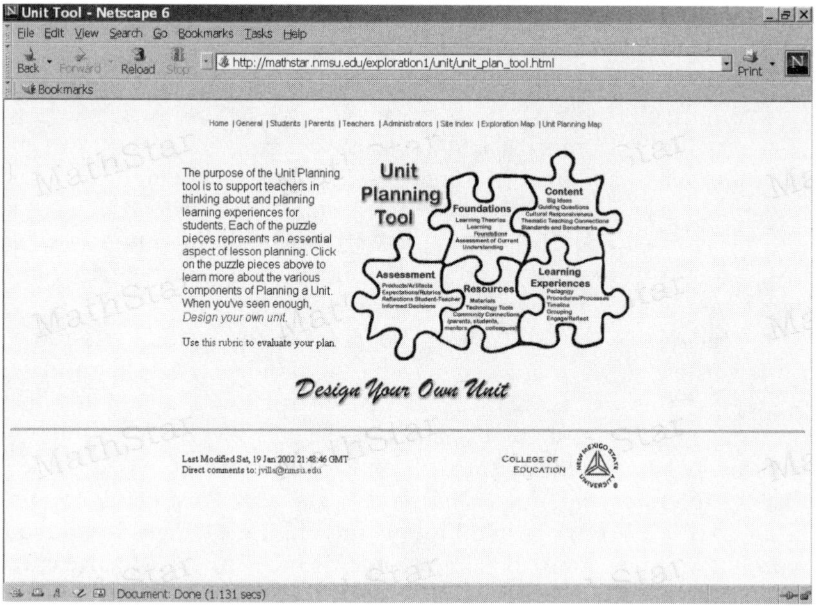

FIGURE 8.2   Unit Planning Tool (mathstar.nmsu.edu)
Source: Used with permission.

checklists, or other forms of alternative assessments for evaluating student learning. Because of the Web, it is also easier to connect students to real-world audiences that can play an important role in assessment at a distance. For example, this is seen in the assessment of students' marketing designs by members of a distant marketing firm. A second role for technology in assessment involves the ease with which teachers, administrators, students, and parents can save and access stored information about student learning. The new computer-based technologies make it easy to store information related to student learning in electronic forms such as a log of an on-line dialog, a student electronic portfolio, records of email communication or student-created Web pages. One can then access, manipulate, communicate, and evaluate the stored information.

How Can the Teacher Assess Communicative Activities Involving Interaction with Real Audiences?

Technology affords the opportunity for students to communicate with a meaningful audience at a distance. Student messages to their email pals can be easily saved within the electronic mail program and analyzed by the student and the teacher in terms of communicative skills. Teachers that involve students in writing to a real audience recognize that student writing is often clearer and contains more detail than their writing when they are just writing for the teacher. Writing for an audience also provides an opportunity for students to generate a lot of their own text. Analysis of student text in these situations also helps teachers and students to analyze common language errors. Such errors can provide information about what kinds of skills-oriented computer-based programs might help them to improve their skills.

Telecommunications environments also support analysis of the levels of participation in chat rooms or bulletin board systems. For example when using the *Web-CT (Web-Course Tools)* program, the teacher can post a question to a bulletin board for all students to answer. Students reply to the question and their answers can be read by all the students. Students can also reply to the teacher or to other students or compose their own questions for the classroom group. The *Web-CT* program saves the answers and the teachers can create saved threaded discussions that support analysis of student conversations. The program also keeps track of how often students log on to the Web-based environment, what sites they visit, and in some cases how long they stay.

How Can the Teacher Assess Student Comprehension of Input?

English language learners need to be exposed to a sufficient amount of language that is understandable to them or they become discouraged about learning the target language. In Sheila Hills's multimedia classroom (highlighted in the first chapter), input was made more comprehensible through the use of a well-designed multimedia authoring program. Specifically, as students developed a presentation on President Washington, their comprehension of historical events was supported by the presence of maps, pictures, and time lines made possible in the *Point of View* software.

In Chapter 4 on listening and speaking skills, students working to improve listening comprehension used a multimedia language program that allowed them to listen to text, click on a related picture, print text or adjust the speed of the spoken dialog. The program could also provide the beginning language listener with simple and more comprehensible sentence structures. Eventually students could listen and comprehend without the scaffolding provided by the computer program. Such environments realize Vygotsky's notion of the zone of proximal development required for learning. Students begin by listening with support and move toward independent listening comprehension.

Simple Dictation. Student listening comprehension can then be examined using *simple dictation,* either provided with the program or developed by the teacher, who could model this dictation on the conversations used in the computer program. The teacher, after getting familiar with the content and context of the conversation, can design additional dictation exercises that will assess student listening comprehension.

Teacher Action Research.   The availability of new computer-based listening and speaking environments lends itself well to teacher action research. An experienced teacher should carefully observe students as they interact with the program and determine if the scaffolding is helping to provide more comprehensible input. The teacher might ask the students which aspects of the multimedia program are most useful to them. Education is one of the few fields in which practitioners are not the ones doing research and developing policy. This is changing as there is growing movement in getting teachers involved in research (Sagor, 1993). One of the best ways to make positive changes in classroom environments is to get teachers involved in asking and answering questions about their own students' learning.

Observation Protocols.   There are also opportunities for the teacher to assess both the classroom and the instructional materials used within an observation protocol such as the Sheltered Instruction Observation Protocol (SIOP) model (Echevarria, Vogt, and Short, 2000). The SIOP provides an observational tool for the teacher to assess their own or another's environment in terms of behaviors theorized to lead to increased comprehensibility of content for ELLs. Behaviors involving preparation, lesson delivery, and review can also be assessed in terms of the level of evidence. For example, comprehensible input is accessed as shown in Figure 8.3).

What is interesting as more and more technology is used in the language learning classroom is the need to apply such assessments not only to teacher and student behaviors but also to the instructional materials themselves. For example, does an environment that includes video examples assist language learners more than just providing them with a series of pictures? What kinds of pictures seem to help students learn language? Such research is only beginning but promises to be important as increasingly powerful computers offer more comprehensive multimedia language learning environments.

FIGURE 8.3   *Excerpt from the SIOP Model*

Comprehensible Input	4	3	2	1	0	NA
Speech appropriate for students; proficiency level (e.g. slower rate and enunciation, and simple sentence structure for beginners)						
Explanation of academic tasks clear						
Uses a variety of **techniques** to make content concepts clear (e.g. modeling, visuals, hands-on activities, demonstrations, gestures, body language)						

Source: Echevarria, Vogt, and Short (1999: 181–182).

How Can a Teacher Assess the Impact of Technology-Mediated Instruction on Cognitive Abilities?

Technology supports high-level cognitive processing even while students are still learning the target language. In Chapter 6 we focused specifically on teaching thinking in the ELL classroom and how technology could provide rich opportunities for thinking with low language demands. In Chapter 3 sheltering strategies for content learning included the use of visual problem-solving environments that engaged students in developing their cognitive abilities. One such example was the use of drawing tools to explore fractions.

Daniel Villa introduced a fraction workspace on a large overhead projection system. He demonstrated how to draw, duplicate, color, and manipulate the unit shapes he drew to create different fraction pictures. The students were able to think about fractions by manipulating these visual objects and then showing what they had discovered. While some students worked on the computer using the computer-based manipulatives, others worked with paper strips, folding them to create different fractions and then comparing their strips to find equivalent fractions. A third group was busy creating fraction war game cards they could use at home to practice naming and comparing fractions. A fourth group met with Mr. Villa to do some group problem-solving using fractions. The problems were based on real-world events like dividing up cupcakes for birthday parties.

Mr. Villa assessed his students' progress by examining what they created using the different media. He could easily assess their understanding of fractions by examining what they constructed. He saved their computer-based and paper constructions for the students' math portfolios. He moved among the groups, often asking students to show him different fractions and equivalent fractions using the computer or paper manipulatives. As a reflective teacher, he also asked himself questions about the lessons, such as the following:

- Did students find it easier to understand equivalent fractions after folding paper and comparing concrete objects?
- Could they transfer their knowledge from hands-on manipulatives to the representational fraction shapes created using the drawing tool?
- After working with fractions and creating fraction problems using different media, did their knowledge hold when presented with new fraction problems?
- Could they generate original problems involving fractions and provide correct answers for these problems?
- Examples of their solving new fraction problems were saved for their portfolios. Students also wrote about their work with fractions and saved examples of their drawn pictures in their electronic math portfolios.

Creating Student Math Portfolios.   At the end of the fraction unit, Mr. Villa sat down with the students and helped them assemble their final fraction portfolio. The student and the teacher chose products that documented the student's growing understanding of fraction concepts such as equivalent fractions, and adding or dividing fractions. Sometimes other adults in the school were asked to look at and comment on student work. The fraction portfolios were shared with the parents during the fall conference period and also displayed at open house.

How Can the Second Language Teacher Assess Student Learning When Students Are Engaged in Task-Based Activities?

In Chapter 2 we introduced the idea of using Web-based activities to support collaborative solutions to tasks. It was suggested that the most effective type of task-based instruction for second language learners requires them to negotiate meaning to accomplish a real-world communicative task. An example was provided involving students in adult ESL classes throughout northern California who participated in a project that asked them to collect and report information on job pay and housing costs in their respective communities. In such a complex learning environment it is not easy for the teacher to assess what students are learning. One way of doing this is to engage students in creating checklists and/or rubrics that they and the teacher can use to analyze both the process and product of the learning task.

Supporting Student Self-Assessment.   In this case, the Web-based task itself was well-structured by the sponsors of the learning project. Students were asked to provide very specific information such as high and low rents for two or three bedroom apartments, and high and low wages for very specific jobs. They were also asked to provide information on the cost of bus fare and the price of a gallon of gas. Because the students were new to self-assessment, the teacher scaffolded the process for them. After dividing her class into small groups, the teacher assigned the students their first assessment task. They must make a careful list of all the information they must find out and, for each of the items, determine how they will find the information. Each group will share their list with the class and ask for feedback. The final checklist indicating what information should be collected will be compiled by the teacher and passed out to the students.

As the students work on the project and compile data from their research, the teacher will work with them to analyze the data. She has made sure that they understand the notions of mean, median, and what to do with outlying data. Their final project will be to explain, based on their information gathering and analysis, where they would like to live and why, based on the data. Working with their teacher they will develop a rubric to evaluate this product. Criteria on the rubric might include completing all of the data requests, providing conclusions based on the data they gathered, accuracy in their mathematics, ability to explain their choices, and ability to suggest alternative suggestions and evaluate them. Groups will then share their final project, not only on-line, but also in the classroom and with their school.

How Do Different Sheltering Strategies Enhance Student Content Learning?

Throughout this book we have provided examples of sheltering strategies for teaching content to English language learners. Sheltered instruction presents academic content in ways that make it comprehensible to the English language learner (ELL). Chapter 3 has a specific focus on sheltering strategies including bridging, modeling, schema-building, text-representation, metacognitive development, and the use of representational manipulatives. The chapter also focuses on how each of these strategies can be supported with technology within a new framework called *TESI (technology enhanced sheltered instruction)*.

For example, *bridging* is a strategy for connecting students' previous experiences and their cultures with new information. The new computer-based maps available on-line support using bridging strategies in a sheltered social studies class. The teachers can bring up these maps and ask students to point to places where they or members of their families have lived.

Graphical organizers can help students to build schemas related to language and concepts. Using a program like *Inspiration* or *PowerPoint*, students can build graphical diagrams with pictures that help support learning content in a new language. The examples given in Chapter 3 included developing a vocabulary graphic and working on notions of community by learning while using an interactive visual representation of a community.

Technology can also be used to support the assessment of student content learning. After hearing a sheltered lecture or reading information enhanced by visuals, the student could be asked to *re-present* the material as a graphical organizer or by building a slide show using *PowerPoint*. For example, a middle school student who is learning English is also learning in a sheltered social studies class about the branches of the U.S. government. He or she is asked to create a *PowerPoint* presentation that explains these three branches and their characteristics. Such graphical representations can also be used to assess student learning. A semi-structured graphical organizer can be created to assess content learning in which students are given spaces to fill in additional information about the three branches of government.

Creating Rubrics.   The teacher might create a four-point rubric for evaluating the student presentation for the topic described above. See Figure 8.4 as an example of a rubric. This example shows one way to create an assessment rubric. The teacher created this rubric by first specifying the elements that would be present in an ideal response to an assignment. This ideal response, a level four, is described in terms of the desired elements. A level three would contain all but one of the elements, and a level two would contain two of the four elements. A level one would indicate the student attempted the project but was only able to complete one or less of the elements.

According to Arter and McTighe (2001), "Performance criteria are guidelines, rules, or principles by which student responses, products or performances are

FIGURE 8.4   *Sample Rubric*

---

4. The student (a) accurately represents the legislative, judicial, and executive branches and the rules and structure associated with each; (b) uses graphics appropriately to enhance textual information; (c) creates at least a five-slide presentation that includes a title page, a page on each of the branches of the government, and a bibliography page that includes references to additional information that supports the presentation; (d) creates a presentation that works and includes transitions and an attractive lay-out.

3. The student meets at least three of the four elements as presented in a level 4 rubric.

2. The student represents at least two of the four elements listed in this rubric.

1. The student attempts the presentation but only partially meets the elements in the rubric.

---

judged. They describe what to look for in student performances or products to judge quality" (p. 4). Criteria communicate goals and achievement levels and make public what is expected of students. A rubric is a particular format for a criteria—it is the written down version of the criteria. The best rubrics according to Arter and McTighe (2001) "are worded in a way that covers the essence of what we, as teachers, look for when we're judging quality, and they reflect the best thinking in the field as to what constitutes good performances" (p. 8).

There are many different types of rubrics. One common distinction is that made between holistic and analytic rubrics. Which form of evaluation should be used is dependent on the purpose of the evaluation. Holistic rubrics give an overall evaluation of a product or performance without analyzing individual strengths and weaknesses. Holistic rubrics are often used when the purpose is to get a quick overall evaluation of the student's abilities. Figure 8.5 is a rubric used for evaluating final essay exams at the college level.

The purpose of this rubric is to provide a fairly quick evaluation of a whole piece of writing at the end of a class. While it is a published rubric that can guide students in preparing for the final written exam, it is not intended to help students continuously improve their writing, or to guide teachers modifying their instruction, as is the case of an analytical writing assessment rubric. An analytic rubric known as the Six-Trait Analytical Writing Model attempts to capture the complexity of good writing and provides scoring rubrics in seven different areas of writing assessment: ideas and content, organization of the writing, voice, word choice, sentence fluency, and conventions (mechanics and spelling). This rubric is available on-line from the Northwest Regional Lab (www.nwrel.org/eval/toolkit98/traits/) and is being used in various districts as part of a comprehensive effort to improve student writing. It demonstrates the power of an analytic rubric to focus attention on different parts of the task at any one time. It also helps teachers to analyze the strengths and weaknesses of different students' writings. This rubric was designed using a five-point scale with clear criteria listed for writing of a high (5), middle (3) or low (1) criteria for each of the seven areas. This scale provides a clear picture of what is an average response, what are a high and low response, and the distance

FIGURE 8.5 *Rubric for Holistic Scoring of Final Exams*

---

4 points | ***Outstanding Rating***

Addresses the topic in depth
Shows understanding of the topic, discusses implications and
   interrelationships
Uses scholarly information or references to support generalizations
Contains theoretical and research information
Projects originality in terms of freshness of ideas and voice of writer
Provides a feeling of conviction and demonstrates insight
Gives pertinent support (examples, details, reasons) that provide credibility
Flow of ideas is easy to follow, transitions are well written
Includes a summarization or conclusion

---

3 points | ***Satisfactory Rating***

Addresses the topic satisfactorily
Shows understanding of the topic
Uses scholarly information or references to support generalizations
Makes points explicit with details, elaboration, and/or examples
Projects writer's voice
Information presented is relevant
Sticks to the topic

---

2 points | ***Unsatisfactory Rating***

Partially addresses the topic
Reflects only partial understanding of the topic
Some detail, elaboration, or support for ideas
Loose organization, hard to follow

---

1 point | ***Fail***

Does not address the topic
Contrived, filling up space
Illogical or irrelevant ideas
Only personal opinion, no support from literature
Poor writing interferes with understanding meaning

between these. Figure 8.6 is an example of a rubric for one of the criteria, Word Choice. Each of the bolded words can be clicked on to provide more information.

How Does One Develop Scoring Rubrics?

There are several different ways teachers can develop their own rubrics. If the evaluators have a clear idea of what a high-quality product should look like, such as an

FIGURE 8.6   *Word Choice*

5

Words convey the intended message in a precise, interesting, and natural way.
- Words are **specific** and **accurate**: it is easy to understand what the writer means.
- The language is **natural** and never overdone: phrasing is highly **individual.**
- **Lively** verbs energize the writing. **Precise nouns and modifiers** create pictures in the reader's mind.
- **Striking words and phrases** often catch the reader's eye and linger in the reader's mind.
- **Clichés and jargon** are used sparingly, only for effect.

3

The language is function, even if it lacks punch; it is easy to figure out the writer's meaning on a general level.
- Words are almost always **correct and adequate**, they simply lack flair.
- **Familiar words and phrases** communicate, but rarely capture the reader's imagination.
- **Attempts at colorful language** come close to the mark, but sometimes seem overdone.
- Energetic verbs or picturesque phrases **liven things up now and then**; the reader longs for more.

1

The writer struggles with a limited vocabulary, searching for words to convey meaning. The writing reflects more than one of these problems:
- Language is so **vague** (e.g., *It was a fun time. She was neat, It was nice, We did lots of stuff*) that only the **most general message** comes through.
- Persistent **redundancy** distracts the reader.
- **Jargon or clichés** serve as a crutch.
- **Words are used incorrectly**, sometimes making the message hard to decipher.
- Problems with language **leave the reader wondering** what the writer is trying to say.

"A" paper or an "A" performance, they can begin by writing down their criteria based on experience. They will need to clearly define the criteria using language that specifies desired outcomes in concrete terms. It is not enough to say "the student should demonstrate creativity in his or her story writing." The rubric writers will need to define what creativity looks like. Does it mean the story has originality and contains unique elements? Can the reader hear the uniqueness of the writer's voice?

Designers will need to decide if the rubric will be a *holistic rubric* that looks at the whole product, or an *analytic rubric* that provides subsections that examine different aspects of the product or performance. You will know when a more analytic rubric is needed. If when trying out a rubric on student work, if you keep wanting to evaluate something that is not on the rubric, you will need to develop more categories for evaluation. Developers of rubrics also need to decide what kind of scale they want to use in the rubric. Do they want a scale of 1–4 (a typical range for many rubrics) or is the task so complex that a scale of 1–6 is or more is needed? Arter and McTighe (2001) provide examples of a six-point mathematics problem-solving scale, a six-point primary reading scale, and an eleven-point developmental writing continuum rubric. You should explore the many different types of rubrics available for guidance on scoring scales.

A second way to begin developing a rubric is to look at student work. This might be a way to start if teachers are not clear on what criteria they are looking for. They may not have considered the reasons they have given a paper or product a certain grade. Teachers could meet together and describe what they think is "A" work, "C" work, and work that fails to meet the desired criteria. Looking at student work provides an excellent opportunity to talk about the many different ways that students solve problems or create products. Insights gained from examining student work can be very helpful in designing classroom assessments.

The teachers design a rubric by looking at and sorting student work. They then can begin to list criteria that seem most relevant at each level of the work. They might also want to consider alternative ways that students have solved problems or presented information and find ways to include a range of different, but *good*, answers in their evaluation. In general, rubrics should include the following:

1. One or more traits or dimensions that serve as the basis for judging students' responses;
2. Definitions and examples to clarify the meaning of each trait or dimension;
3. A scale of values (or a counting system) on which to rate each dimension; and
4. Standards of excellence for specified performance levels accompanied by models or examples of each level. (Herman, Aschbacher, and Winters, 1992)

Teachers should also note that they do not have to start from scratch. There are now many sites on the Web that provide multiple examples of excellent rubrics that can be modified by the teacher, school, or district. Try the following website from Ontario, Canada, which provides extensive examples of rubrics: http://www.odyssey.on.ca/~elaine.coxon/rubrics.htm.

How Can the Level of Student Autonomy in Learning Be Assessed?

Technology provides valuable support for the development of student-centered learning environments. There are places for students to write, record, draw, and assemble learning records and reflections using electronic journals, email communications with the teacher, and electronic portfolios. In addition to computer-based writing spaces, students can use video to record and then evaluate their own presentations. Students can participate in designing rubrics for their work and learn how to self-assess using rubrics. They can be asked to reflect on their own learning and communicate with their teacher on how they are doing on a project on a weekly or more frequent basis. While working in class, the teacher can stop and ask students to write down a few questions they have right now about what they are learning and then send those questions to their teachers. Students working in a communicative writing environment as described in Chapter 5 (reading and writing) can assess their own reading and writing skills and self-select computer-based skills programs to use to improve their own areas of language need.

How Can the Teacher Assess the Development of English Language Skills (Reading, Writing, Speaking, and Listening)?

As mentioned in the previous discussion on comprehensible input, multimedia-based language learning programs include microphones and means of listening to native language speakers and then comparing your speaking to the native speakers. Many of these programs also store information about each student's progress, how long it took to master a unit of dialog, and how often additional support such as pictures or sound were used to support comprehension. These comprehensive computer programs not only help students build language skills, they also provide important assessment information to the teacher.

Student Self-Assessment of Language Skills in a Bilingual Environment.
Gardner (1996) suggests ways to guide learners to assess their own strategies and abilities to communicate in a second language. He points to a study by Murphey (1995) in which students were paired randomly to explain language items to each other, and, after some negotiation, to give themselves a score for how well they did it. In their learning logs some of these students report finding this procedure to be useful, enjoyable, and challenging. Although this procedure was used in a class, it could also be used by English language learners at a distance. It also adds an assessment dimension to an activity students are already enjoying on *Dave's ESL Café*. In a student discussion section on this site, students can ask questions about grammar and receive corrections and suggestions from students around the world.

Gardner (1996) provides a number of specific strategies for his Chinese students who are learning English to use for assessing their own listening/viewing/reading comprehension. While his examples apply to the use of television and video in Chinese and English, the strategies can be used in other locations in which bilingual media are found, such as the southwest borderlands (Spanish/English) or the U.S. states that border on Canada (French/English). For places in which bilingual popular media, either written or video/television, are not readily available, the bilingual teacher can collect videos or movies, record television shows, or bring in print media to the classroom in the target language. The self-assessment exercises involve watching the news in one language and then in the other and having students compare their comprehension in each language. Gardner also suggests his students watch a movie while covering up the subtitles in their native language, then make up their own subtitles in the target language and finally compare the subtitles they wrote with the ones provided in the movie.

The following is an adaptation of an example by Gardner (1996, p. 23) of a self-assessment of reading comprehension for his bilingual students:

Self-Assessment of Reading Comprehension

Exercise 4:
- The purpose of this exercise is for you to discover how good you are at reading for meaning. You can do this self-assessment at home or in class.
- You need any handout that has an English and Chinese (or Spanish or French, etc.) version. This could be a publicity handout or information from a government office.
- Read all the instructions before you start.
  1. Only look at the English version.
  2. Summarize the main points. Underline any important information.
  3. Now read the Chinese (or Spanish or French, etc.) version.
  4. Is your summary correct? Did you find the most important information?
  5. Are there any points you missed?

Scoring
For each main point that is correct, give yourself 1 point.
For each main point that you got wrong, give yourself 0 points.
For each main point that you missed, subtract 1 point.

You can now calculate your score as a percentage using the following formula: (Number of correct points divided by the number of points times 100).

Are you satisfied with your score?

You have to make your own decision about the scores but here are some suggestions:
- More than 76% is good.
- 50% to 75% is OK, but try again with a different document.

• Less than 50% indicates you are having problems understanding the English version. Try working on a single paragraph at a time and checking your comprehension by reading the version in your native language. If there are English words you don't understand try your dictionary.

Additional Skills Assessment.   In the areas of reading and writing assessment, many types of assessments can be used to assess student comprehension. For example, students can be asked to read a passage and then retell a story, draw a cartoon, or create an outline or graphical map of what they read. Another excellent assessment of comprehension is to have a student read a set of directions and then follow them to create a product such as reading or hearing directions and then drawing a simple map, making a paper construction, or cooking something. Cloze exercises are also helpful in assessing student comprehension skills. Write a cloze exercise related to the topic students are studying and at their appropriate language level. Then leave out every fifth word or so. Evaluate how well the students can fill in the missing words. Simple quizzes can also be used for building skills and background knowledge. Try having the students themselves write the quizzes for each other.

How Can a Teacher Assess Student Learning Styles and Strategies? How Can a Teacher Assess His or Her Own Teaching to Ensure That He or She Is Teaching to All Modalities and Learning Styles?

Computer-based multimedia environments provide an excellent way to support students with different learning styles as they participate in classroom learning projects. For example in Chapter 1, Ms. Lujan-Pincomb's elementary students not only worked with written language, but also used kinesthetic and visual skills to draw pictures of their insects. Students participating in multimedia groups in Ms. Hills's middle school class were valued for the different learning abilities they demonstrated. Those with high artistic intelligence could provide the graphics, those with strong linguistic abilities could write the text, and those with interpersonal skills could actually organize the group in order to successfully finish the project.

Chapter 7 concentrates on incorporating understandings of different learning styles and preferences into teaching practices for English language learners. Multimedia is shown as a particularly valuable media for providing multiple ways for students to learn and demonstrate their learning ranging from creating images, to using sound, text and/or animation. A student still learning English might be able to assemble powerful images and/or video that demonstrate key ideas in a concept area. An interesting assessment in terms of learning styles is for the teacher to assess her or his own classroom in terms of whether different learning styles are being supported. An instrument for teachers to use to assess how well they are meeting learning styles of their students is provided in Figure 8.7.

FIGURE 8.7   *Teacher Self-Assessment: Learning Styles/Teaching Styles*

In order to accommodate a variety of learning styles, students in my classroom have the opportunity to . . .

	*Often	*Sometimes	*Never
1. Make choices			
2. Use visual materials			
3. Listen to lectures			
4. Study independently and quietly			
5. Study in groups			
6. Present oral responses			
7. Present written responses			
8. Present information in graphical formats			
9. Create individual projects			
10. Participate in group projects			
11. Engage in discussion			
12. Share in planning			
13. Take oral tests			
14. Take written tests			
15. Be creative			
16. Listen to music			
17. Work at his/her own level			
18. Work at his/her own speed			
19. Correct mistakes			
20. Learn by doing			
21. Make up and ask questions			
22. Self-assess their own learning			
23. Use multimedia materials			
24. Learn with technology			

*20 or more responses in the Often and Sometimes columns indicate you are probably accommodating the learning styles of your students most of the time; 15 or more responses in the Sometimes and Never columns indicate that some of your students may not have the opportunity to use their best learning modality.

How Can the Teacher Assess the Level of Collaborative Learning in Face-to-Face and Distance Learning Environments?

The use of technology for social constructivist problem and project-based learning can have a significant impact on the way the classroom is organized. Research (Dwyer, Ringstaff, and Sanholtz, 1990; Marx, 2000) suggests that as teachers utilize technology to support student-directed learning, the classroom environment itself begins to change, as do the roles of teachers and students. One of the common changes is increased use of students as peer teachers. One teacher in an ACOT (Apple Classroom of Tomorrow) study noted that after two years of integrating technology in her classroom, she finally realized that she had 24 other teachers to help her.

Using Video for Assessment.   We recently videotaped a middle school classroom for several days prior to the teacher making a major change in the classroom management structure of the class. Our intention in working with the teacher to change her instructional management was the school's request that we help the teachers use the four to five classroom computers in the classroom. These computers frequently sat unused in the back of the classroom. The principal was concerned that her investment in classroom-based technology was not being used. We hypothesized that part of the problem is that the teachers had no experience in differentiating assignments. They had learned as students that teaching required everyone do the same thing at the same time.

The sixth-grade teacher had been using traditional methods including reading and lecturing to students, calling on one person at a time, and assigning traditional worksheets, in spite of the fact that there were four computers in her classroom which were often not used. The teacher had been introduced to a new type of instructional design based on problem-based learning. (See Chapters 6 and 7 for a detailed discussion of problem-based learning and how to implement it in the classroom.) In this new instructional management approach, the students are provided with a series of tasks that they must complete by rotating through them. The tasks include the use of computers, individual assignments, and collaborative learning projects. There were several different kinds of activities going on at the same time. The teacher was interested in assessing how well her students worked together in this new environment.

We videotaped the class during several days after the implementation of a problem-based approach. The first unit centered on construction. While some students read newspaper articles, others worked together to design buildings, some using cardboard and construction materials and others working with *KidCad* on the computer. The students were introduced to the project in terms of the kind of work people do on the job. The students were interviewed as they worked with the project approach and asked to explain how it was going for them. They were asked to assess how well they worked in their groups and to meet with their supervisor if the group was experiencing any problems. There was a significant change in the classroom, most clearly seen by watching the before and after videotapes. There is no way that an observer can avoid seeing the increased interest and interaction of the students, the increases in student responsibility, and the way reorganizing a classroom can increase computer use for learning. One student commented, "Now I feel more important. I feel like my parents. I have a job to do, and it has to be done on time." The teachers commented on the additional planning time required for this approach, but were also excited about the students' increased engagement in learning.

Assessing Participation in On-Line Communities.   Assessing collaboration in a distance learning environment requires different strategies. The teacher needs to monitor the on-line work including the email and other types of on-line communications between the participants. If students are involved in synchronous chats, it is important that the teacher facilitates the chats carefully using techniques such as a round robin (hearing from each person in order) or calling on specific students in the on-line classroom so that equitable participation is ensured. A careful analysis of the logs of chats or the reading of emails provides information about the level of collaboration being used by the on-line group. Sometimes it is necessary to break large groups of 20 or so into smaller subgroups of 3 or 4 students who will work on-line on projects in order to facilitate additional small group learning. An effective strategy is to give these students tasks that they can complete collaboratively at a distance. A facilitator can be assigned to each group and be asked to summarize the on-line work and send this information to the instructor. It is also useful to rotate facilitators so that all students gain leadership skills in on-line work.

How Can Technology Help Meet the Affective Needs of Students?

How computers are used for teaching and learning affects how well the use of technology meets the affective needs of English language learners. Some research has indicated that the use of integrated learning packages in which students are plugged into sequential tutorials often does not work well, especially for English language learners. This might be because they have problems with the language, not the concepts being taught. However, when students use the computers for self-selected skills practice (as discussed in Chapter 5), they find these computer environments a safe place to try out new language skills in a private place. The computer is endlessly patient with them, provides frequent feedback, and lets them build confidence in their skills before trying them out in public. The basis for supporting affective needs of students with technology is related to how much in control of the technology the students feel. The following description of a sheltered language art class illustrates this.

> It was always exciting to see the diverse learners that would show up the first day of Mr. Bustamente's sheltered language arts class at the middle school. He was lucky to have six computers in his classroom that students could use. He welcomed the students and told them that this

year they would be able to learn about each other as they learned to use computers. During the first class, he asked the students what they would like to learn about each other and wrote their suggestions on the board. Then he helped them turn their ideas into questions.

Mr. Bustamente introduced students to the use of *Word,* the writing process software available in the classroom, by modeling the use of the questions as part of an interview with another student. He asked which students had used a computer before for writing and he paired them up with students who were unfamiliar with computers. The student partners first worked at their desks using paper and pencils. The next day he asked the students to go to the computer and create their interviews using a word processor. After they finished this word processing task, he introduced them to the paint tool and told students to paint a picture related to what they had learned about the other student. They were then shown how to copy the picture into their interview and the interviews were posted.

Later in the week students were introduced to the use of digital cameras for taking pictures of each other. Working in new groups, the students were asked to create a newsletter about themselves that included pictures of each other and pictures of things they liked around the school. Later, students began a current events newsletter. The students worked with Mr. Bustamente to develop a rubric for evaluating their news publications. This project was so successful that the school newsletter soon became a project of the sheltered class.

Students also created databases and charts during this "getting to know you" unit. By the end of the unit, the students were all feeling comfortable with each other, with the computers they would soon be using for improving their writing, speaking, listening, and reading skills,

---

FIGURE 8.8   Using a Checklist to Evaluate the Class Newsletter

---

0 = no evidence of meeting criteria
1 = begins to meet criteria
2 = meets or exceeds criteria

_____ Correct spelling and grammar
_____ Attractive format (can follow easily, consistent look and feel)
_____ Appropriate use of graphics (graphics enhancing meaning of text, graphics makes reading it more inviting or friendly)
_____ News is current (within last month, not old news)
_____ There is a diversity of information (evidence of news from various sources, reflection of diverse viewpoints)

Comments: Points: _____ / 10

---

and with the classroom. The teacher and anyone walking into the classroom could feel that the affective environment was good. Mr. Bustamente used the checklist in Figure 8.8 he developed with his students to evaluate their newsletter.

Additional evidence for this positive climate can be gathered by using assessment tools that ask students to evaluate how they feel about the school and classroom. See Technology Resources in this chapter for suggestions on where to find out more about emotional learning and classroom climate.

How Can Students' Understanding of Target and Native Cultures Be Assessed?

Cummins and Sayers, in their book *Brave New Schools* (1995), discuss how the use of telecommunications activities between students in different cultures can help students develop cultural literacy. Chapter 7 in this book discusses the interconnections between language, culture, and community. The use of electronic key pals is one strategy that provides students with the opportunity share their culture and to learn the culture of the language they are trying to acquire. After students have participated in a project that involves learning about and communicating with students in another culture, the teacher will want to assess what they have learned, not only in terms of language but also in terms of the target culture. This can be done in a variety of ways. Saved records of emails and/or chats between the cross-cultural students can be analyzed both in terms of growing language skills and increased understanding of partner student culture. In terms of culturally responsive teaching, teachers may also want to assess themselves in the three areas suggested in Chapter 7.

1. Do students have an opportunity to bring their experiences or knowledge into their learning?
2. Can students construct their own knowledge through guided activities and can they provide input into how their work will be evaluated?
3. Are diverse ways of learning and demonstrating learning valued?

Does the ELL Learning Environment Provide Appropriate Feedback and Assessment?

This last attribute of learning environments takes us back to the initial Nintendo Principle with which this chapter began. The use of technology for immediate feedback is perhaps most obvious in the use of skills-oriented games and tutorials which constitute an important role in learning language. These games range from tutorials to new specific skills games like Davidson's new grammar and vocabulary games. Yet these specific skills environments are not the only way in which technology can be used to provide support for continuous assessment. In fact, the teacher is cautioned that in order to meet students' affective needs, it is important to provide students with opportunities to create using technology. The products they are creating can be easily evaluated using rubrics designed by the teacher and/or the students. Technology programs, from word processors to painting and drawing tools, to multimedia and hypermedia tools, provide valuable support for students to demonstrate in diverse ways what they have learned. Integrating technology ultimately has broader implications for the second language teacher that involves changes in the organization of the classroom and the roles of teachers and learners. Many of these changes will, we believe, facilitate a more communicative and more thinking-centered environment than the traditional teacher-directed classroom.

Conclusion

Teachers of English language learners need a variety of assessment strategies to accurately evaluate their students' progress in acquiring the new language and learning content. Electronic portfolios, computer-based checklists and rubrics, peer review sheets, cloze tests, learning logs, and multimedia projects are a few of the many ways computers can be utilized to give students feedback on their work and evaluate their progress.

As we discussed each of the attributes of successful language learning environments, we described assessment strategies that seemed applicable in each situation. Taken together, these strategies address the Nintendo Principle suggested in the opening section of this chapter. We hope the teacher will continue to ask: Is there enough feedback in each of learning opportunities provided so that students know how well they are doing?

This chapter suggests that you, the teachers of English language learners, assess your students' learning in terms of the characteristics we have suggested for successful language learning and answer for yourself if there is sufficient appropriate feedback and ongoing assessment. Technology-based and new forms of alternative assessments are new areas in education and we encourage you to try some of the different strategies suggested in order to learn what works best for you and your students. We would be interested in hearing about these experiences from you.

Summary of Key Ideas

1. The chapter begins by describing the Nintendo Principle as a guiding principle for thinking about and designing instruction. This principle states that for every instructional activity there must be embedded within it enough feedback that students always know how they are doing.

2. There are a number of problems with traditional standardized testing, including (a) measuring the kind of knowledge that is becoming less relevant today (isolated facts) and not the kinds of problem solving required in an increasingly complex world; (b) testing individual students repeatedly with tests that were designed to

give a rough picture of program or school success; and (c) testing students on information that they were not taught.

3. A growing alternative assessment movement is addressing concerns about standardized and norm-referenced tests. Researchers suggest that alternative assessments are variants of performance assessment that allow students to generate rather than choose a response. They also summarize alternative assessment as being instructionally based, relatively nonintrusive, providing students with multiple opportunities to demonstrate what they know, and a kind of assessment in which students are evaluated on what they can produce, explain, or show, rather than what they can recall.

4. Several scenarios show the power of technology to support assessment. Technology has a dual role in expanding assessment opportunities. First, the existence of technology environments support more student-generated learning projects. It is easier to use alternative assessment strategies to evaluate the kinds of products and presentations that are made possible with the use of technologies. Technology also supports student collaborative and project-based learning. Second, technology makes it easier to store information related to student learning in digital form, whether it is a log of on-line work, a student electronic portfolio, records of email communication, or student-created Web pages or multimedia projects.

5. The second part of the chapter organizes assessment strategies within the context of attributes of successful language learning environments. Examples of learning related to each attribute are presented together with types of related assessments.

Learning Activities _____

1. Assessment is a complicated issue. Consider possible answers to some of the many questions that abound in the literature.
   • Can multiple-choice tests evaluate higher-level thinking?
   • Does current testing encourage broad but shallow coverage in all content areas?
   • Why do teacher tests provide different results than standardized tests?
   • Which are more accurate indicators of performance?
   • How can one test for understanding of concepts or big ideas?
   • Are entrance tests such as the Scholastic Assessment Test actually predictive of performance in college?
   • Are they more predictive for mainstream white students than for language or ethnic minorities?
   • Do current tests measure deep knowledge, both procedural and declarative, or only the ability to recall unrelated bits of information?
   • Do tests of content reflect the latest subject matter standards?
   • Is there a mismatch between locally developed goals and nationally designed standardized tests?
   • Are the kinds of skills tested in schools the same kinds of skills used when people go to work?
   • Does success on school tests transfer to success in the real world?

2. Brainstorm some of your favorite teaching strategies in your content area. For each of these teaching strategies consider appropriate assessment strategies that will help

you evaluate the impact of your teaching on student learning. This would be a good activity to do in small groups in order to get multiple perspectives on assessment.

3. Begin to develop your own folder or toolbox of assessment tools—surveys, forms, rubrics, websites, and so on. This would be an excellent activity to do in relationship to creating a digital assessment portfolio or even a class CD-ROM that contains all kinds of assessments that are useful for English language learners.

4. Herman, Auschbaher, and Winters (1992) summarize important and common characteristics of alternative assessment strategies. They include the following:
   - Ask students to perform, create, produce, or do something.
   - Tap higher-level thinking and problem-solving skills.
   - Use tasks that represent meaningful instructional activities.
   - Invoke real-world applications.

   Consider each of these strategies and pick one you'd like to use for assessment. Design a learning activity and appropriate assessment using the strategies in this chapter for a content area you teach.

5. The use of rubrics is a widely recognized and valued method of assessing student writing and oral production. In a project-based course in which student groups use the Internet and educational software to complete specific tasks, is it possible to use a rubric for assessment purposes? In small groups, brainstorm a student activity centered on a commercial or educational website or software program. First, identify the desired learning outcomes of the activity and then create a rubric that could be used to assess student attainment of these outcomes.

Technology Resources _____

Hyperstudio 3.2 for Windows. (1999). Torrance, CA: Knowledge Solutions.
Kid Cad. Torrance, CA: Davidson.
Microsoft Office (2000). Redmond, WA: Microsoft.

Technology Resources on Standardized Testing

This site provides information for parents about standardized testing: http://www.kidsource.com/kidsource/content/standardized.testing.html.
The Educational Testing Service itself has suggested that there is *Too Much Testing of the Wrong Kind; Too Little of the Right Kind in K-12 Education.* For more information visit their site at http://www.ets.org/research/pic/testing/tmt2.html.

Technology Resources on the Assessment of Language Learning

The National Clearinghouse for ESL Literacy Education (NCLE) (http://www.cal.org/ncle/) is the National Clearinghouse for ESL Literacy Education (NCLE), the only national information center focusing on the language and literacy education of adults and out-of-school youth learning English, works to support those providing such services.
Launched in 1993 with funding from the United States Department of Education (USDE), the Center for Advanced Research on Language Acquisition (CARLA) (http://carla.acad.umn.edu/) at the University of Minnesota supports a number of coordinated programs of research, training, development, and dissemination of information related to second language teaching,

learning, and assessment. The center has been designated as one of nine National Language Resource Centers, whose role is to improve the nation's capacity to teach and learn foreign languages effectively.

Links to Language Assessment Resources (http://carla.acad.umn.edu/slalinks.html) and Technology and Second Language Learning (http://carla.acad.umn.edu/technology.html) can also be found on the CARLA site.

Internet Resources on Emotional Learning and Classroom Climates

http://www.eq.org/K12_Schools/. Excellent resource on emotional learning for K–12 schools.

http://myhero.com/home.asp. A welcome site that celebrates the best of humanity. Heroes who are doing positive work are celebrated on this page and discussion and interaction is welcomed.

http://eqi.org/. A comprehensive site on emotional intelligence from the academic and practitioner's viewpoint.

http://www2.southwind.net/~furtweng/rsi/index.html. A low-cost and comprehensive set of questionnaires for assessing school and classroom climates and effectiveness.

References

Allen, G., and Thompson, A. (1994, March). *Analysis of the effect of networking on computer-assisted collaborative writing in a fifth grade classroom.* Paper presented at the annual meeting of the American Educational Research Association. (ERIC Document Reproduction Service No. ED 373 777).

Arter, J., and McTighe, J. (2001). *Scoring Rubrics in the Classroom: Using Performance Criteria for Assessing and Improving Student Performance.* Thousand Oaks, CA: Corwin Press.

Berlak, H., Newmann, F., Adams, E., Archbald, D., Burgess, T., Raven, J., and Romberg, T. (1992). *Toward a New Science of Educational Testing and Assessment.* New York: State University of New York Press.

Brown, A. (1995). The advancement of learning. *Educational Researcher* 23 (8): 4–12.

Brown, H. D. (1994*). Teaching by Principles: An Interactive Approach to Language Teaching.* Englewood Cliffs, NJ: Prentice Hall Regents.

Brown, J. S., Collins, A., and Duguid, P. (1988). *Situated Cognition and the Culture of Learning* (Report No. IRL 88–0008). Palo Alto, CA: Institute for Research on Learning.

Brown J. D., and Hudson, T. (1998). The alternatives in language assessment. *TESOL Quarterly* 32 (4): 653–675.

Canale, M., and Swain, M. (1980). Theoretical bases of communicative approaches to second language teaching and testing. *Applied Linguistics* 1 (1): 1–47.

Chao, C. (1999). Theory and research: New emphases of assessment in the language learning classroom. In J. Egbert and E. Hanson-Smith (Eds.), *CALL Environments: Research, Practice, and Critical Issues* (pp. 243–256). Alexandria, VA: TESOL, Inc.

Cummins, J. (1996). Foreword. In J. M. O'Malley and L. V. Pierce (Eds.), *Authentic Assessment for English Language Learners: Practical Approaches for Teachers.* Reading, MA: Addison-Wesley.

Cummins, J., and Sayers, D. (1995). *Brave New Schools: Challenging Cultural Illiteracy Through Global Learning Networks.* New York: St. Martin's Press.

Darling-Hammond, L. (1991). The implications of testing policy for quality and equality. *Phi Delta Kappan* 73 (3): 220–226.

Darling-Hammond, L. (1994). Performance-based assessment and educational equity. *Harvard Educational Review,* 64: 5–29.

Darling-Hammond, L. (1997) *The Right to Learn: A Blueprint for Creating Schools That Work.* San Francisco: Jossey-Bass.

Dwyer, D. C., Ringstaff, C., and Sanholtz, J. H. (1990). *Teacher Beliefs and Practices: Patterns of Change.* Cupertino, CA: Apple Classrooms of Tomorrow, Apple Computer, Inc.

Echevarria, J., Vogt, M. E., and Short, D. (2000). *Making Content Comprehensible for English Language Learners: The SIOP Model.* Boston: Allyn and Bacon.

Eisner, E. W. (1994). *Cognition and Curriculum Reconsidered* (2nd ed.). New York: Teacher's College Press.

Eisner, E. W. (1999). *The Kind of Schools We Need.* Portsmouth, NH: Heinemann.

Garcia, G. E., and Pearson, P. D. (1993). Assessment and diversity. *Review of Research in Education* 20 (1): 337–389.

ETS (Educational Testing Service). (2000). Available on the Internet. http://www.ets.org/research/pic/testing/tmt2.html.

Gardner, D. (1996, Spring) Self-assessment for self-access learners. *TESOL Journal* 5 (3): 18–23.

Gardner, H. (1985). *Frames of Mind.* New York: Basic Books.

Geisinger, K. F., and Carlson, J. F. (1992). *Assessing Language-Minority Students.* Washington, DC: ERIC Clearinghouse on Tests, Measurement, and Evaluation. (ERIC Document Reproduction Service No. ED 356 232).

Harmon, M. (1995). The changing role of assessment in evaluating science education reform. In R. G. O'Sullivan (Ed.), *American Evaluation Association: Vol. 65. Emerging Roles of Evaluation in Science Education Reform* (pp. 31–52). San Francisco: Jossey-Bass.

Hart, D. (1994). *Authentic Assessment: A Handbook for Educators.* Menlo Park, CA: Addison-Wesley.

Herman, J. L., Aschbacher, P. R., and Winters, L. (1992). *A Practical Guide to Alternative Assessment.* Alexandria, VA: Association for Supervision and Curriculum Development.

Huerta-Macías, A. (1995). Alternative assessment: Responses to commonly asked questions. *TESOL Journal* 5 (1): 8–11.

Knapp, L., and Glenn, A. (1996). *Restructuring Schools with Technology.* Boston: Allyn and Bacon.

Kulm, G., and Malcolm, S. (Eds.). (1991). *Science Assessment in the Service of Reform.* Washington, DC: American Association for the Advancement of Science.

Lacelle-Peterson, M., and Rivera, C. (1994). Is it real for all kids? A framework for equitable assessment policies for English language learners. *Harvard Educational Review* 64 (1): 55–75.

Lam, T., and Gordon, W. (1992). State policies for standardized achievement testing of limited English proficient students. *Educational Measurement: Issues and Practice* 11 (4): 18–20.

Madaus, G. F. (1991). The effects of important tests on students: Implications for a national examination system. *Phi Delta Kappan* 73 (3): 226–231.

Madaus, G. F. (1994). A technological and historical consideration of equity issues associated with proposals to change the nation's testing policy. *Harvard Educational Review* 64 (1): 76–95.

Marx, S. (2000). Unpublished doctoral disseration, New Mexico State University.

Mathematical Sciences Education Board. (1993). *Measuring What Counts.* Washington, DC: National Academy Press.

Mathies, B. K. (1994, February). *Technology in Authentic Assessment. Portfolios: Addressing the Multiple Dimensions of Teaching and Learning.* Paper presented at the annual meeting of the American Association of Colleges for Teacher Education, Chicago. (ERIC Document Reproduction Service No. ED 376 117).

Murphey, T. (1995). Tests: Learning through negotiated interaction. *TESOL Journal* 4 (2): 16.

National Commission for Excellence in Education. (1983). *A Nation at Risk.* Washington, DC: U.S. Department of Education.

National Council of Teachers of Mathematics. (1989). *Curriculum and Evaluation Standards for School Mathematics.* Reston, VA: Author.

National Council of Teachers of Mathematics. (1993). *Standards for Teaching Mathematics.* Reston, VA: Author.

National Research Council. (1996). *National Science Education Standards.* Washington, DC: National Academy Press.

Newsweek. (2000). The New America, September 18, p. 48.

Norton, P., and Wiburg, K. (1998). *Teaching with Technology.* Fort Worth, TX: Harcourt Brace.

Oakes, J. (1985). *Keeping Track: How Schools Structure Inequality.* New Haven, CT: Yale University Press.

O'Malley, J. M., & Valdez Pierce, L. (1996). *Authentic Assessment for English Language Learners: Practical Approaches for Teachers.*

Piaget, J. (1972). *The Principles of Genetic Epistemology* (W. Mays, Trans.). New York: Basic Books.

Rosa, A., and Montero, I. (1990). In L. C. Mjoll, (Ed.), *Vygotsky and Education: Instructional Implications and Applications of Sociohistorical Psychology.* New York: Cambridge University Press.

Sagor, R. (1992). *How to Conduct Collaborative Action Research.* Alexandria, VA: Association for Supervision and Curriculum Development.

Sheingold, K., and Frederiksen, J. (1994). Using technology to support innovative assessment. In B. Means (Ed.), *Technology and Education Reform: The Reality Behind the Promise* (pp. 111–132). San Francisco: Jossey-Bass.

Sternberg, R. J. (1994). Diversifying instruction and assessment. *Educational Forum* 59 (1): 47–52.

U.S. Congress, Office of Technology and Assessment. (1992). *Testing in American schools: Asking the right questions* (OTA -SET-519). Washington, DC: U.S. Government Printing Office.

Vygotsky, L. S. (1962). *Thought and Language.* Cambridge, MA: MIT Press.

Vygotsky, L. S. (1978). *Mind in Society: The Development of Higher Psychological Processes.* Cambridge, MA: Harvard University Press.

Wiggins, G. (1993). Assessment: Authenticity, context, and validity. *Phi Delta Kappan* 75 (3): 200–214.

Wilson, K. G., and Davis, B. (1994). *Redesigning Education.* New York: Holt.

Index